Capture America's Majestic Beauty
with **30 Easy Projects**

NATIONAL PARKS
IN *watercolor*

KOLBIE BLUME

Author of *Stunning Watercolor Seascapes*
and *Wilderness Watercolor Landscapes*

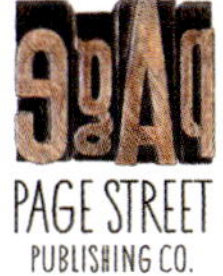

PAGE STREET
PUBLISHING CO.

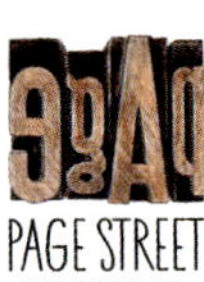

Copyright © 2025 Kolbie Blume

First published in 2025 by
Page Street Publishing Co.
27 Congress Street, Suite 1511
Salem, MA 01970
www.pagestreetpublishing.com

Distributed by Macmillan, sales in Canada by The Canadian Manda Group.

29 28 27 26 25   1 2 3 4 5

ISBN-13: 979-8-89003-252-2
Library of Congress Control Number: 2024945234

Edited by Krystle Green
Cover and book design by Molly Kate Young for Page Street Publishing Co.
Artwork and photography by Kolbie Blume

Printed and bound in the United States of America

Contents

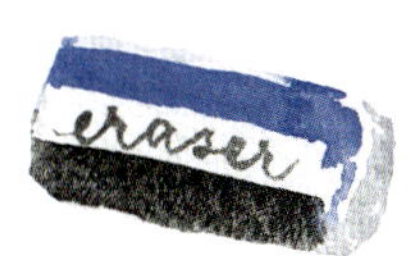

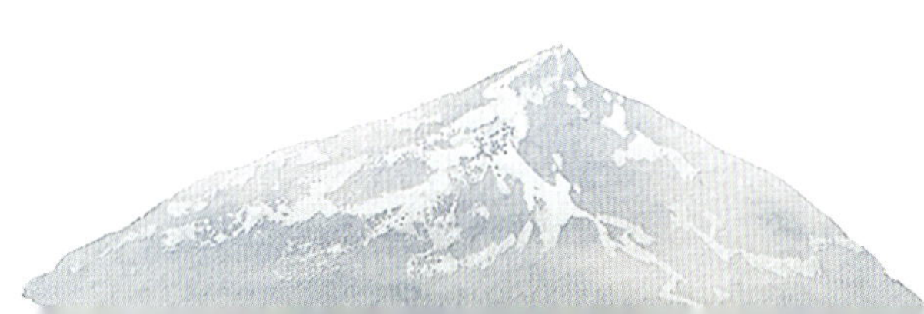

introduction

There's a sentiment I heard a few years ago that completely changed the way I view my painting practice: *You're a painter. It's okay that your painting looks like a painting.*

Especially since I've primarily painted landscapes for the better part of a decade, it's so easy to get lost in whether or not your work looks realistic enough to be, well, *good*, you know?

. . . Then you try painting not just landscapes, but amazing, recognizable vistas—breathtaking scenes we yearn to witness in real life? If you're wondering whether painting national parks is intimidating for me, the answer is unequivocally YES.

Here's the thing about photorealistic painting: It's an incredibly technical skill, and I admire the hell out of anyone who can sit for dozens if not hundreds of hours to make their paintings look *just right*.

And that is just *one* way to paint. It's okay to be a painter who paints kind of quickly and imperfectly. It's more than okay to look at your painting and realize, *Well, turns out I'm not a camera!*

You're definitely not a camera, my friend, and *that is a good thing*. The world has a lot of cameras and a lot of photos of these iconic places. What it *doesn't* have is the painting you're about to create.

Truth? One of the best ways to honor our planet's most beautiful, natural creations—like the ones in the U.S. National Parks—is to lean into the sheer amount of *wild imperfection and luck* it took to form them. It's okay to stumble and scribble your way into creative experiences. The whole point of preserving national parks in the first place is not to tame them, but to let them be free in all their chaotic glory—and to let humans be a small, messy part of something bigger than themselves for a while.

Remember that creativity is for *you*. The goodness you're bringing through your art isn't really about the painting itself—it's about the courage you're creating by being completely terrified of that blank page, and giving it a shot anyway. That's where the magic is, because that's where you discover just how much more inside you there is to explore.

The painting isn't the masterpiece. *You* are the masterpiece. Your life, and the desire you have to experience the world around you, is the masterpiece. Painting is just one way you get to celebrate how miraculous it is to be here . . . to belong. (And, I promise, no matter how mediocre or messy or unqualified you feel, *you belong here.*)

So, are you ready for a watercolor adventure? Me too, and I'm so glad you're here. Let's take a stroll through some of the world's most astounding places, yeah?

Cheers,

P.S. I always love being your biggest cheerleader, online and in real life. If you'd like to share your work on Instagram, make sure to tag @ThisWritingDesk and #WildernessWatercolorClub!

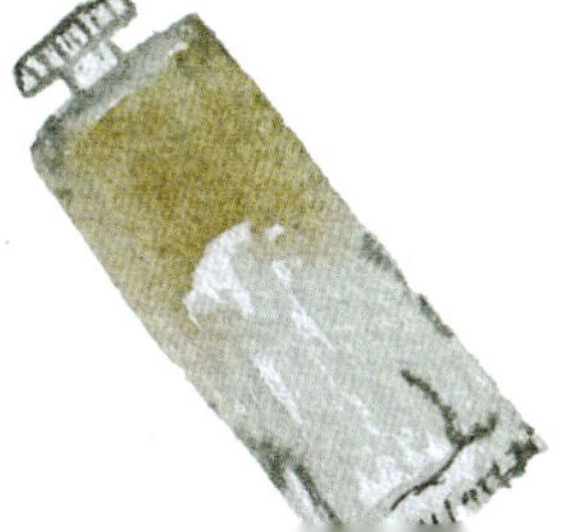

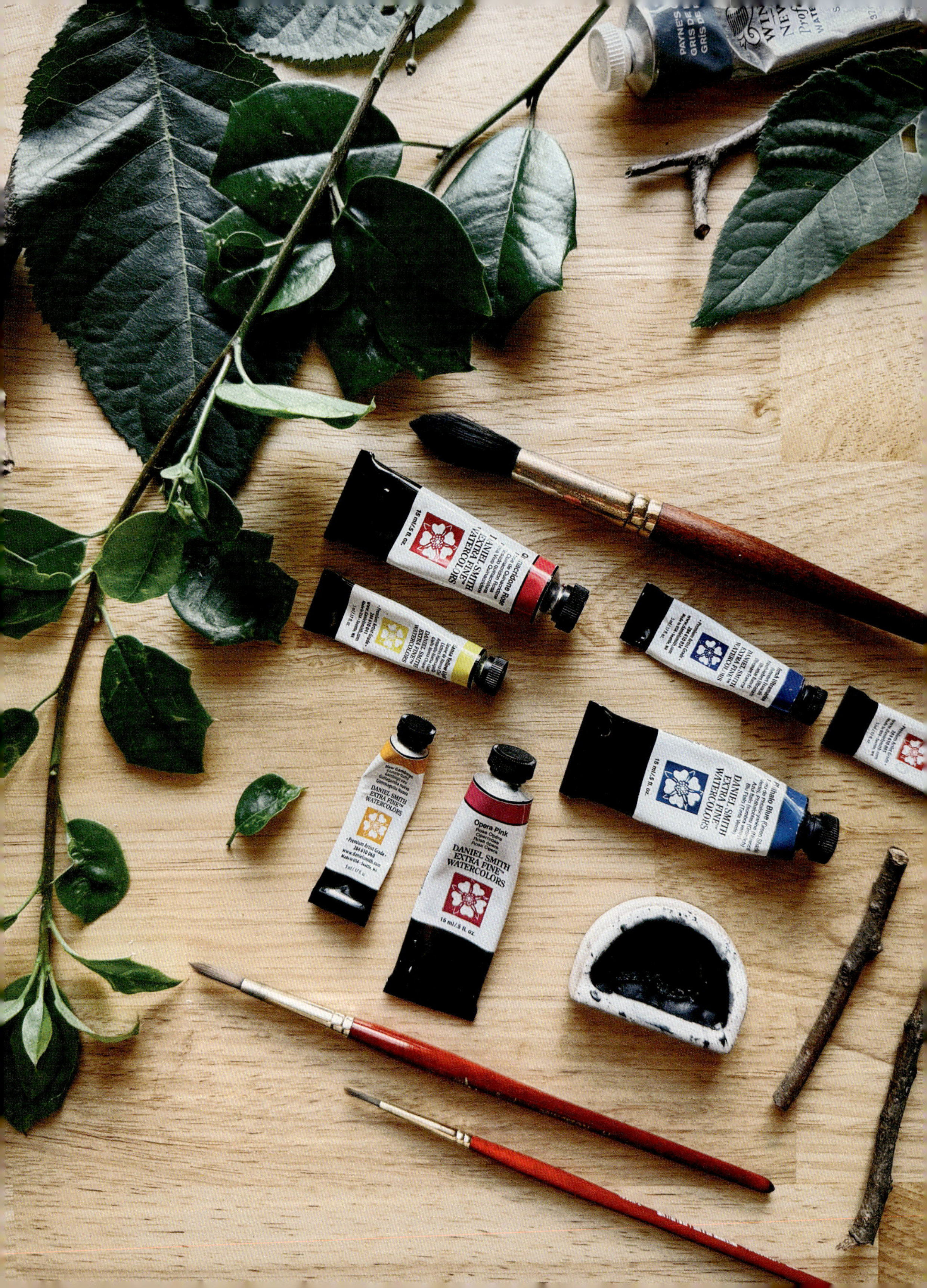

getting started

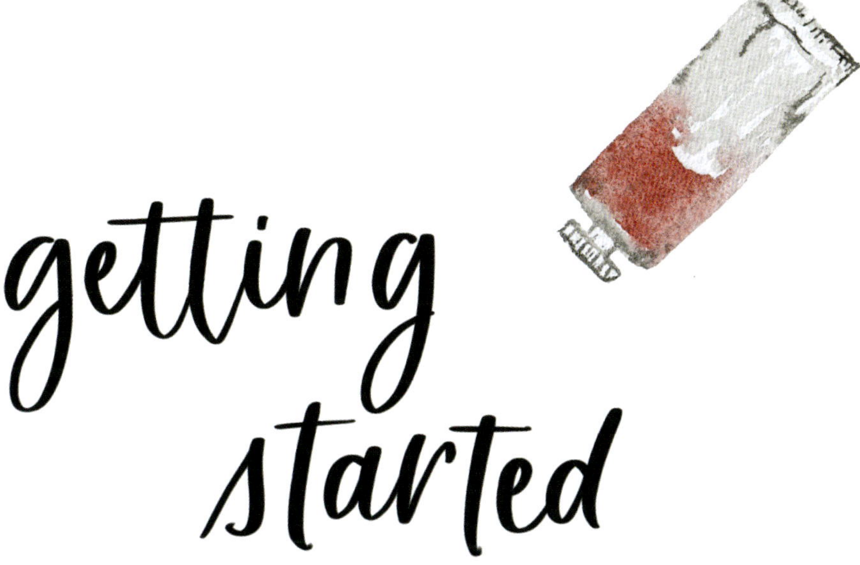

"If you hear a voice within you say, 'You cannot paint,' then by all means paint, and that voice will be silenced."

— Vincent Van Gogh

Still not sure where to start? That's why I'm here! Before diving into the projects, let's take a look at the supplies and techniques you'll need to prepare for the adventures ahead. This chapter explores watercolor concepts and tools that will be referenced throughout the rest of the book, so if you're ever confused, these pages hold a treasure trove of helpful information.

Oh, before you go, remember you can always find wonder and joy in creativity wherever your skills are, no matter what supplies you're using (or not). This chapter is a resource, not a requirement list. Take what helps, leave behind the rest, and trust that you're a real artist either way!

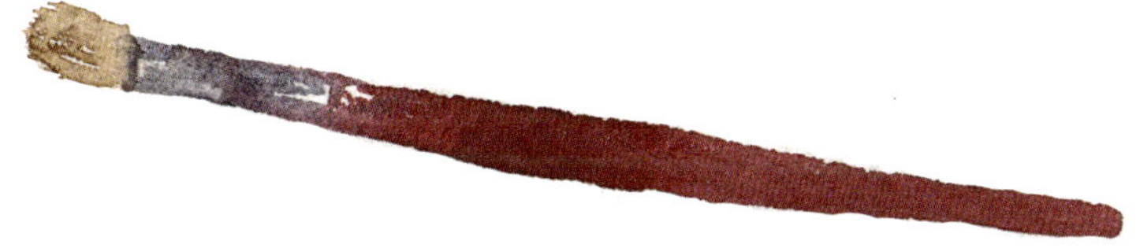

SUPPLIES

Which watercolor supplies you invest in can make or break your experience, especially when it comes to the projects in this book. There are two things you need to remember:

1. You don't need all the fancy supplies and tools to create a magical experience for yourself. Promise! You can have the most wonderful time even if you're using old, chipped crayons and bargain watercolor palettes.

2. Your creativity is a worthy investment because *you* are a worthy investment. You are absolutely qualified to use supplies that feel luxurious, like a gift, simply because it would bring you joy.

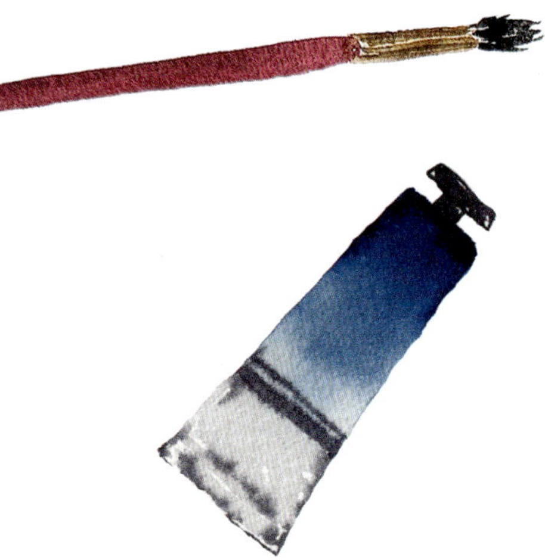

Paper

Making sure you're painting on high-quality watercolor paper can make a big difference in helping watercolor techniques actually work.

I highly encourage you to invest in cold-press (textured) watercolor paper, at least 140 lb (300 gsm). Student-grade quality (made from wood pulp or only a small percentage of cotton) will work okay if it's heavy enough, but artist-grade paper (acid-free, 100% cotton) is the best option, even for beginners.

Student-grade recommendation: Canson® XL® Watercolor paper, Fabriano® Studio

Artist-grade recommendations: Arches® Cold Pressed Watercolor paper, Baohong® Watercolor cold-press paper

Sketchbook recommendation: Arches Travel Journal, Hahnemühle

Paint

The quality of your watercolor paint also plays a role in how well these techniques and projects will work for you. High-quality paint will last a lot longer and make your experience feel more like a gift than a chore.

My recommendation typically is to purchase watercolor in tubes (where it's more of a paste), squeeze your colors onto a palette, and let it dry for up to 24 hours before use. You can also purchase pre-dried watercolor palettes through most well-known artist brands, which work well if you want a lot of colors in one set.

Either way, to begin using your watercolor, use a spray bottle or drops of water directly on the paint and leave for a few seconds before using a wet brush to activate and start painting!

For this book, I chose to use a limited palette (only a few colors) to practice color mixing and to demonstrate the vast range you can get without breaking the bank.

Student-grade recommendation: Winsor & Newton™ (WN) Cotman Series

Artist-grade recommendations: Daniel Smith (DS) Extra-Fine™ Watercolor, WN Professional Watercolors™

My palette for this book:

- DS Watercolor Essentials Set (French Ultramarine, Phthalo Blue [Green Shade], Pyrrol Scarlet, Quinacridone Rose, New Gamboge, Hansa Yellow Light)

- DS Opera Pink

- WN Payne's Gray

- Dr. Ph. Martin's® Bleedproof White™ (white gouache)

Brushes

Because watercolor is such a delicate medium, we want our brushes soft, flexible, and versatile—which is why I nearly always recommend a set of round watercolor brushes for beginners.

Student-grade recommendation: Princeton Artist Brush Co.™ Select™ Series

Artist-grade recommendations: Princeton Heritage™ Series, Princeton Neptune™ Series

My brushes in this book:

- Princeton Neptune size 12 round brush

- Princeton Heritage size 2 round brush

- Princeton Heritage size 6 round brush

- DIY **foliage brushes** and a DIY **masking fluid brush** (both old round brushes repurposed for various watercolor techniques)

Other Supplies

I also recommend a **ceramic or porcelain palette** for smooth watercolor mixing (a thrifted dinner plate works great for this!), paper-friendly tape to tape down your paper while painting (**washi tape**, **masking tape**, etc.), a **pencil**, an **eraser** (a kneaded or putty eraser is especially handy for sketches, which we'll talk in Starting with a Sketch [page 20]), **two cups of clean water** (one to stay clean during painting), and a **small towel**.

WATERCOLOR BASICS

Watercolor can be so intimidating—but the good news is that even the most complicated skills can be broken down into simple, doable steps! In this section, let's chat about the most basic watercolor techniques (wet-on-wet and wet-on-dry), then expand on them so you can feel prepared to creatively explore these iconic National Park sites.

> **Note:** Painting is a skill, and it takes time to build skill—remember that the more you paint with curiosity, the more you'll figure out how watercolor works best for you! You're doing a great job already, even if all you do is make a big mess.

Painting on Wet Paper

Also called the **wet-on-wet technique**, painting on wet paper is one of two main ways to use watercolor—and it's probably the most unique to watercolor, creating those characteristic blend-y washes. Any time you paint on wet paper, the paint will blur and spread across the water, at least a little.

The wet-on-wet technique can be tricky to control because it's inherently *not* in your control—making it simultaneously magical and frustrating! One helpful rule is the *more water* at play (in the paint, on your brush, on the paper), the *less control* you will have over the results.

So, if you want a light, **luminous** wash with plenty of random blooms and swirls interspersed with white space, use a watery brush with watery paint on watery paper.

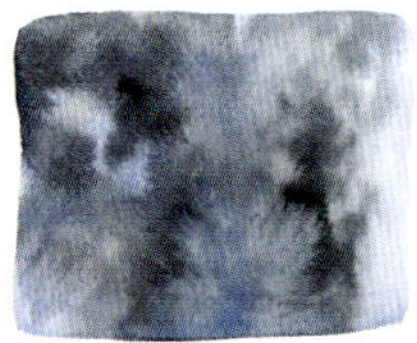

luminous, blendy wash

The wet-on-wet technique is perfect for creating a **gradient** with watercolor, which is a subtle shift from one color to the next. Start with a wash of clean water, then tap one color along the top ridge of the wash, allowing the color to gradually blend down, creating a **monochrome** (single color) gradient. Rinse your brush, load with a different color, and then tap along the bottom of the wash, allowing the second color to gradually blend upward to create a gradient with two colors.

> **Note:** This technique is so helpful for creating shadows along mountain ridges or colorful skies!

If, on the other hand, you want a little more control over the paint (to create a blurry but still recognizable subject or to keep the blurry paint in place rather than having it flood the wash), use less water on your brush, in your paint, and on your paper. To help with the visual, you can also think of this more-controlled form as the **dry-on-wet technique**—the paper is still wet, but the brush or the paint are significantly drier.

To help with the dry-on-wet technique, you can create what's called a **thirsty brush** by rinsing a brush with clean water, and then blotting on a towel to remove the excess water, leaving the bristles slightly damp, before dipping into paint that's not so watery. You can also dip into watery paint and blot the brush on a towel once or twice before painting, leaving just a bit of watercolor on the brush before painting.

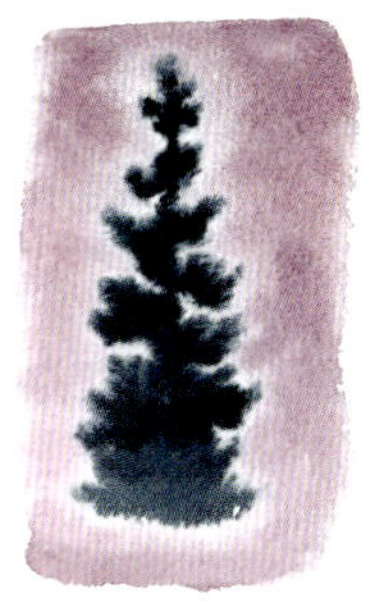

dry-on-wet marks to paint a blurry tree

Considering the consistency of the watercolor will also help. A commonly used resource for watercolor consistency is called the **tea-to-butter scale**—comparing the percentage of water in the paint by how alike it is to a common substance. The more watery the paint, the less control you'll have over it. Using watercolor, the consistency of tea will probably not be helpful for the dry-on-wet technique because it's so watery, but watercolor the consistency of butter will likely hold its shape a lot more effectively.

gradient steps

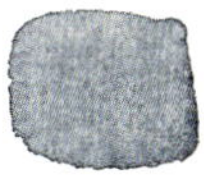 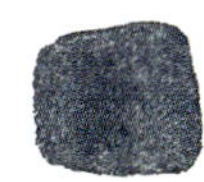   

butter (90% paint, 10% water)   *cream* (75% paint, 25% water)   *milk* (50% paint, 50% water)   *coffee* (25% paint, 75% water)   *tea* (10% paint, 90% water)

tea-to-butter scale

Painting on Dry Paper

The other most basic watercolor technique is the **wet-on-dry technique**, which is painting on dry paper. The wet-on-dry technique is characterized by defined shapes and textures—you have much more control over the paint, which can sometimes make it even scarier! The most important thing to remember when you don't have the buffer of a wet wash is that doable is better than perfect—that means embracing messiness, uncertainty, and the inevitability of mistakes.

The wet-on-dry technique can be useful for building texture, and the tea-to-butter scale can help with this too. Painting with watercolor the consistency of tea (very watery) will help you build light, subtle layers and texture (especially when layering shadows and crevices on mountains or rocks). In watercolor, layering paint over a dried wash is called glazing.

Painting with watercolor the consistency of butter (quite thick, not a lot of water)—also called the **dry-on-dry technique** or the **dry brush technique**—will help you build rough, gritty textures because the paint will skip over the dry paper. (This is especially useful for painting rocky textures over multiple layers!)

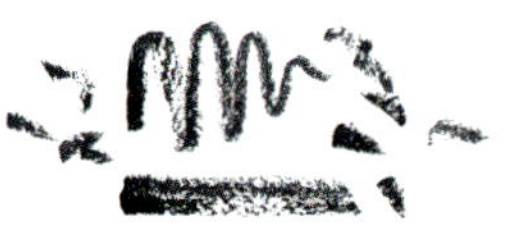

dry-on-dry texture

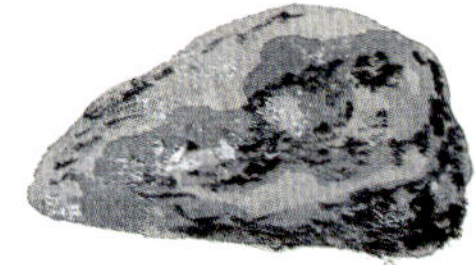

rocks with textured layers

You can also use the wet-on-dry technique to more naturally blend different layers on top of or over each other by **feathering** the paint down in long, wispy strokes of your brush on dry paper, creating a dry brush texture in the white space or into another layer rather than leaving behind a defined line. (Feathering comes in handy when painting sloping, grassy textures on hillsides or making a distant layer kind of disappear into the paper.)

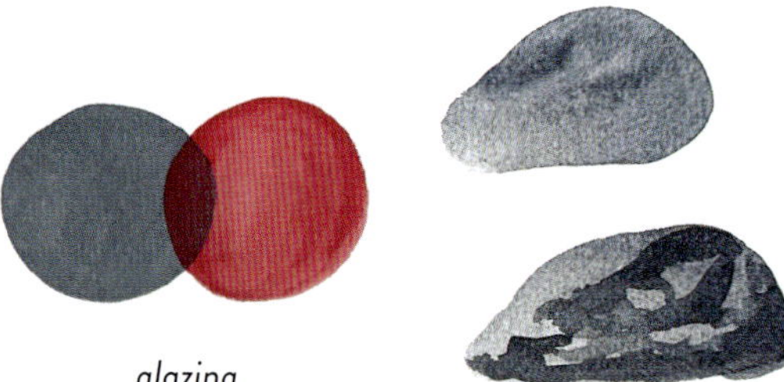

glazing

rocks with glazed layers

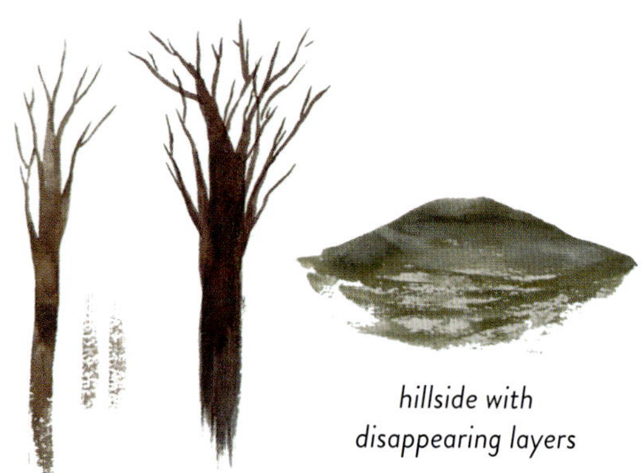

feathering

hillside with disappearing layers

Mark-Making

One common theme in this book is that **you are not a camera—you are a painter**! That means leaning into the natural human imperfections that make your paintings uniquely *you*. There's no better way to exercise curiosity with your imperfections than **mark-making**, a time-honored tradition among artists of all mediums. Mark-making is pretty much exactly how it sounds—a practice in making marks of all kinds, without always knowing what the end result is supposed to be. Your goal as an artist isn't to perfectly capture anything. It's more than good enough to *imply* detail through various forms of movement, texture, and color.

Sometimes, it's easier to begin with a few recognizable marks and then experiment with them—like **lines**, **S-curves**, and **C-curves**. Most shapes can be simplified into these three categories, so as you practice recognizing them in the wild and in your mark-making, you'll be able to easily paint more things! (A tip: Use more or less pressure on your paintbrush when making lines or curves to vary the thickness, and watch as that transforms your marks.)

S-curves especially are everywhere in nature (also called a zigzag, depending on the sharpness of the curves) and make for a great default shape when creating natural movement.

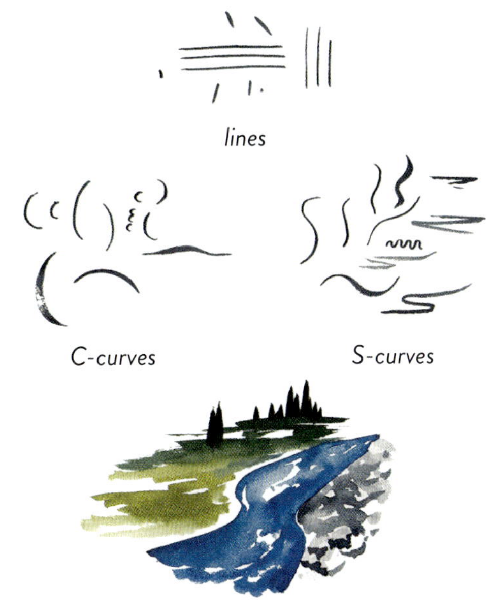

lines

C-curves

S-curves

rivers, mountains, trees

You can also move beyond these three basic marks and experiment more randomly—remember that the more you practice leaning into your imperfections, the more comfortable you'll be painting without a specific goal in mind. A personal favorite of mine is a **brush footprint**—a mark you can make by pressing down the length of your brush to get a rough outline! Very useful for distant tree shapes.

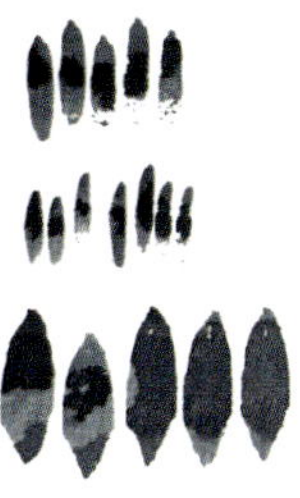

brush footprints

Foliage Texture

Especially when painting the scenic views in national parks, you need to be comfortable implying certain textures rather than painting individual subjects (like leaves, flowers, or distant trees) for more cohesive and doable scenes. Intentional mark-making can be an effective tool for mimicking the movement of various landscape elements without getting too bogged down in the details. One way to achieve a natural foliage texture is through **scumbling**, which is essentially making random marks close together through quick movements of your paintbrush. Depending on the kinds of small marks you make, the texture may look slightly different. Wispier lines will create a sharp texture, while more rounded curves will create a softer texture.

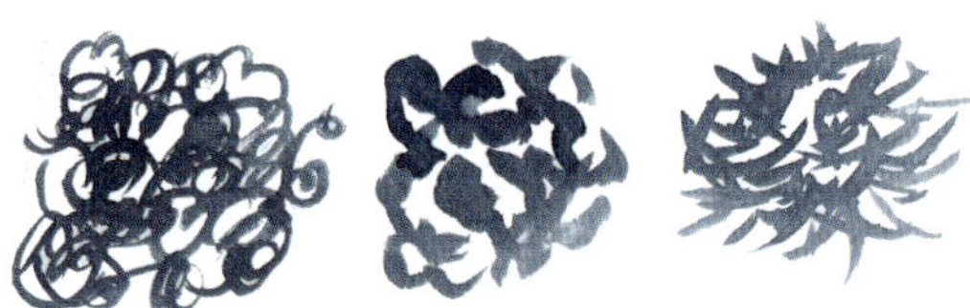

scumbling in three different ways

You can also create a foliage texture by creating your own **foliage brush**. Take an old round paintbrush (I used a Princeton Neptune Round Size 10, but you can use whatever you have on hand), and use a pair of scissors to cut up the bristles to various lengths. Load your brush with somewhat watery paint, and then tap on the paper to create a foliage texture. The texture may look different depending on how you move your hand—have fun, and experiment with it! The benefit of a foliage brush is its unpredictability. Because you have less control over the shape of the strokes due to the randomness of the bristles, you can more easily create imperfect movement and interesting marks. I like to make foliage brushes of all sizes (small, medium, and large), and while you can purchase them, my DIY foliage brushes get the best results.

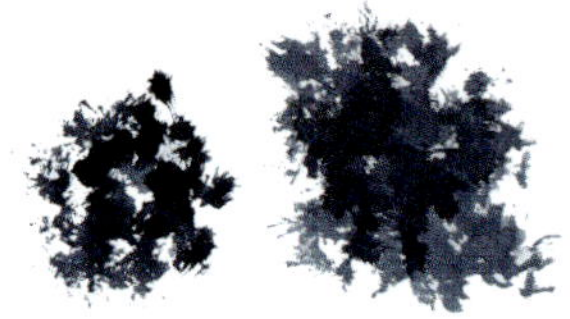

foliage brush marks

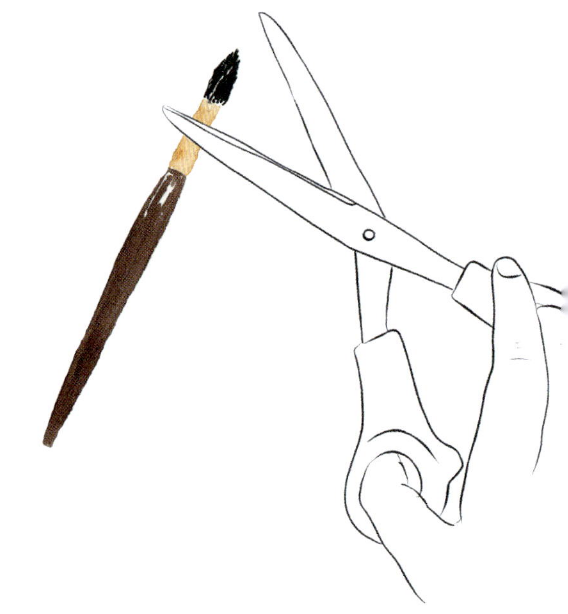

White Space

Another unique aspect of watercolor is its **transparency**—historically, rather than using white paint to create white or luminous subjects, you can carefully preserve or bring forward the white of the paper to shape your subjects. This can be an especially tricky technique, and it's worth noting that I often use white gouache (a medium similar to watercolor, except it's more opaque) to aid this process.

The most straightforward way to create light subjects with watercolor is the **negative space technique**—carving out the light by painting around it, leaving behind white space. Carving out negative space works with both the wet-on-wet and the wet-on-dry techniques.

If simply eyeballing where the negative space should be and painting around it feels too tedious, **masking fluid** is another useful tool. Typically, masking fluid is liquid latex (though there are latex-free versions), and working with it is notoriously difficult. I find the most effective way to use masking fluid is with an old paintbrush you don't particularly care about, designating it as your masking fluid brush. Get the bristles wet, then coat them with just a bit of liquid soap, ensuring the masking fluid can easily wash off the bristles when you're done. Then, dip the soap-coated masking fluid brush into the bottle of masking fluid, and paint over the areas you'd like to stay white on your paper. Let the masking fluid dry (usually at least 30 minutes) until it's tacky and not wet. Then, paint your layers as normal, and let them dry completely before rubbing away the masking fluid with your finger or an eraser to reveal the white space.

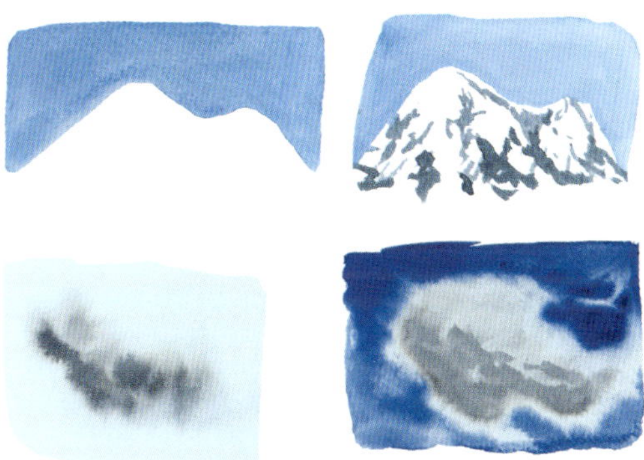

negative space examples

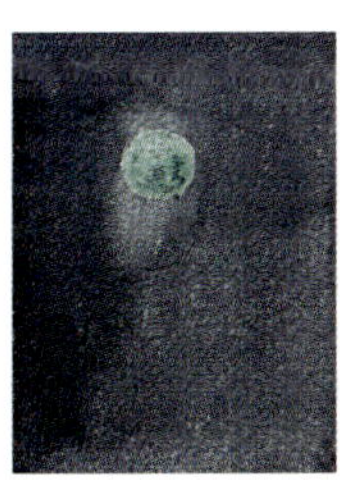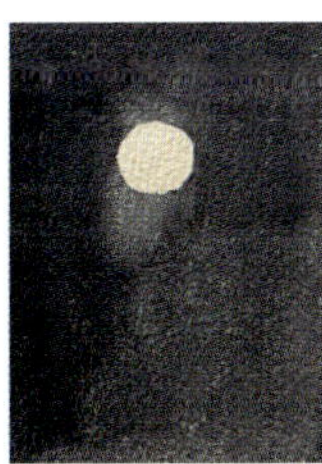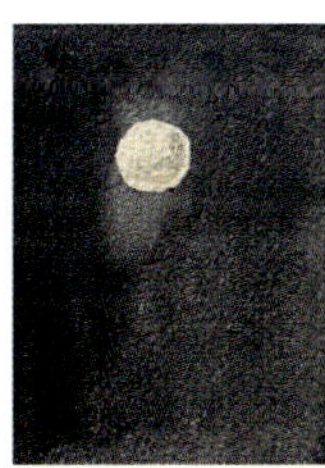

The masking fluid preserves the white space for the moon while painting the sky

Last, you can use a thirsty brush (page 11), and press firmly into your brushstroke on top of a wet wash to lift paint from the page, creating white or lighter spaces. This technique is particularly effective if you want blurrier white spaces or to create subtle texture inside an already wet wash of color. You can also press firmly with a towel to lift color from a wet wash.

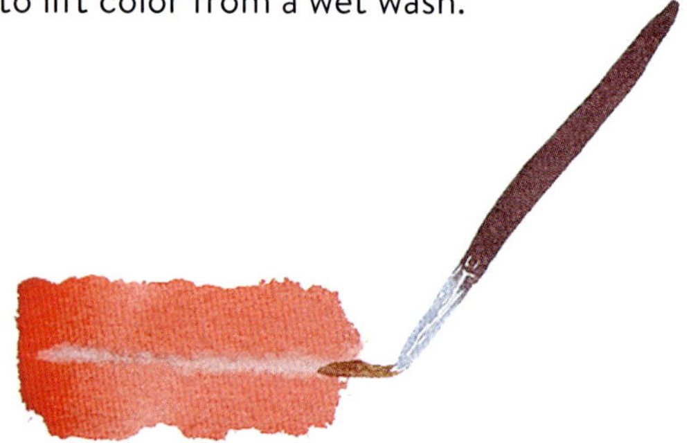

COLOR

Color Value

Color value indicates the lightness or darkness of a single hue—this will be very important when we talk more about layering and composition (see Composing a Scene [page 20]). The way to adjust color value with watercolor is by changing the water-to-paint ratio. More water in the mix makes the value lighter, and more paint makes the value darker. (This is also how you adjust the consistency of watercolor, as discussed in the tea-to-butter scale on page 11.)

The Color Wheel

Color theory is wild because with just three colors—especially when you start with the three primaries: red, yellow, and blue—you can mix hundreds of unique shades.

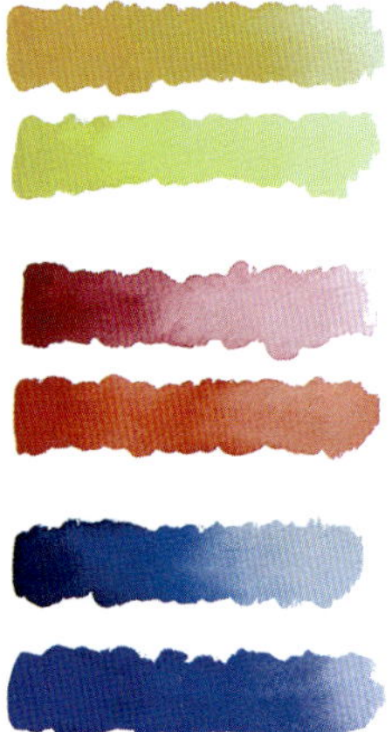

Start with two primary colors in about equal amounts to create the secondary colors.

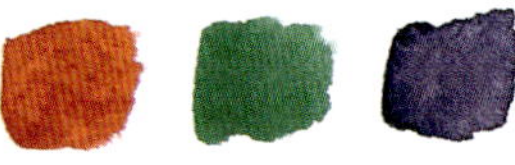

orange, green, and violet

Then, add a bit more of each primary to secondary mixes to create the tertiary colors.

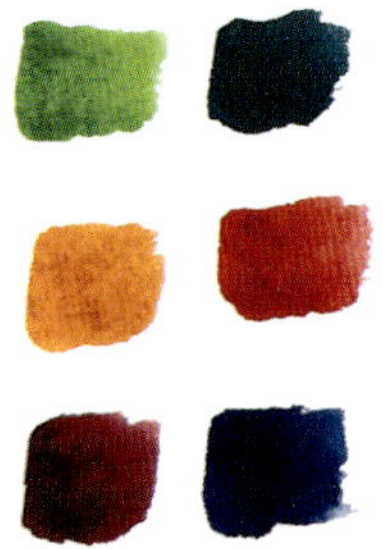

yellow-green, blue-green
yellow-orange, red-orange
red-violet, blue-violet

Put them all together to create a 12-color wheel.

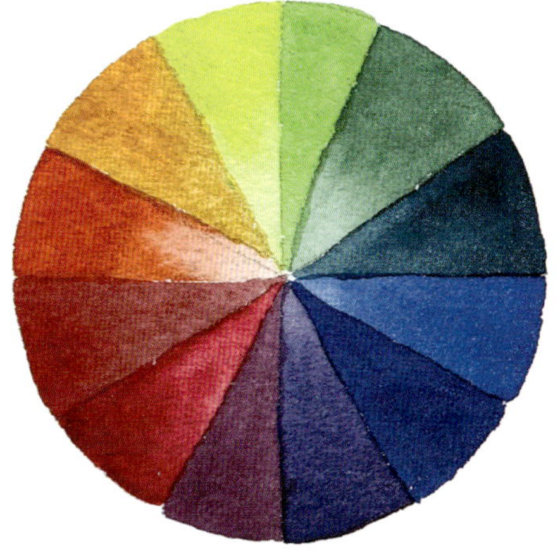

12-color wheel with Hansa Yellow Light, Phthalo Blue (Green Shade), and Quinacridone Rose as the primary colors

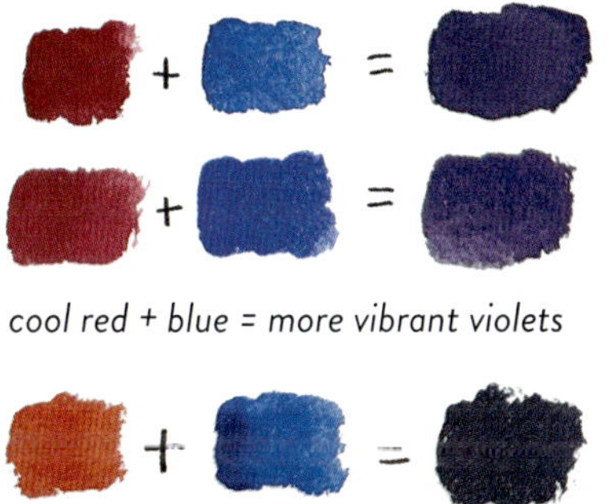

cool red + blue = more vibrant violets

warm red + blue = more earthy violets

Probably the most important tip to remember about mixing paint colors by hand is that not all primary colors mix the same. For example, depending on which red you use with which blue, you'll create widely different violets. That's why my palette in this book includes two sets of primary colors: a warm set and a cool set. Typically, warm primary colors create more earthy, muted tones, and cool primary colors create more vibrant tones.

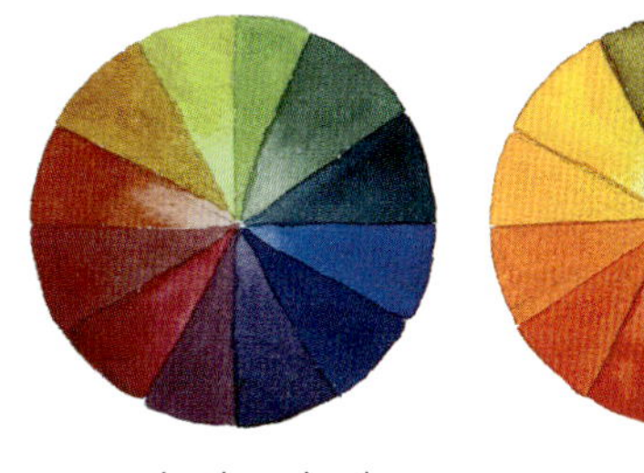

cool color wheel

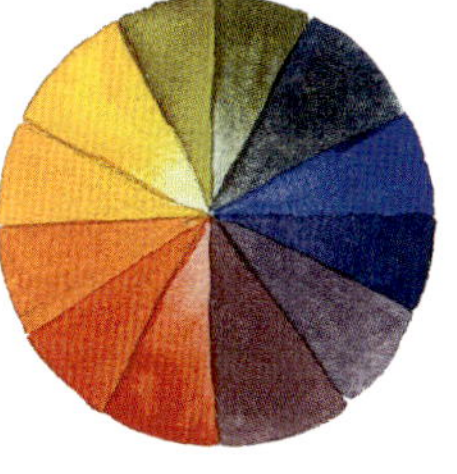

warm color wheel

Color Bias (Warm vs. Cool)

Let's chat about what I mean by warm vs. cool primaries—meaning, color temperature, or **color bias** (which is my preferred descriptor). Color exists on a spectrum, which often means hints of overlapping hues exist even in a primary color. When a primary color is warm or cool, that means it leans more toward one secondary color vs. another (rather than landing squarely in the middle of the two). That's why it's called a color bias—because the hue is biased toward one end of the spectrum. If we break down the colors into the overlapping hues, a warm or cool primary will consist of the main primary color plus a hint of a stowaway, which tips the scales.

In our limited palette, the warm primaries are New Gamboge, Pyrrol Scarlet, and French Ultramarine, because they all either lean toward a warm secondary color, and/or they have a warm stowaway.

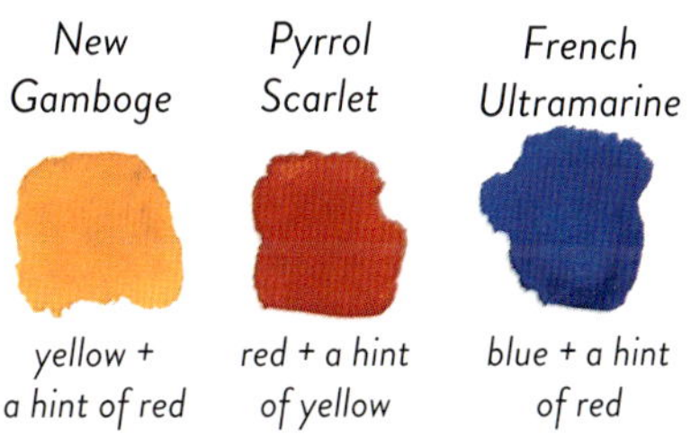

New Gamboge

Pyrrol Scarlet

French Ultramarine

yellow + a hint of red

red + a hint of yellow

blue + a hint of red

The cool primaries are Hansa Yellow Light, Quinacridone Rose, and Phthalo Blue (Green Shade), because they all either lean toward a cool secondary color, and/or they have a cool stowaway.

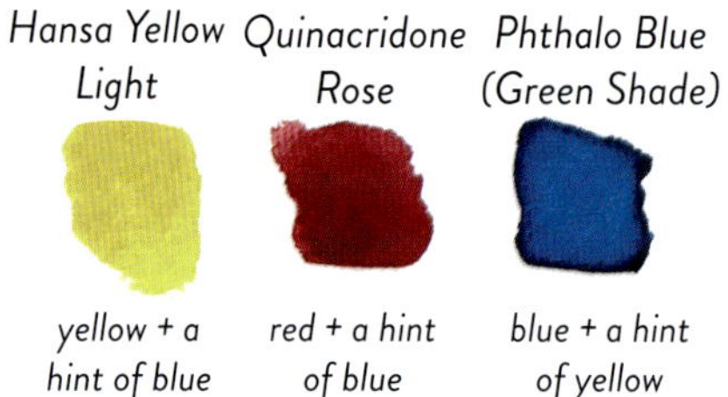

Two big things from this section: First, remember your creative practice is about you and what you enjoy—color mixing and matching can be quite tedious, so you should always feel free to paint with whatever colors feel fun and inspiring for you, even if they're not exactly "realistic"! Second, *you can absolutely learn color theory*—even just a few basics will take you a long way.

Over the next few sections, we'll go over color value and how that applies to watercolor painting specifically, the color wheel and basic color mixing with a limited palette, and color mixing/matching—including knowing your warm and cool tones and how they apply to mixing neutrals that'll make your national park scenes sing.

Color Mixing + Neutrals

Color bias plays a big role in demystifying mixing neutrals (browns, grays, etc.) with just a set of primaries. One general rule is that **complementary colors** (colors that are opposite each other on the color wheel) neutralize each other's hue. That rule also applies to the stowaways when mixing primaries that are strongly warm or cool. It's a bit like a math equation—if you want a vibrant mix, you have to make sure both the primary and the stowaway primary will play nicely together, otherwise you'll neutralize a bit of the hue. If you want a more muted, earthy neutral, you *want* the stowaways to be complementary and to neutralize the main hue.

Gauging color bias with the naked eye is tricky—if it's not tracking right now, don't worry about it! One way to quickly identify which color mixes can yield you the most interesting neutrals is by making a color chart. As opposed to a color wheel, a color chart gives you a method for mixing all the colors in various amounts without worrying about any specific order.

Start with three primaries (maybe mix and match warm and cool this time), and then make a 3 x 3 square grid (9 squares total). Assign each primary to a vertical and horizontal axis. Mix the colors according to which horizontal and vertical color aligns with each square. Each set of two primary colors will mix twice, so adjust the percentage each time, alternating which primary hue has the highest amount in the mix. Color charts aren't about creating exact measurements—they're about experimenting with your palette and discovering all sorts of interesting hues you might not have stumbled on otherwise! You can make the chart as big as you'd like; adjust the grid size to the number of colors you're mixing.

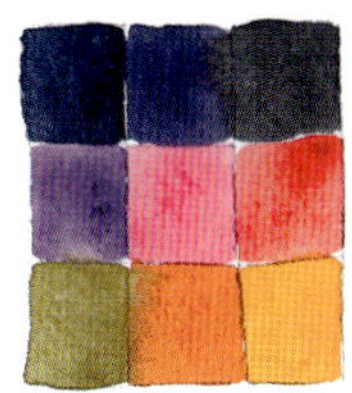

color chart with New Gamboge, Opera Pink, and Payne's Gray

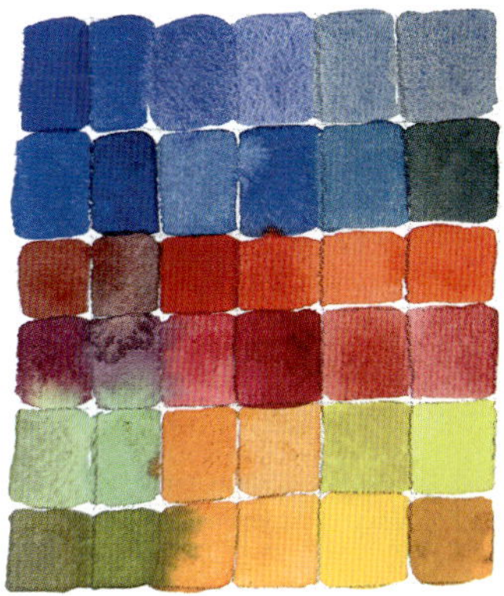

color chart with New Gamboge, Hansa Yellow Light, Quinacridone Rose, Pyrrol Scarlet, French Ultramarine, and Phthalo Blue (Green Shade)

A couple reliable color mixes you'll use a lot in this book:

Pyrrol Scarlet + New Gamboge + French Ultramarine (in various amounts) to make **brown**.

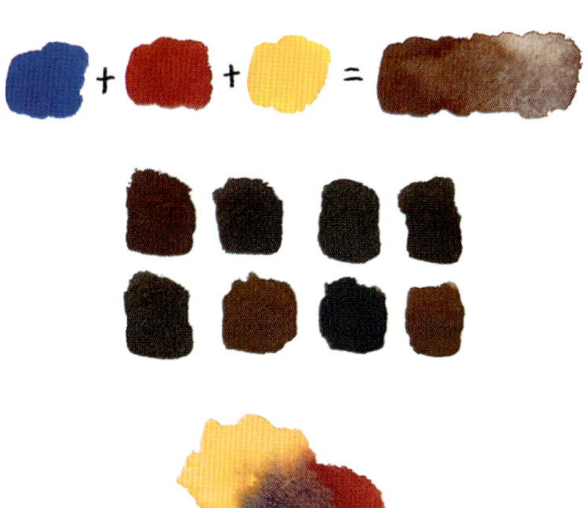

Phthalo Blue (Green Shade) + Pyrrol Scarlet to make **Payne's Gray.** (Although, I also keep my own tube of this so I don't have to mix it all the time.)

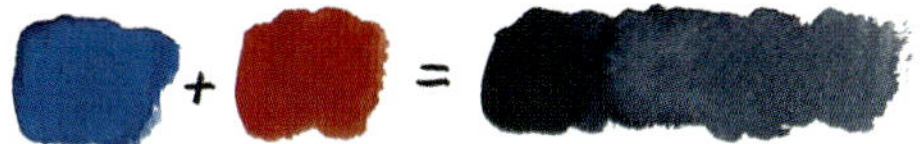

Phthalo Blue (Green Shade) + Pyrrol Scarlet = DIY Payne's Gray (deep, shadowy blue)

Any time you want some kind of neutral color, you can also just mix whatever's on your mixing palette, and see what you get!

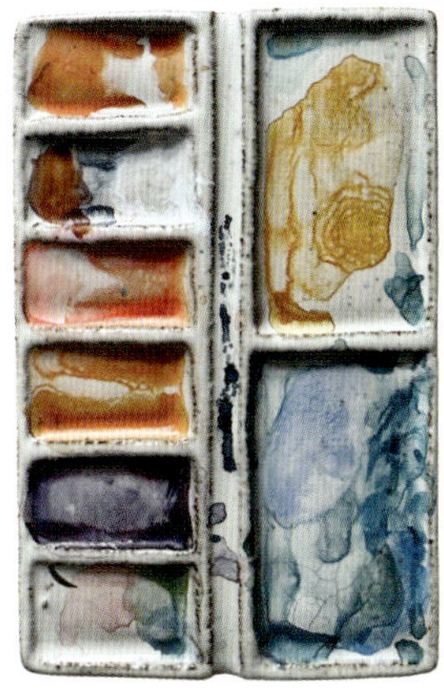

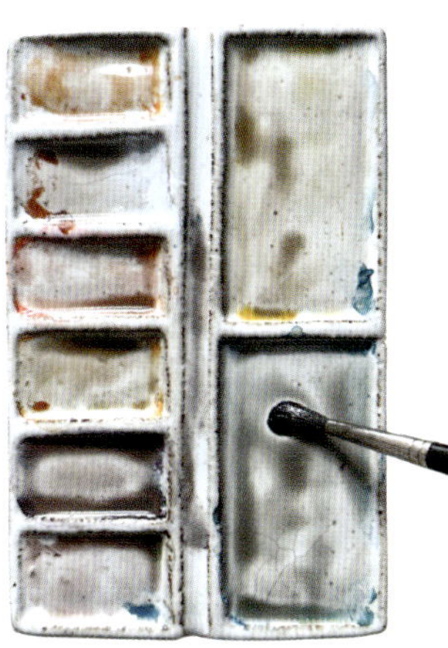

COMPOSING A SCENE

Along with our theme of *you are not a camera* throughout this book, before we dive into composition, remember that your main goal as a painter of national parks isn't accuracy—it's figuring out what you can *simplify* to make the scene both doable and recognizable as a *painting*. Trying to capture too much information and realism will actually make your paintings worse because they'll be confusing and cluttered. So, not only is it good for your soul to make a simplified painting plan—it's also good for your painting! On that note, let's take a look at some resources you can use to simplify these breathtaking national park scenes (and other landscapes you decide to paint in the future).

Starting with a Sketch

Contrary to popular belief, not every painting must start with a sketch. Though most projects in this book do have a loose pencil sketch for reference before painting, I find freehanding layers a wonderful way to let go of perfectionism and lean into the natural movement of your hands. I painted landscapes freehand for many years before I started adding sketches!

Still, beginning with a simple sketch can be a useful way to add a kind of scaffolding for your painting so you don't get lost along the way. I highly recommend keeping detail out of your sketches—basic lines and curves to separate layers or only sketching one or two subjects that require more detail will suffice.

Though most pencil lines will probably not show through the layers, make sure to use a light hand when sketching these projects. You can also use a kneaded or putty eraser to gently roll or tap along any pencil sketch to further lighten before painting. Once paint covers your sketch, it will be difficult to remove the graphite.

Layers

Landscapes can be reliably broken down into three different layers: the **background**, the **midground**, and the **foreground**.

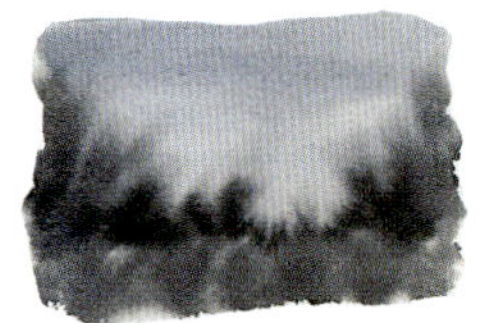

background   *midground*

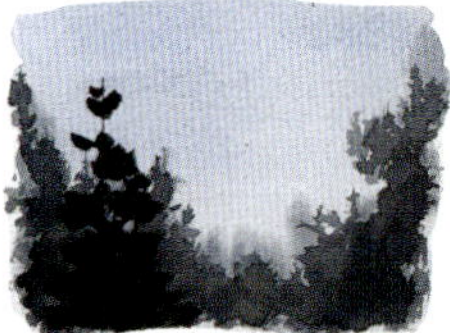

foreground

Typically, and this will be true for most of the scenes in this book, the background layers will be lighter and more muted with very little detail, while the foreground layers will be darker and more vibrant with more detail. Sometimes, that will mean *intentionally simplifying* the background layers to act mainly as a contrast to the more detailed foreground layer. You're not trying to prove that you can paint anything; your goal is to identify which layer is the star of the scene and focus your efforts on that, while sometimes simplifying other layers on purpose.

At times, even though the foreground is closest in the scene, it's not actually the star of the show—which means intentionally simplifying the foreground and adding the most detail to whichever other layer has the element you're trying to highlight with your painting. One good rule is to choose one layer to have the most detail, then simplify the other two.

Order of Operations

When beginning to paint a landscape scene with watercolor, there are certain rules to keep in mind so you don't accidentally get too dark or too detailed too quickly. Because of watercolor's transparency, it's much easier to start lighter and more abstract and then build detail later, to maintain light in your painting. Watercolor can easily become overworked, and unlike other mediums, you can't really just paint over it to start over! For that reason, I've co-opted a math term and created my own watercolor "order of operations" for general painting to help give you a place to start: light to dark; wet-on-wet to wet-on-dry; blurry to defined; and muted to vibrant.

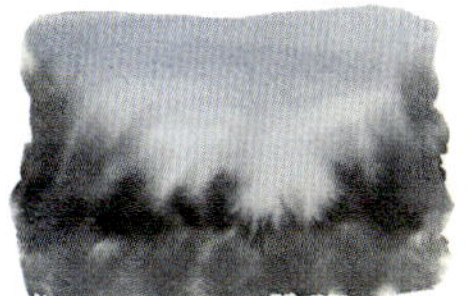

simplified background layer

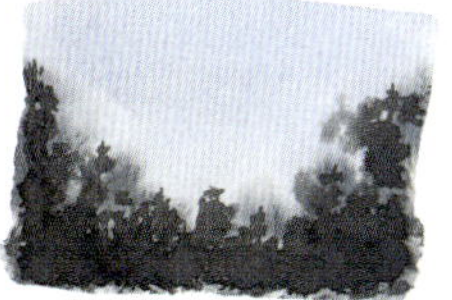

slightly more detail

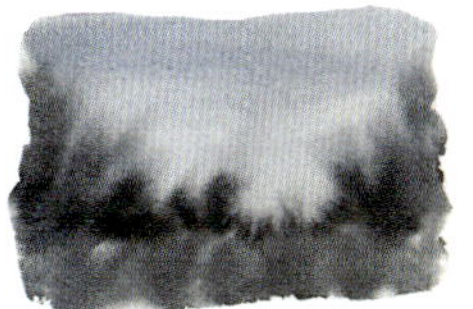

background layer is blurry and light value, wet-on-wet technique

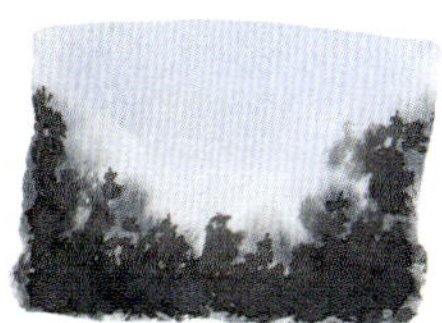

midground layer is slightly darker value, wet-on-dry technique

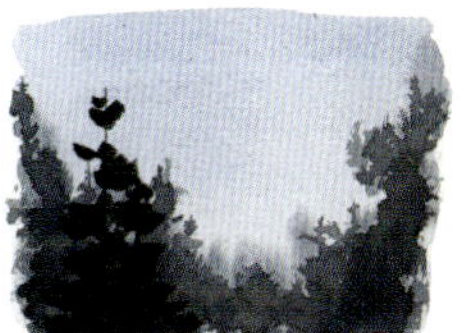

most detail in the foreground

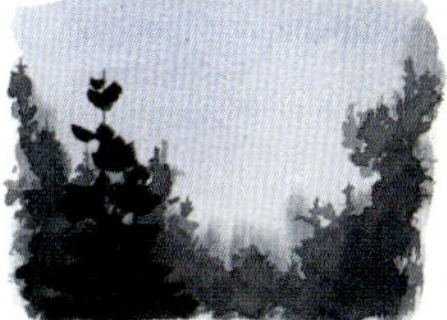

foreground layer is darkest value with the most detail

When building layers together in a scene, sometimes it's helpful to start with an **underpainting**. For the purposes of this book, an underpainting is a light-value wet-on-wet wash that gives a kind of abstract, luminous color and value outline for the rest of the painting. Typically, I'd start with whatever the lightest part of the painting will be for the underpainting, let it dry, and then gradually add detailed and more vibrant layers around the light spaces.

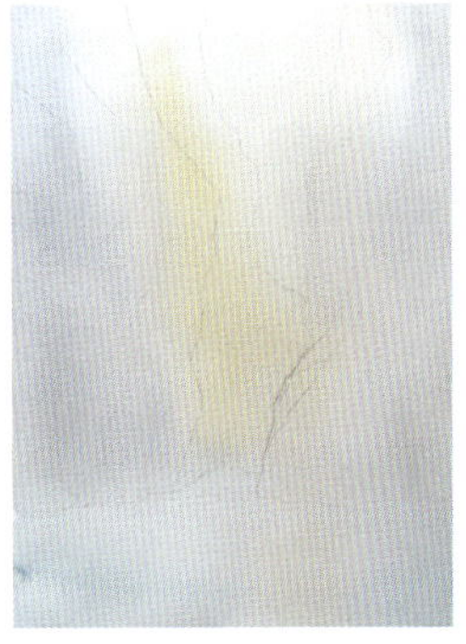
underpainting

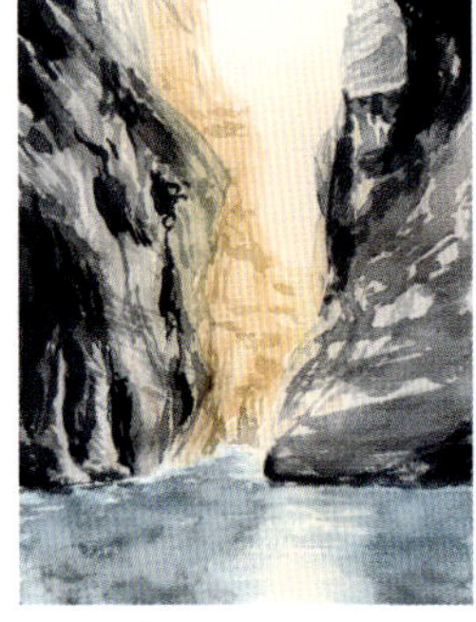
final painting

Composition Ideas

How the overall subjects and layers come together can play a big role in the effectiveness of a painting, and figuring out what looks "best" can be overwhelming! Here is a scenic composition idea that can help you determine where to place layers and elements in your own paintings.

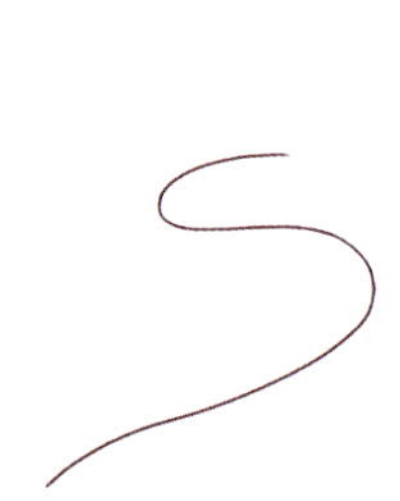

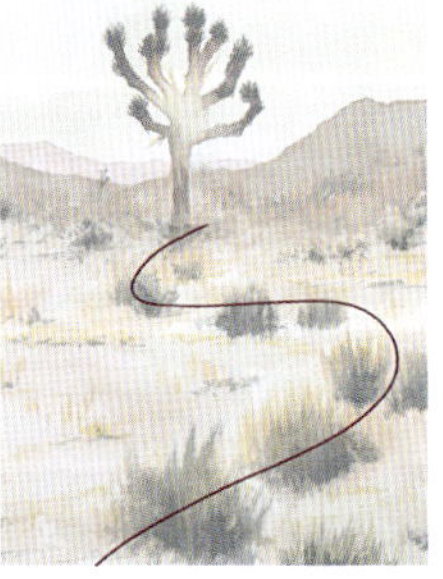

PAINTING NATURE

Like composing a scene, painting the landscape and wildlife elements characteristic in these national park scenes will be much more effective when you allow it to be simple!

One of the easiest ways to add an animal or plant to a scene is to use a **silhouette**, which is basically just the outline of a figure or form filled in with hazy, shadowy color. You can use one color for silhouettes, or you can mix multiple colors directly on the page by starting with one color, and then dropping another into the mix. This method can result in richer color variation.

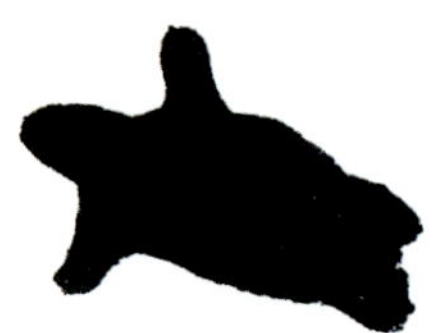

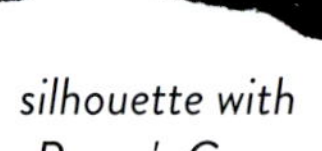
silhouette with Payne's Gray

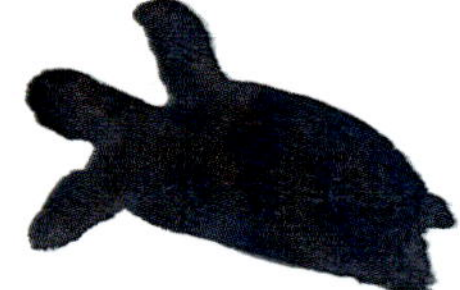
silhouette with Pyrrol Scarlet as a base, then drops of Phthalo Blue (Green Shade) to create a varied shadow

If you want the form to be a little more visible, you can still simplify using the order of operations and color values to block in the details without getting too bogged down. Start with a light-value wash of colors, let it dry, and then add a few darker shadows to sharpen up the form.

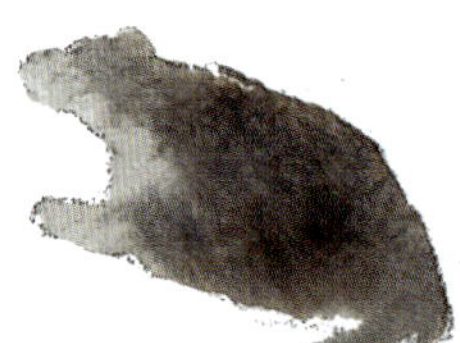
layer one: light, blurry wash

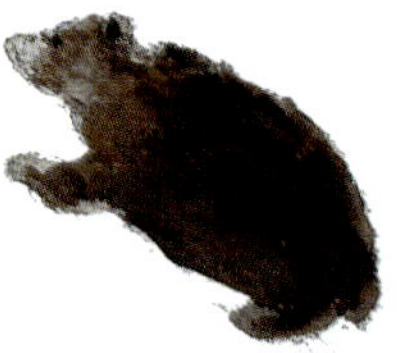
layer two: dark, dry details

Mark-making can play a crucial role in adding rich movement to layers without too much information. Remember that your goal with landscape painting is to *imply detail* rather than capture it with precision. Let grassy fields mostly be swaths of texture with just a few key blades of grass. Forests can mostly be foliage texture with a few treetops to bring them together. Even individual evergreen trees can mostly be random marks with sharp elements rather than individual needles. Try to identify the movement or texture you want to mimic and focus on that rather than letting all the extra stuff get in the way.

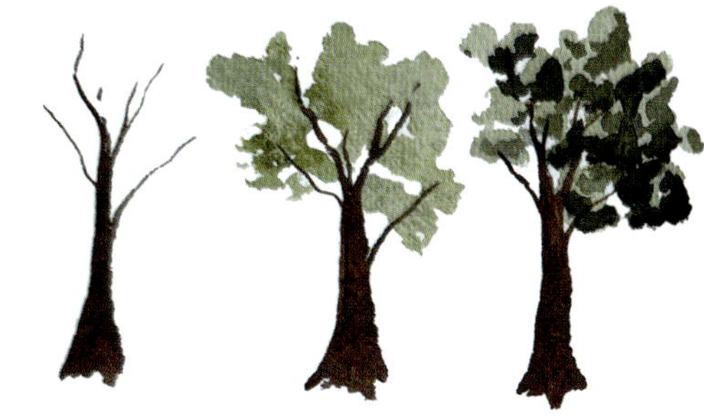

deciduous trees

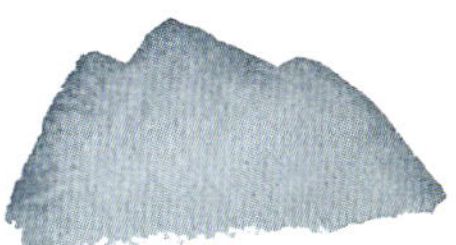
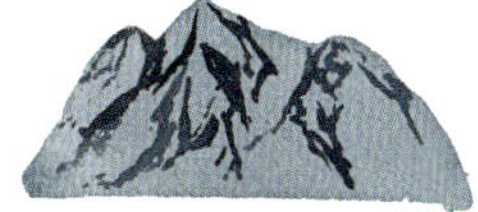

mountain crags and shadows

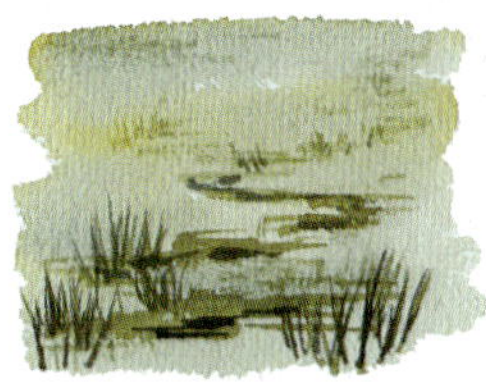

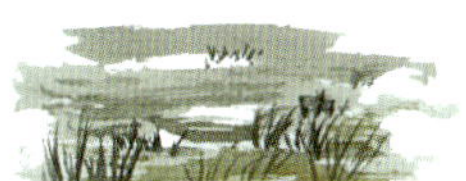

grassy plain

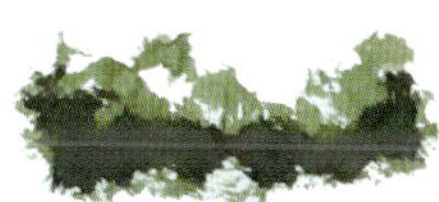
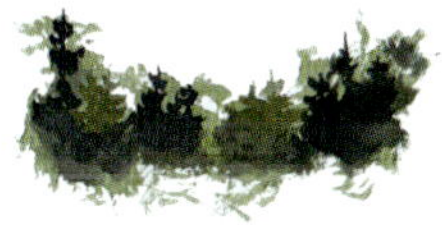

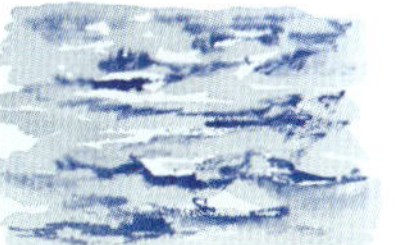

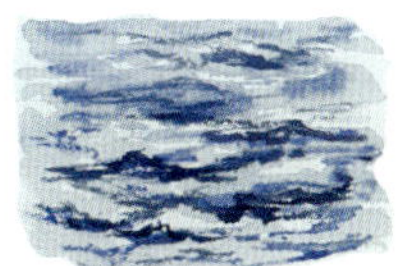

choppy water

Want some ideas for simplifying common landscape elements? Take a look!

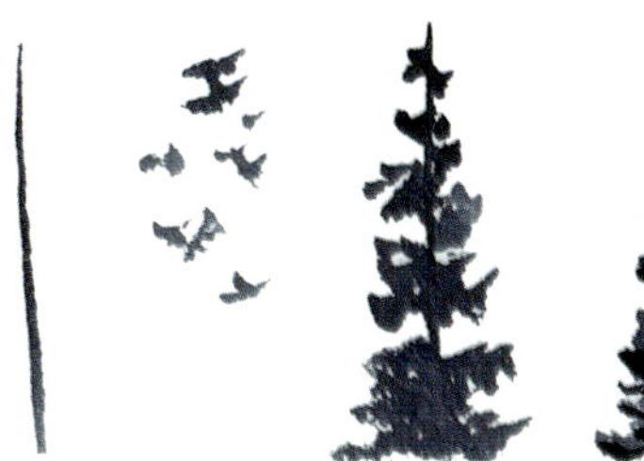
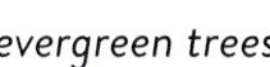

evergreen trees

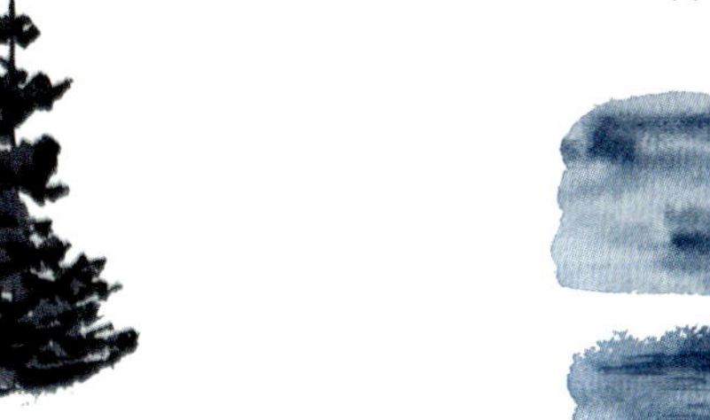

smooth water

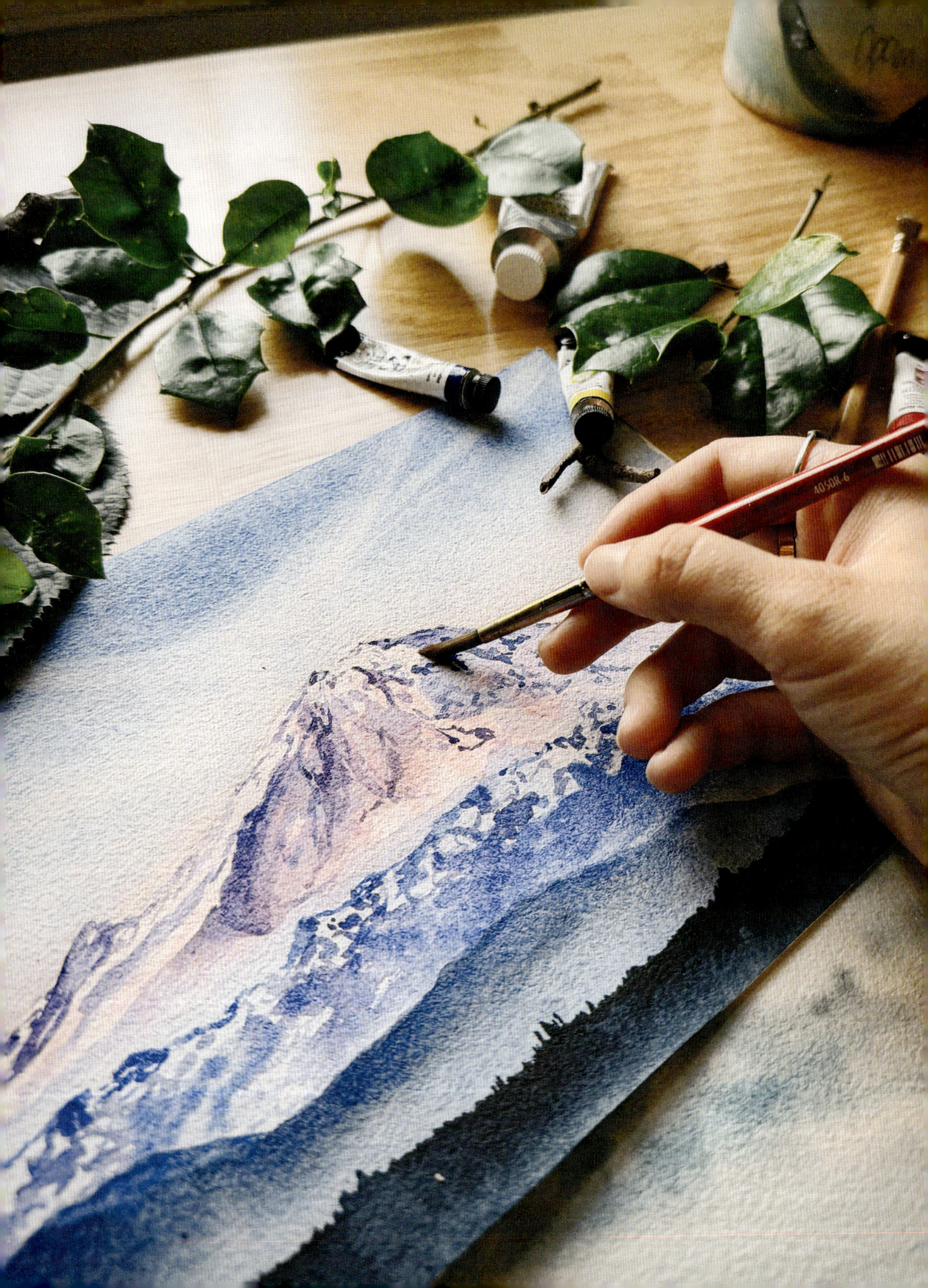

meandering on the mountain

Stillness and a sense of adventure go hand in hand when meandering through mountainsides, and America's national parks are full of some truly awe-inspiring views. Whether you're in the valley staring up at towering peaks or in the thick of the rocky layers, painting the national parks in this chapter will help you step into all kinds of creative discoveries.

When painting mountains with watercolor, slow layers of texture, color, and value are key—just like climbing a mountain happens one step a time, painting a mountain happens one stroke at a time. The middle may seem like a mess, but you may just stumble into some truly breathtaking scenes if you trust the process and let the mountains speak through you!

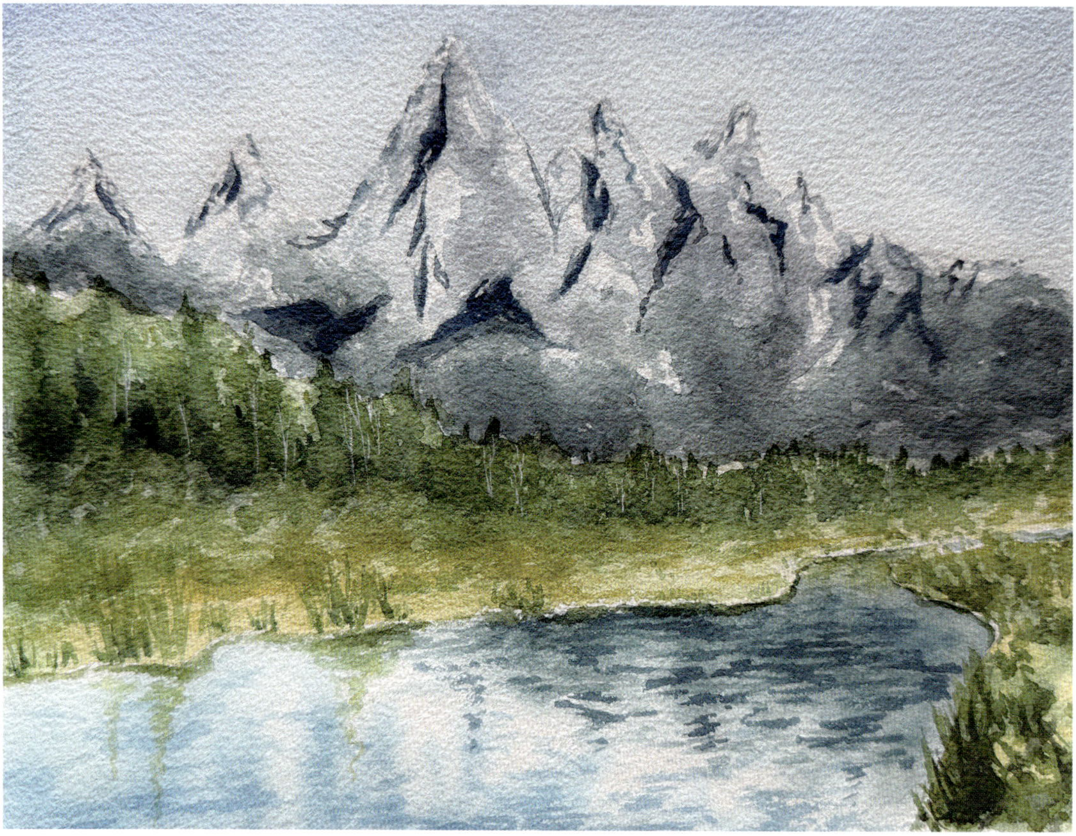

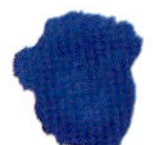

GRAND TETONS

BRUSHES
Round sizes 2, 6, and 12; Foliage brush

COLOR PALETTE
French Ultramarine, Phthalo Blue (Green Shade), Payne's Gray, New Gamboge, Hansa Yellow Light, white gouache

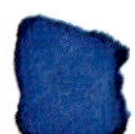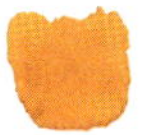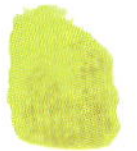

With sharp, craggy peaks that stand like a crown on the landscape, the Tetons are about as iconic as it gets when it comes to famous mountains in the United States. Let's practice melding contrasting textures and layers into one cohesive scene, seemingly straight out of a fairytale.

STEP 1: THE SKETCH

First, sketch the scene with the iconic craggy peaks in the background, nearly touching the top of the page in some parts. Then, sketch a river using two S-curve strokes (page 13) with a wide mouth along the bottom of the page, gradually growing smaller and closer together, meeting about one-third up from the bottom on the right.

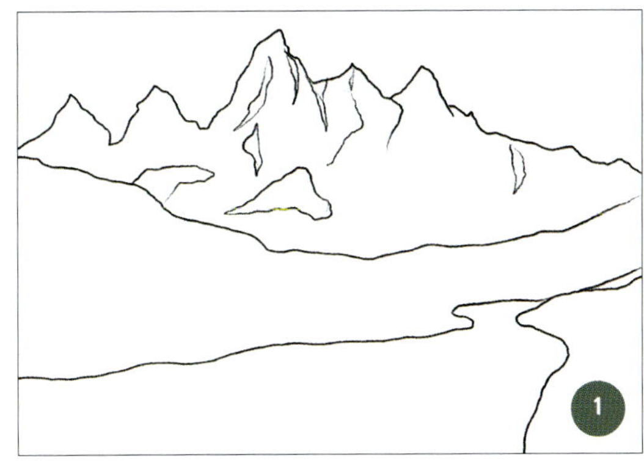

STEP 2: THE SKY

Create a watery mix of French Ultramarine and Phthalo Blue to get a more balanced sky blue. With a size 12 round brush, wet the sky with clean water, carefully painting around the mountain peaks. Drop in the watery sky-blue mixture, tapping clean water around some of the mountain peaks to create even more loose, airy blends. Let dry.

STEP 3: THE MOUNTAIN

Next, use a light-value (watery) mix of Payne's Gray with a bit of French Ultramarine to paint the base layer of the mountain with a size 6 round brush. Leave behind random areas of white space, especially around the mountain peaks. Make sure some of the negative space marks (page 15) are long, skinny, and sideways, though not all of them need to look like that. While still wet, tap in a few drops of watery Payne's Gray (without the French Ultramarine) for added color variation in the layer.

(continued)

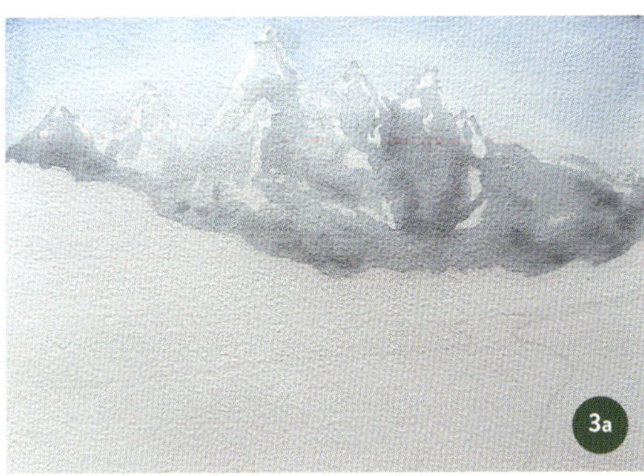

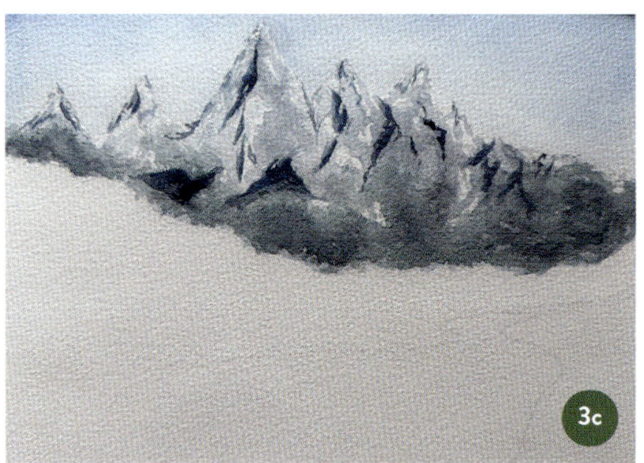

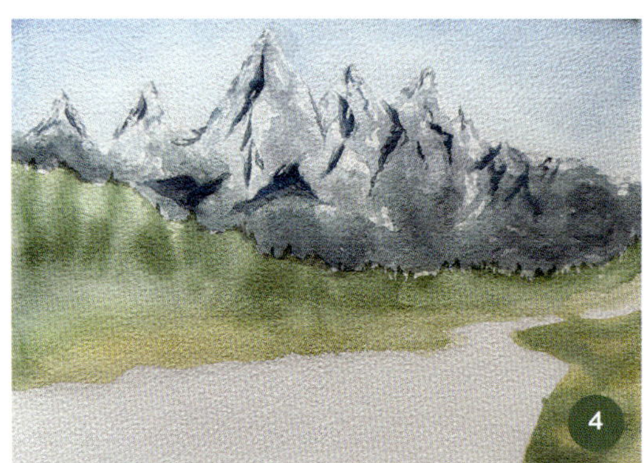

While the page is still damp (doesn't need to be very wet anymore, but doesn't need to be dry, either), use a foliage brush to tap a forest green (French Ultramarine + Payne's Gray + New Gamboge) texture in a sloping curve along the bottom of the background mountain peak.

Finally, use a size 2 round brush to add contrasting crags and shadows to the mountain peaks. Start with medium- and light-value Payne's Gray, then grow darker. The darkest shadows give the mountain peaks their shape. Think skinny, jagged C-curves (page 13) at an angle with varying thickness, which you can change by using more or less pressure on your paintbrush (see Mark-Making [page 13]). Don't overthink it! It's a mountain—it's meant to look random and wild.

STEP 4: THE TREES

Now, paint a base layer for the trees and landscape below the mountain layer and by the river. Wet the areas around the river with clean water, then drop in various yellow-greens (more so by the river) and darker greens (closer to the mountains). You can mix greens using any combination of New Gamboge, Hansa Yellow Light, Phthalo Blue, and French Ultramarine that are fun and interesting to you. Use a foliage brush or the edge of a round paintbrush to create tree texture along the top ridge, where the green layer meets the mountain.

While still wet, you can also use a size 2 round brush to paint a few long, skinny strokes of medium-value green along the top left of this layer, to imply the shape of the evergreen trees contrasting against the horizontal movement of the grass below it. This layer is supposed to be messy! The point is to imply movement and color to build depth for the details ahead. Let dry.

STEP 5: THE RIVER

Moving onto the river, start with a clean layer of water in the river area, then use a size 2 round brush to tap in a mix of Payne's Gray + a small bit of New Gamboge (for a grayish green) along the right side of the river. Leave a jagged area of white space, then tap in the sky-blue mixture along the bottom left edge of the river. Because we're using the wet-on-wet technique (page 10), the colors may bleed together—most important here is to make sure there's still a bit of jagged white space to mimic a watery reflection of the snowy peaks. Use a thirsty brush (page 11) or a towel to lift any stray paint that covers too much white space. Then, while the river is still wet, tap in a bit of yellow green just along the top right of the river.

Let dry, then use the same watery colors with a size 2 round brush to paint subtle ripples on the river's surface. Use loose zigzag strokes. It's okay to be scared! You're not ruining anything! You can also skip this step if you prefer.

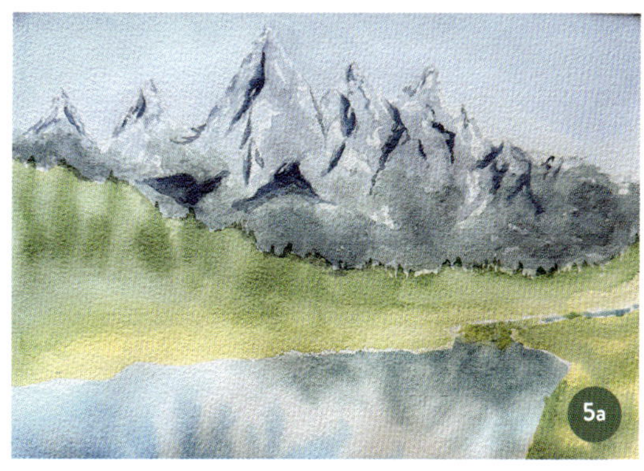

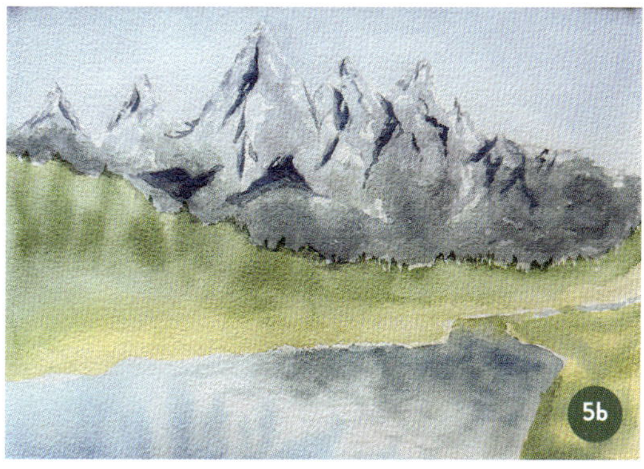

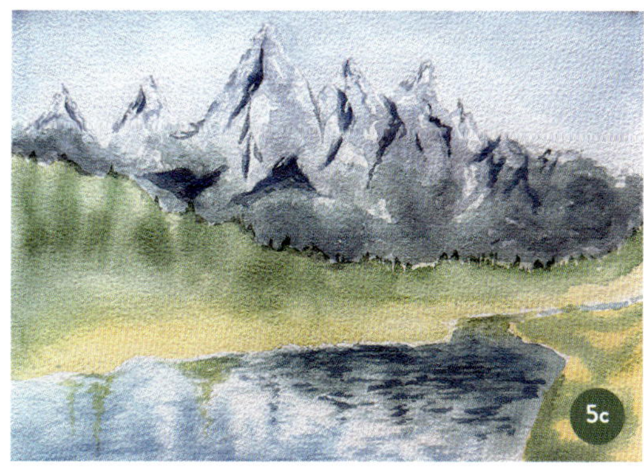

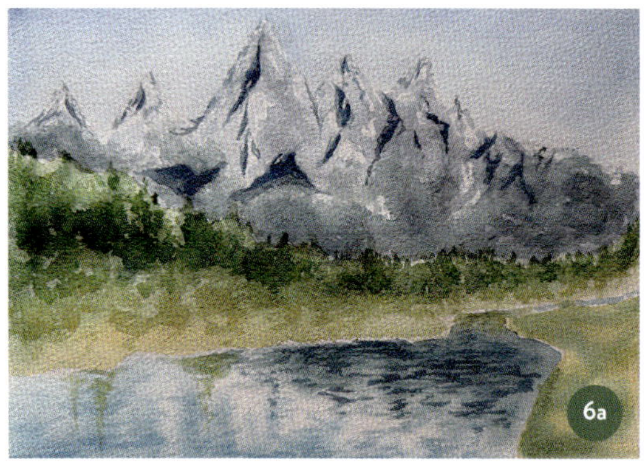

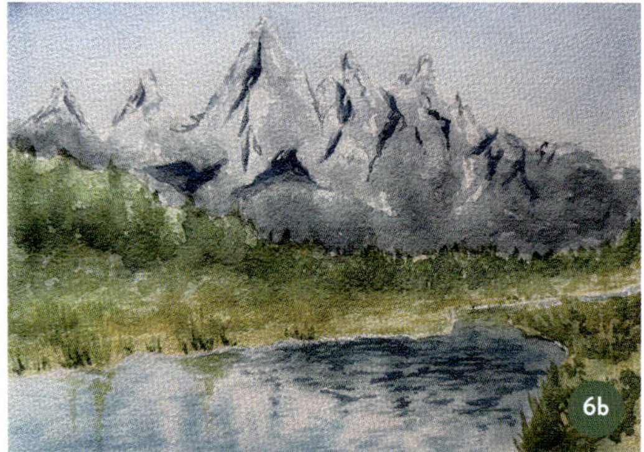

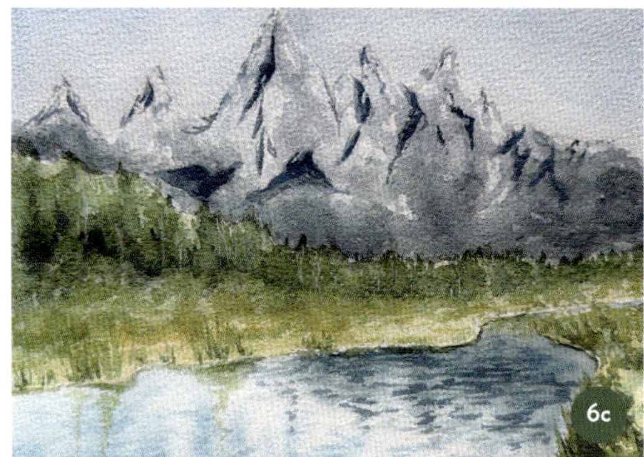

STEP 6: THE TREES, PART TWO

Last, add more texture to the landscape and trees. Use a foliage brush and various greens (more yellow and horizontal toward the river; darker, more green, and more vertical toward the mountain) to create a more defined grassy area and a tree line. Then, use a size 2 round brush to paint some quick, thin vertical lines near the river area and along the right side bank to mimic blades of grass. Remember that this doesn't have to look completely realistic—the main event in this project is the mountain, so it's okay to simplify the landscape down to mainly texture, value, and colors with just a few key details (like blades of grass and ripples in the water). Use thin strokes of white gouache throughout the trees to imply trunks, and add a few spots of Payne's Gray with the foliage brush to deepen the shadows in the trees. Then, add some final shadows with a size 2 round brush along the river bank.

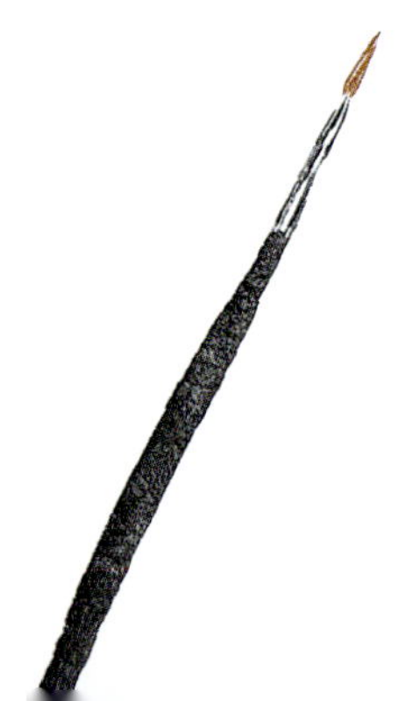

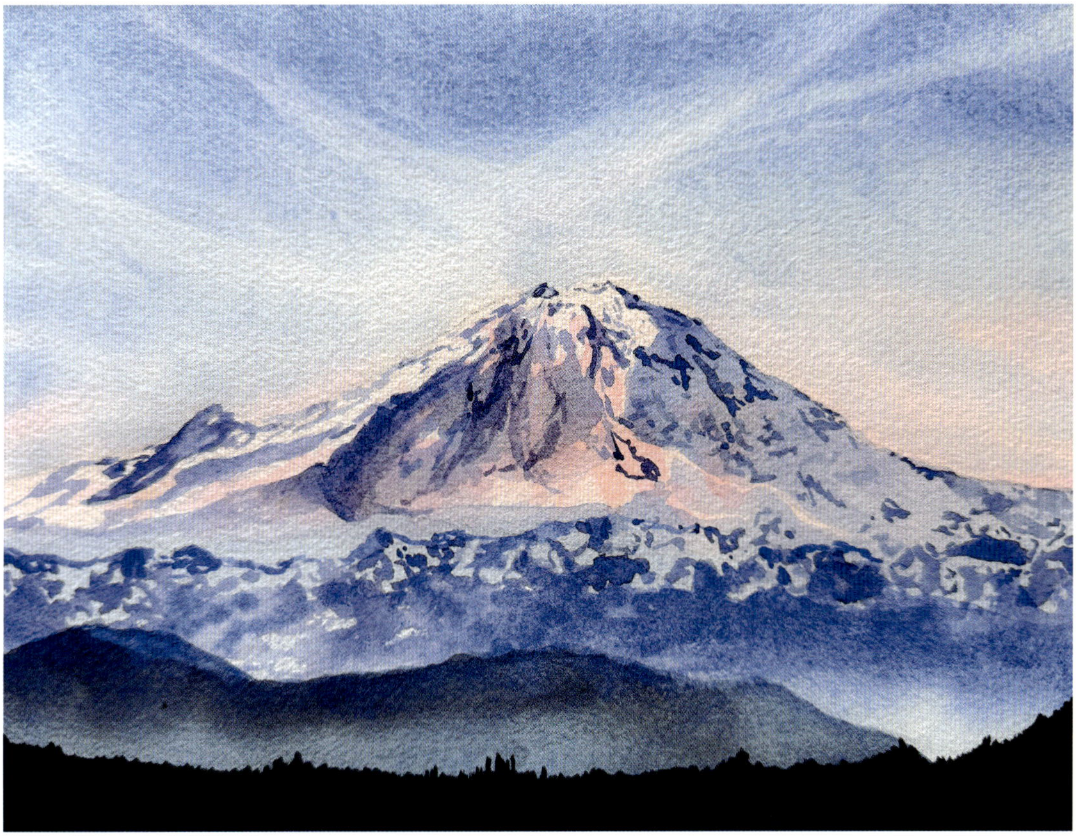

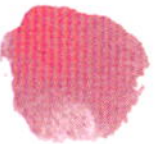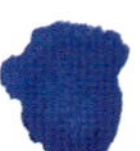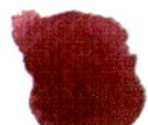

MOUNT RAINIER

BRUSHES
Round sizes 2 and 12; Foliage brush

COLOR PALETTE
Opera Pink, New Gamboge,
French Ultramarine, Payne's Gray,
Quinacridone Rose

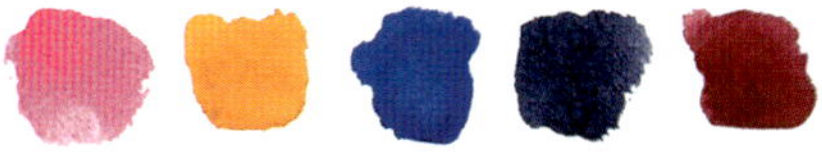

A beacon of the Pacific Northwest, Mount Rainier is another iconic peak that brings a sense of wonder and adventure to life. Let's capture the scene at sunset, where shifting light and shadows breathe life into the rocky layers. Simplifying here will be key—you don't need to capture every single detail to make the mountain sing!

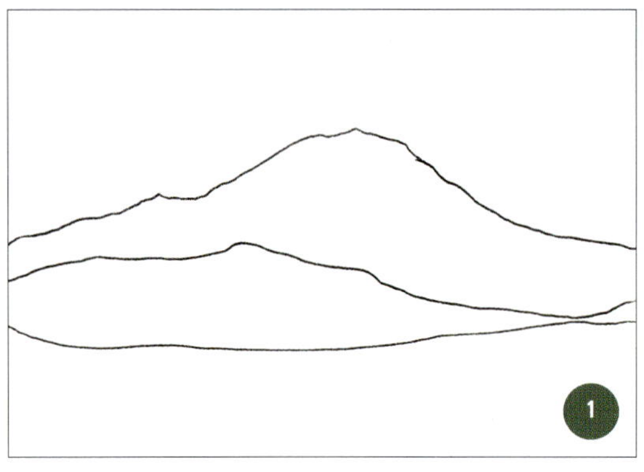

STEP 1: THE SKETCH

Sketch the mountain layers before painting, especially since Mount Rainier has a recognizable shape to its peak. Start with the main peak, slightly rounded and jagged, landing a bit off-center from the top third of the page. Then, sketch a smaller mountain ridge just beneath, and a final layer curving upward and sloping along the bottom fourth of the page.

STEP 2: THE SKY

Create a watery coral mixture with Opera Pink and a bit of New Gamboge (more pink than orange). Wet the top two-thirds of the page with clean water, then drop in the watery pink along the main peak, bleeding into the sky around the mountain area. Let dry, then wet just the sky area with clean water. Use a foliage brush to tap in French Ultramarine along the top of the page and fading down so it's lighter in value near the mountain peak. Rinse your brush, then use a thirsty brush (page 11) to push and lift soft white curves in the blue sky, adding texture and movement behind the mountain. Make sure small hints of pink are showing along the mountain ridge, either by adding in a bit more pink or by lifting away the blue. Let dry.

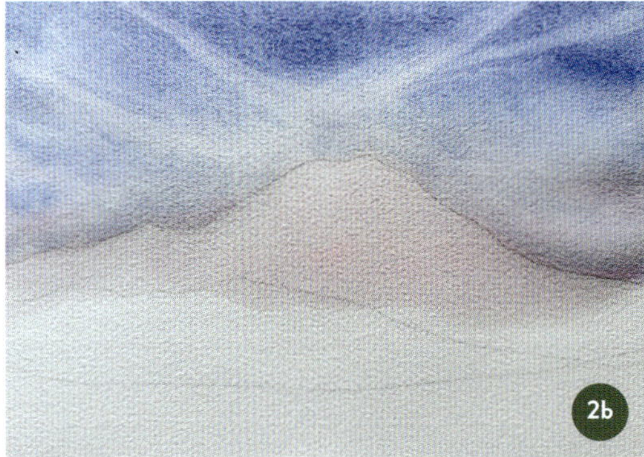

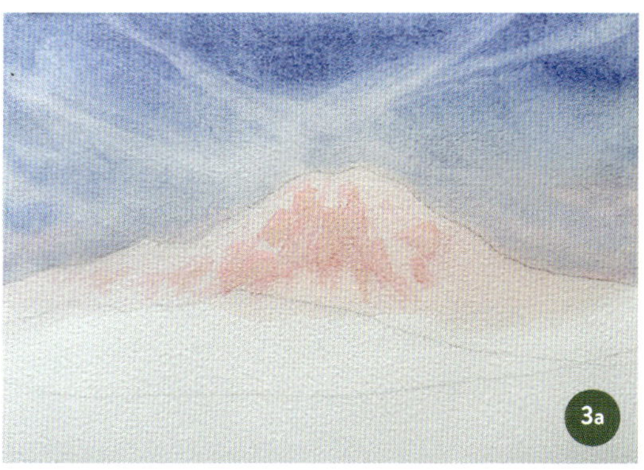

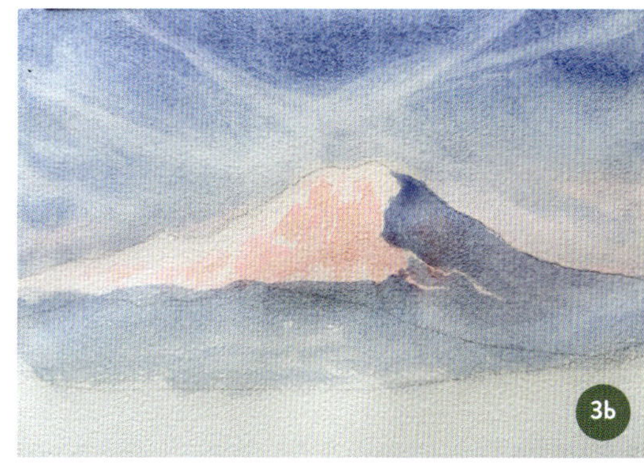

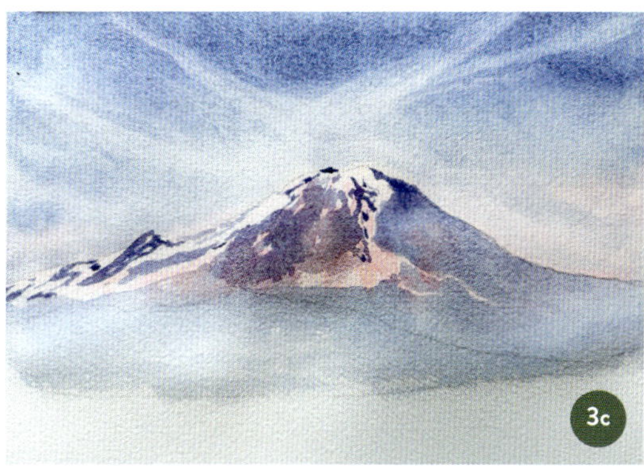

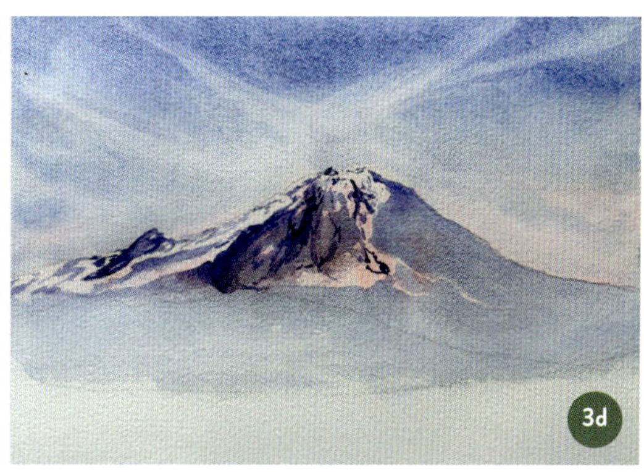

STEP 3: THE MOUNTAIN

Add slightly more paint to the coral mixture from Step 2, then use a size 2 round brush to create some subtle shadowy textures in the center of the main peak, making random marks and leaving behind bits of dry space. Tap in some watery New Gamboge while the pink areas are still wet for added movement.

Mix Payne's Gray and French Ultramarine to create a watery bluish gray color, then use a size 12 round brush to paint a craggy shadow coming down from the right side of the mountain and across the bottom, leaving the left side and some small veins of dry space pink and white. Use a dry brush (page 12) to feather (page 12) the bottom of the shadow layer into the page below. Add a bit of Quinacridone Rose to the shadowy blue mix to make it more of a blue-violet color, then use a size 2 round brush to paint more craggy shadows on the left side of the mountain, always ensuring to leave behind bits and pieces of the light layer beneath. Slope most of the shadows at an angle. Add more paint to the mix to create a darker value, then darken some of the edges of the shadows (while wet or dry) to give a shape to the ridges coming down from the mountain peak.

(continued)

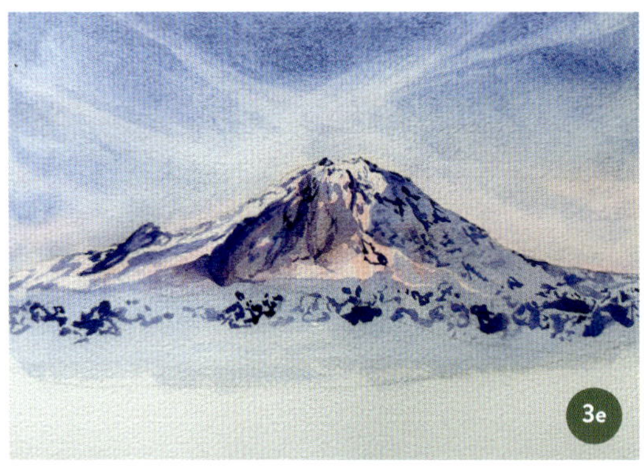 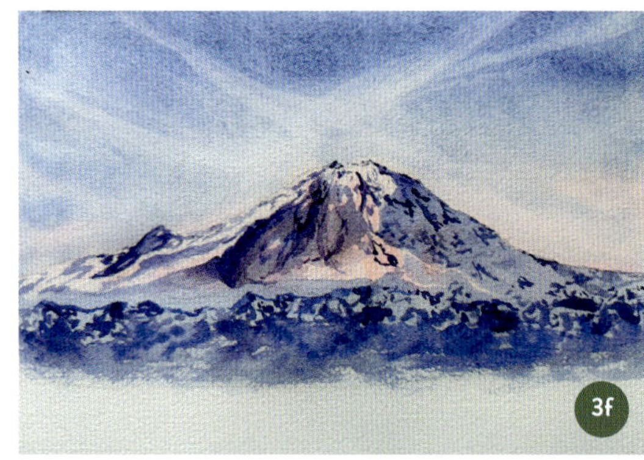

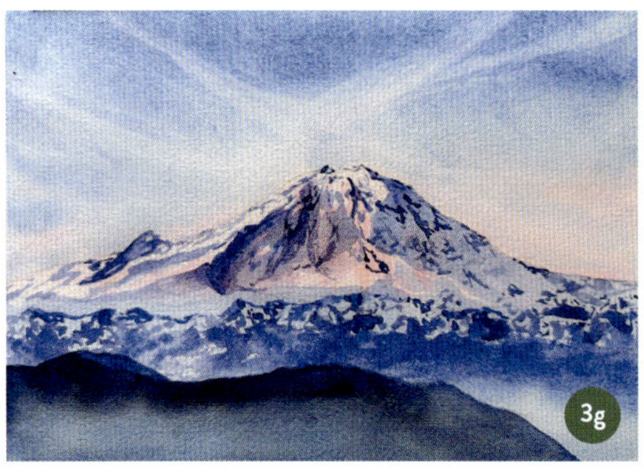 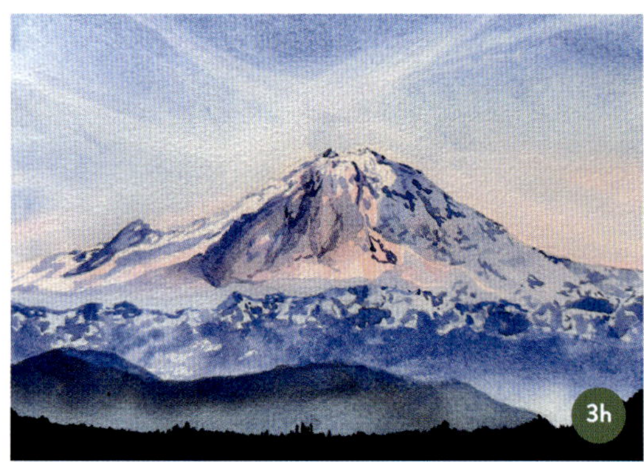

Then, use either a foliage brush or a size 2 round brush to add scumbling (page 14) marks along the base of the mountain with lots of dry space around the marks. Fill in the bottom of that mountain layer with more blues (that blue-violet mixture + French Ultramarine), feathering the layer with a dry brush into the page below. This is supposed to look textured and messy!

Let dry, then use a Payne's Gray + French Ultramarine mix to paint a third mountain layer coming from the left side of the page, varying in direction but ultimately sloping down, contrasting against the fading white space from the previous layers. Let dry, then create a final mountain layer with a dark-value Payne's Gray reaching to the bottom of the page. This time, use a foliage brush or the side of a size 2 round brush to create a subtle tree texture along the ridge of the final layer.

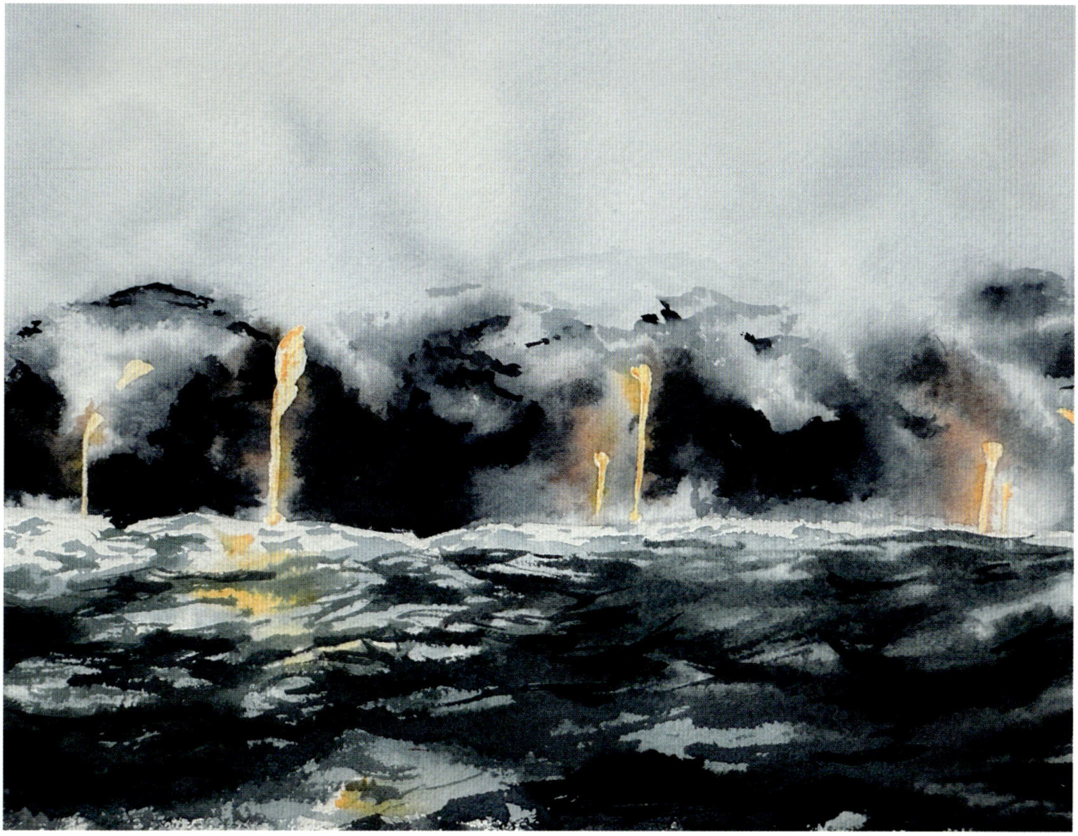

HAWAI'I VOLCANOES

BRUSHES
Round sizes 2, 6, and 12; Foliage brush; Masking fluid brush

COLOR PALETTE
Payne's Gray, French Ultramarine, New Gamboge, Opera Pink, Phthalo Blue (Green Shade), Hansa Yellow Light

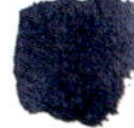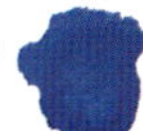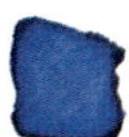

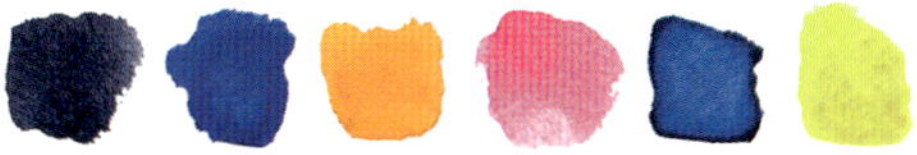

Note: This project uses masking fluid.

Though not quite as tall as other majestic peaks, the brilliant lava flows from Hawai'i Volcanoes National Park are just as mesmerizing, creating waves of steam flooding the rocks. Pay special attention to the values and layers in this project. By starting light and blurry, gradually building toward bright and sharp, we'll piece together this stunning scene.

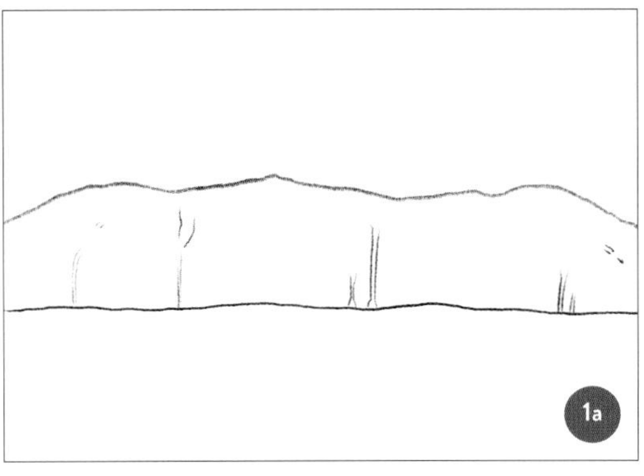

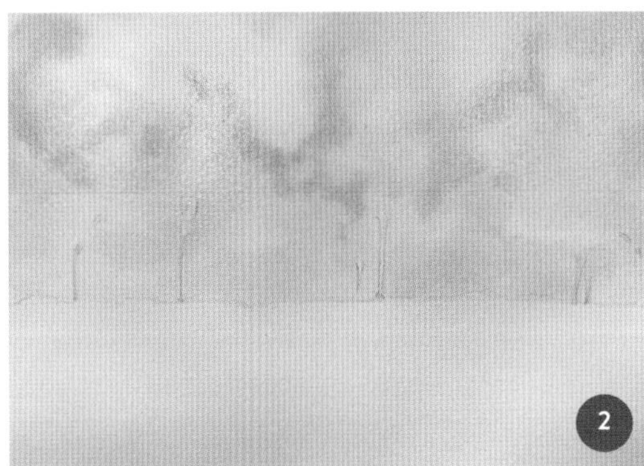

STEP 1: THE SKETCH

Start with a low mountain layer taking up the third center of the page, separating the sky and the water. Make the top mountain ridge slightly jagged. Sketch a few lines for thin streams of lava flowing out of the rock, a bit thicker and curved toward the top then flared at the bottom, as if the lava is hitting the lip of the rock before streaming down in a straight line.

Next, use your masking fluid brush prepped with soap and masking fluid (page 15) to paint the lava streams, reserving that white space for later. Let dry for 30 minutes or until tacky.

STEP 2: THE SKY

With a size 12 round brush, layer a wash of clean water across the whole page, then drop a quite watery mix of Payne's Gray + French Ultramarine into the wash, creating a subtle hint of muted blue for an under-painting. Let dry completely, then rewet the sky and the mountain with clean water. Mix a slightly darker-value (though still quite light) muted blue with French Ultramarine and Payne's Gray, then use a foliage brush in taps of swooping curves to create a foggy, cloudy texture. Leave plenty of the lighter layer beneath, especially in the top center of the sky and the bottom of the mountain.

STEP 3: THE MOUNTAIN

While the previous layer is still wet (rewet if necessary), mix a medium-dark value Payne's Gray (somewhat dark, though still a bit watery) and use a foliage brush to tap into the wet wash, especially along the bottom of the mountain. Leave behind tendrils of white space, using a towel or thirsty brush (page 11) to lift stray paint if necessary. Right now, we're creating the steam from the lava flows by painting the rock and leaving behind white space, all in a wet wash so it stays blurry! This will be easier to do if the Payne's Gray is a slightly thicker consistency and if the page isn't sopping wet (more water = less control). Leave this layer wet for now.

Create fiery orange mixes with New Gamboge and Opera Pink, then use a size 2 round brush to tap directly into the wet Payne's Gray around the masked lava flows. We want the lava to appear like it's glowing on the mountain, and adding an orange haze in this layer will strengthen that glowing effect! It's okay if part of the layer starts to dry—dried paint lines will just add to the interesting texture happening between the rock and the steam.

While this layer is still wet, add more paint to the Payne's Gray to make it darker, and use a foliage brush to darken some of the mountain, especially near the bottom. If necessary, rinse and use a clean foliage brush to blend some of the strokes into the mountain by tapping around the edges.

(continued)

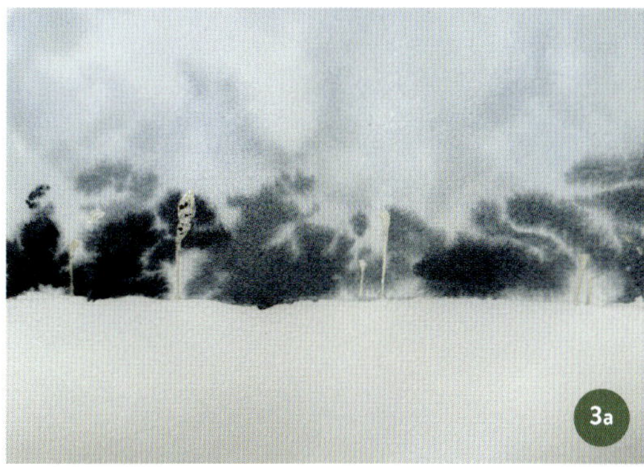

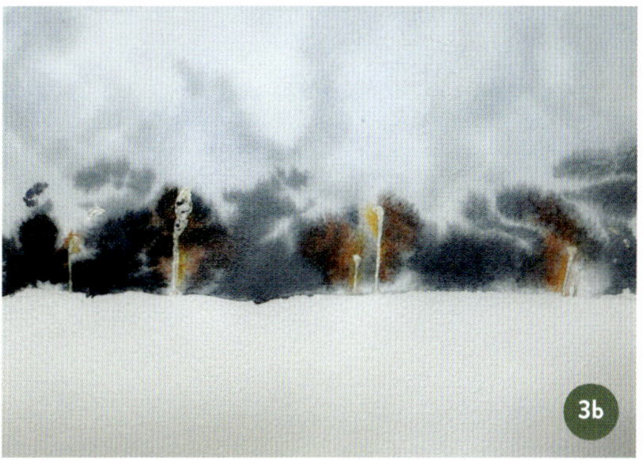

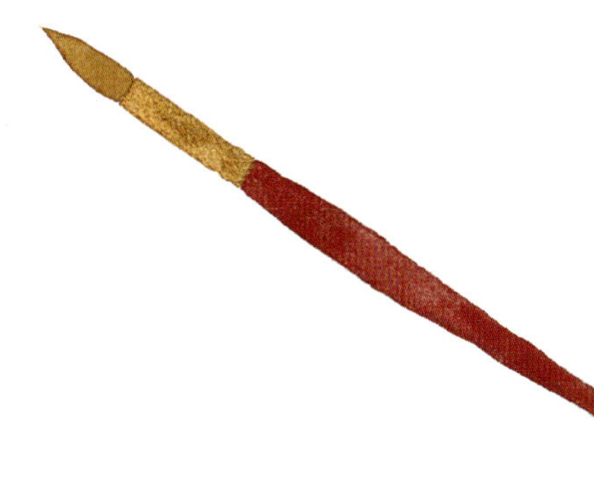

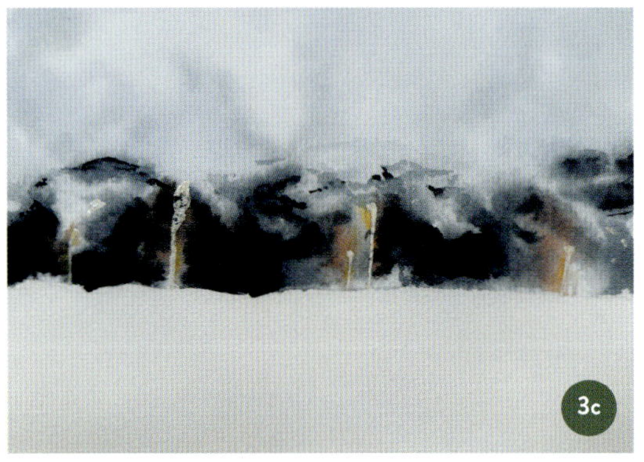

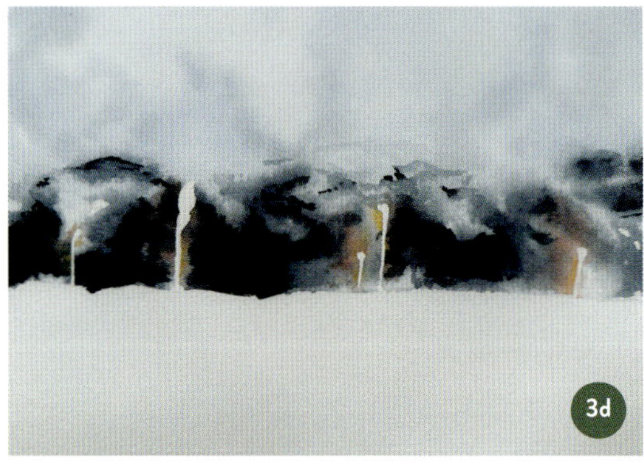

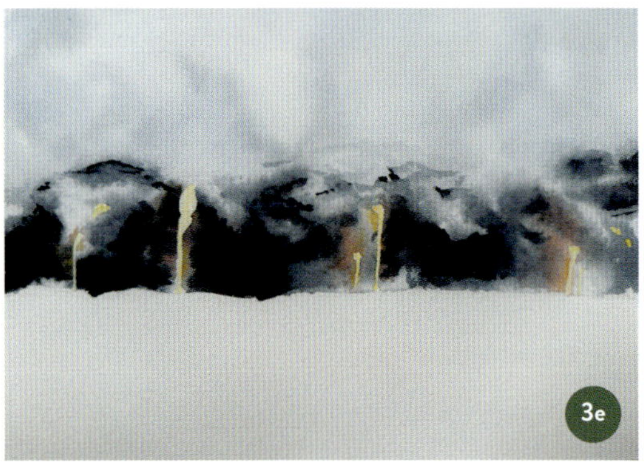

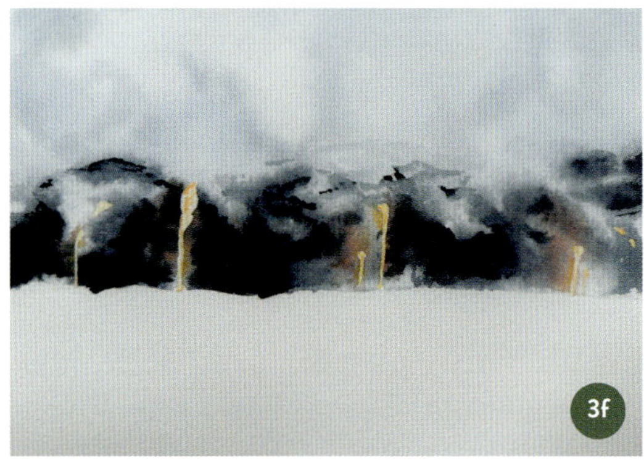

We want the ridge of the mountain with steam rolling down it to be hazy and not fully formed! Let dry, then use a size 6 round brush to darken a few spots on the mountain even more, and add some sporadic dry marks to contrast against the blurry layers beneath, making the rock look more like a rock. Less is more here.

Let dry completely, then remove the masking fluid by gently rubbing it away with your finger or an eraser (page 15). Use a size 2 round brush to wet the small lava flows, then tap light-value (watery) fiery orange mix into the streams. Let dry, then use a size 2 round brush to add one or two small, darker, more defined orange marks to the lava flows for a small and subtle contrast. Let dry.

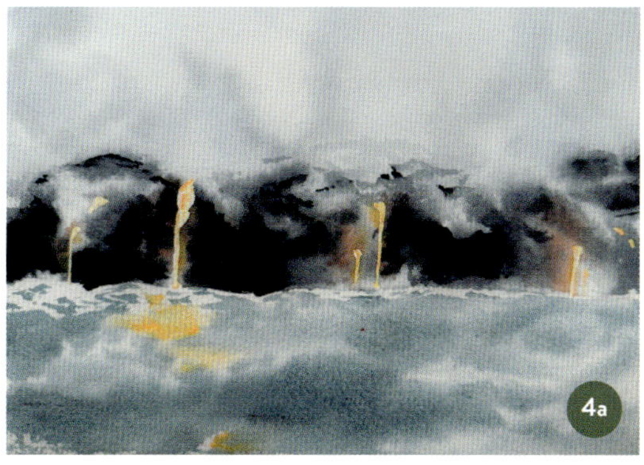

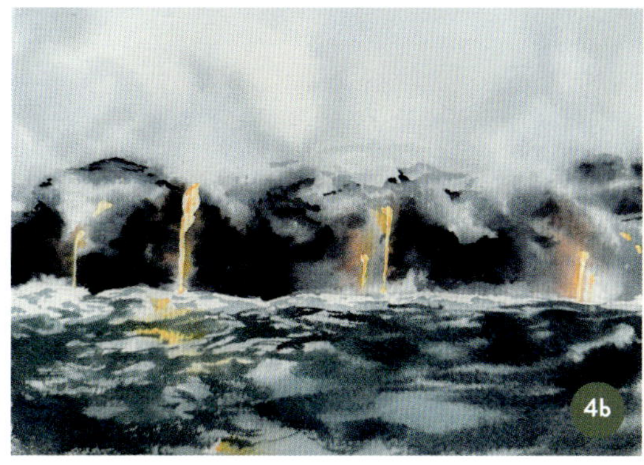

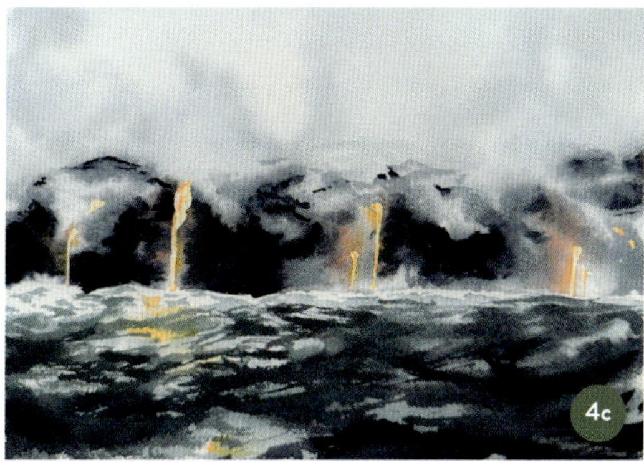

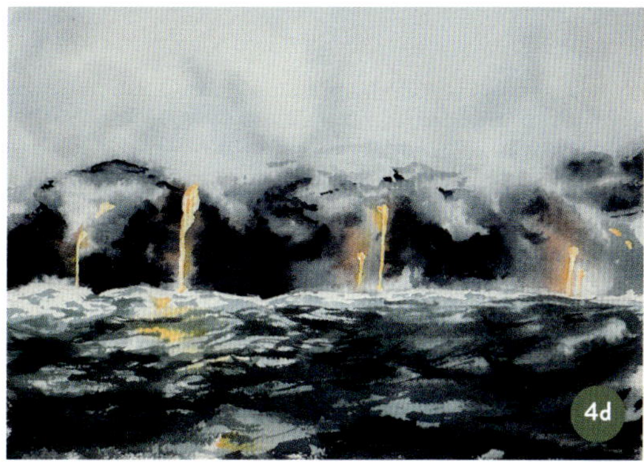

STEP 4: THE WATER

Use a size 12 round brush to layer a wash of clean water in the ocean area, leaving behind some dry space near the mountain for white waves. First, use a size 2 round brush to tap fiery orange into the sea, directly beneath one of the lava flows. Then, use a foliage brush with a medium-value (pigmented but somewhat watery) muted turquoise mix (Payne's Gray + Phthalo Blue + a hint of Hansa Yellow Light) to create a choppy wave texture into the wash, painting around the fiery orange reflection and leaving behind a few swirls of white space. Paint some wave-like marks into the white dry space near the rocks to add to the crashing wave effect. While still wet (though some parts may start to dry, which is completely fine), repeat with slightly darker-value muted turquoise. To maintain a distance perspective, make the wave strokes larger toward the bottom of the page (the foreground), and smaller and more compact toward the center of the page (the midground). Leave behind plenty of the lighter previous layer. Repeat again with slightly darker-value paint, again while the layer is still somewhat wet. Let dry completely, then repeat one final time with wet-on-dry strokes (page 12) of muted turquoise to sharpen the contrast even more.

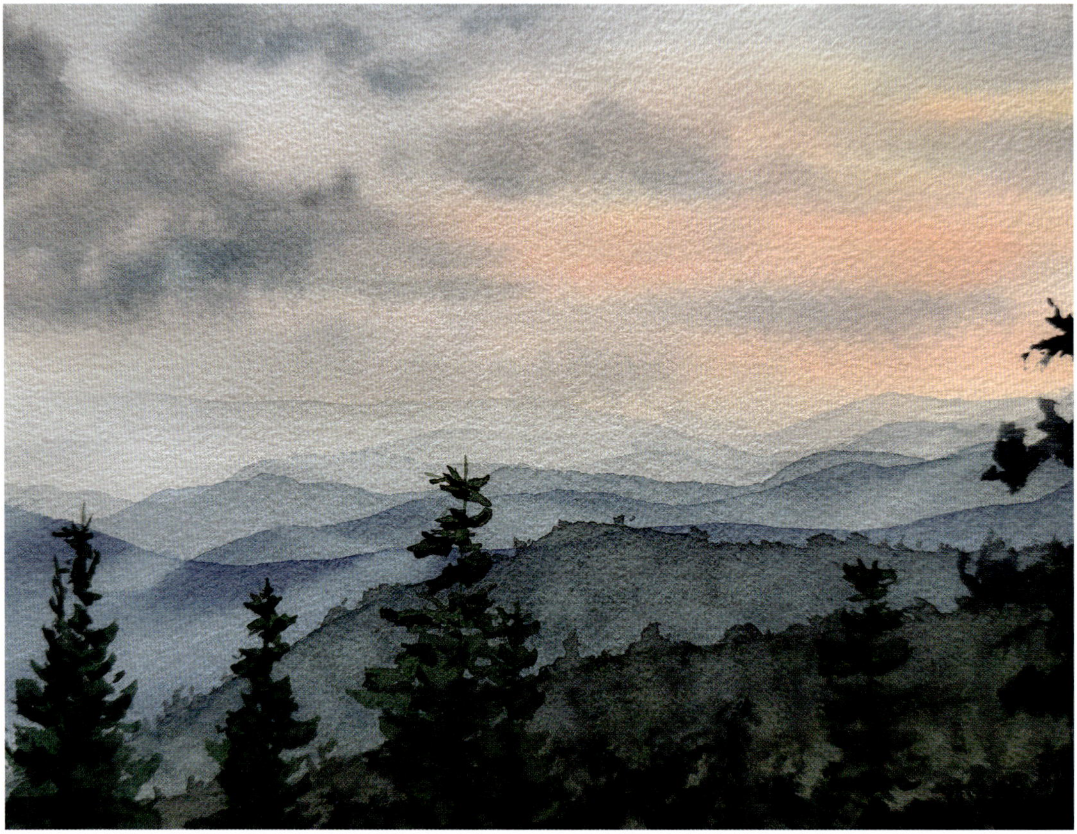

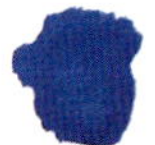

GREAT SMOKY MOUNTAINS

BRUSHES
Round sizes 2, 6, and 12; Foliage brush

COLOR PALETTE
French Ultramarine, Phthalo Blue (Green Shade), New Gamboge, Hansa Yellow Light, Opera Pink, Payne's Gray

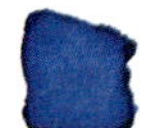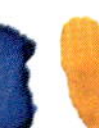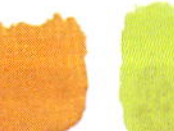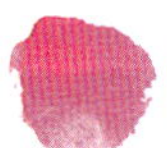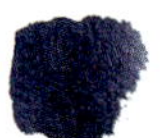

Known widely as America's most visited national park, the Great Smoky Mountains are as breathtaking as they are beloved. Let's capture their ethereal blue haze through layers of rolling mountains and trees. Patient layers will be key here. Remember to start light, then gradually grow darker to heighten the contrast (and the mystery)!

STEP 1: THE SKY

Start with a quite light sky, with little hints—wisps—of blue, yellow, and orange. Before painting, create light-value mixes of French Ultramarine and Phthalo Blue as well as a coral color, using New Gamboge, Hansa Yellow Light, and Opera Pink. Then, add water to the mixture to make it quite light. Wet the whole page with clean water, and use a large wash brush (round size 12) to paint a few loose strokes from the top right sides of the page into the center. Load your brush with some watery New Gamboge and repeat, leaving the top right of the sky with subtle stripes of orange and yellow.

While still wet, rinse the brush and load it up with the watery blues as well as watery Payne's Gray. Start on the left hand side this time, and gently brush toward the center, being careful not to cover up the orange and yellow strokes on the other side. Add a few strokes of watery Phthalo Blue as well, for a fun variation in the blue. Let dry completely.

(continued)

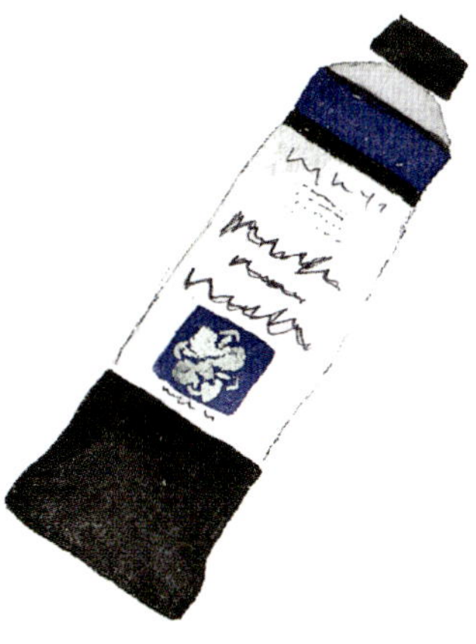

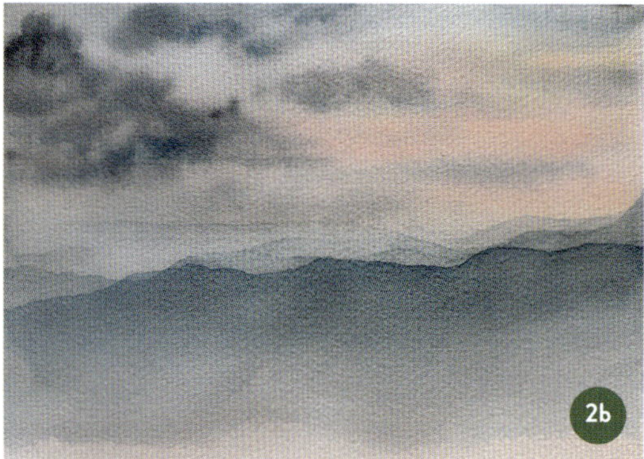

Rewet the page with clean water, then let it sit for 30 to 60 seconds. Load up a size 6 round brush with a medium-value Payne's Gray (not very watery, but not too dark), then dab your brush along the top left to paint a medium-sized cloud and some wispy, cloud-like shadows. This is supposed to be blurry! The idea here is to paint dry-on-wet (page 11), using as little water as possible on the brush and in the paint to minimize the paint blending all over. If necessary, use a thirsty brush (page 11) and push gently to lift any runaway paint and avoid a muddy sky. You can also use a clean towel to mop up any still-wet surface and try again! Tap some French Ultramarine into the still-wet cloud to add more depth. Let dry completely.

STEP 2: THE MOUNTAINS

Next, build up the mountain range, starting with quite light values (watery paint) and gradually growing darker (by adding a little more paint to the mixture). Create a watery puddle of Payne's Gray and Phthalo Blue to get a hazy blue mixture, then use a large wash brush loaded with the gray-blue mix to paint the first background mountain layer. Lay the watery paintbrush flat against one side of the page to create a thick, watery stroke, and slowly move across the page, adding slightly jagged movements to create a realistic mountain ridge. Once across the page, add more water to the brush, and bring that layer down a couple more inches, feathering (page 12) the edge into the bottom of the page.

Let dry completely (this is important!), then add a bit more Payne's Gray to the mixture to create a slightly darker-value color. You can use a piece of scratch paper to swatch beforehand. Load up the wash brush with the slightly darker (but still watery) blue-gray mixture, then repeat with another mountain layer just below. Make sure this one has variations—we don't want the layers to look the same! Let dry completely, then repeat the process a few more times, with slightly darker-value paint each time. As you get closer to the front, add a bit more Phthalo Blue, to make the layers more vibrant, and use a thirsty brush (page 11) to lift some of the paint and create subtle layers of white space to mimic fog or streams of light.

STEP 3: THE TREES

Let dry completely, then paint two layers of distant trees. Add just a dab of New Gamboge to the blue mix previously used to paint the mountain layers, making it a grayish green color. Then, use the foliage brush to create a mountain layer with a tree texture along the ridge. Rinse the brush and use a thirsty foliage brush to lift some textured strokes within the layer. Let dry, then repeat with slightly darker and more green paint by adding just a bit more New Gamboge.

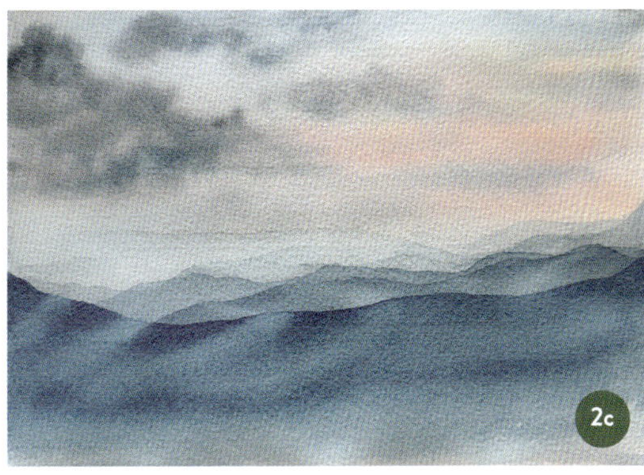

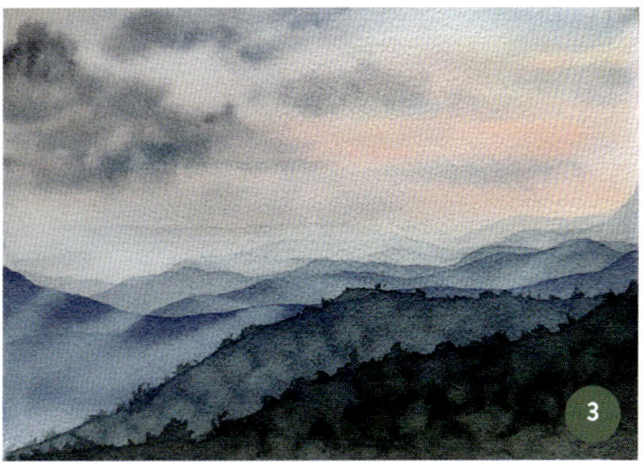

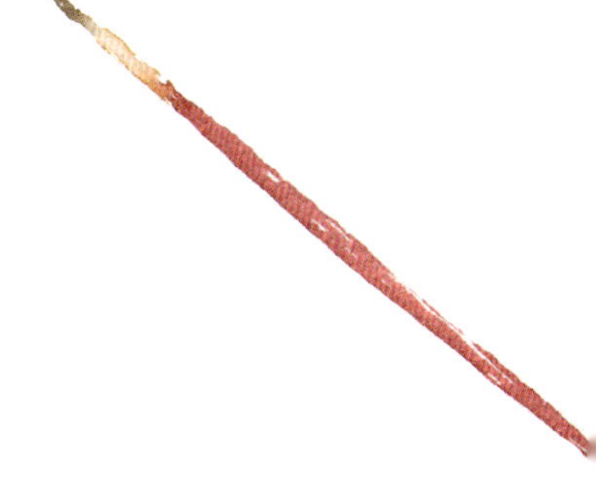

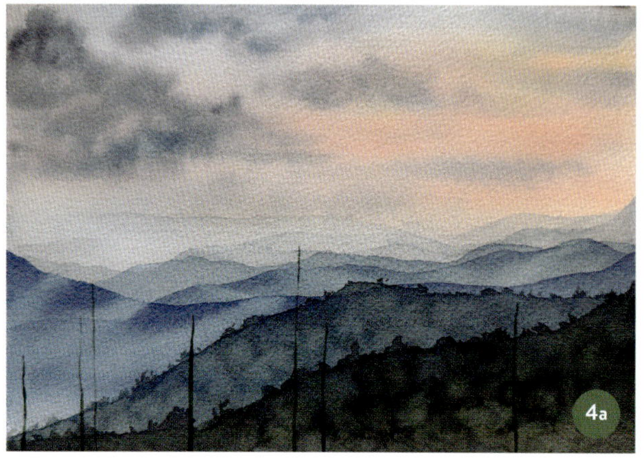

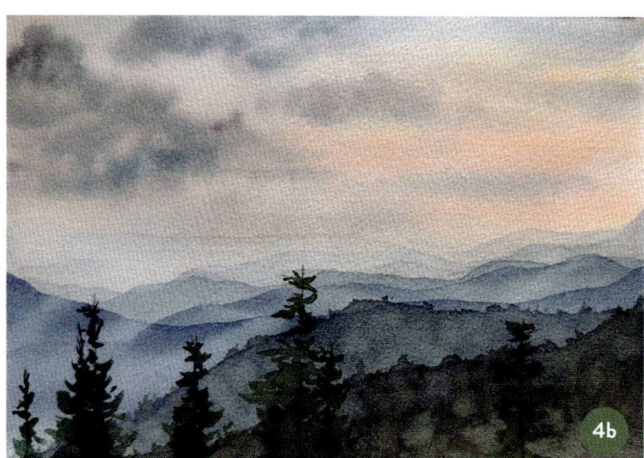

STEP 4: THE TREES, PART TWO

When that layer is dry, use a size 2 round brush to paint a few thin tree trunks along the bottom of the page, varying in size and placement. (The more wonky or uneven, the better!).

Then, use a foliage brush with a medium-value forest green (New Gamboge + French Ultramarine) to paint the tree shapes. Start from the center of the trunks, and lightly flick or press the brush to create various marks, sometimes pointing up, sometimes pointing down. Remember that trees are supposed to be wild—the goal is to have fun with your brush, and it will definitely look like a tree!

Let dry, then add Payne's Gray to the forest green mix, and repeat using the round size 2 detail brush, making sure to leave behind bits of the previous, lighter layer on the trees. Repeat one more time with even darker paint along the bottom edges of the boughs of the trees, and then use a foliage brush to add just the side of one larger tree along the right of the page. This tree should be the darkest in value and the largest overall, to help snap the layers and distance effect into place.

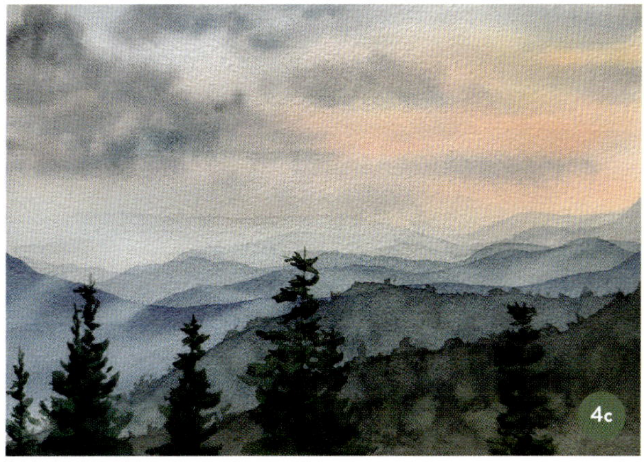

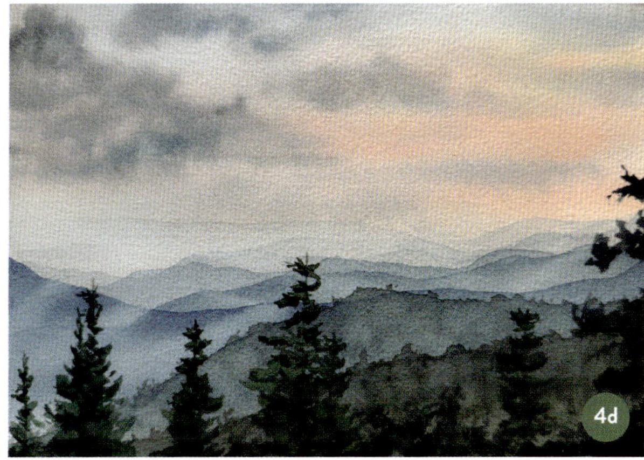

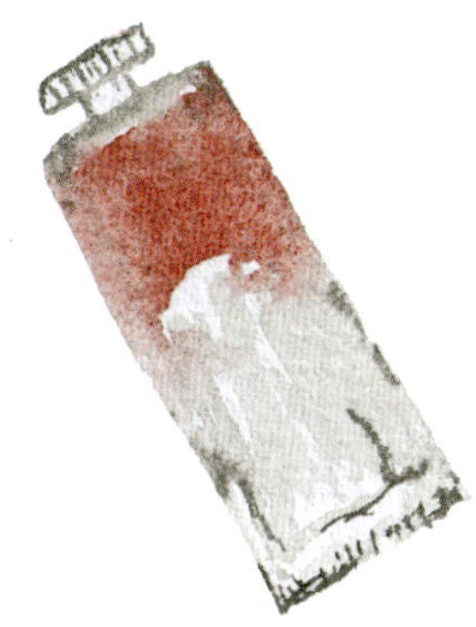

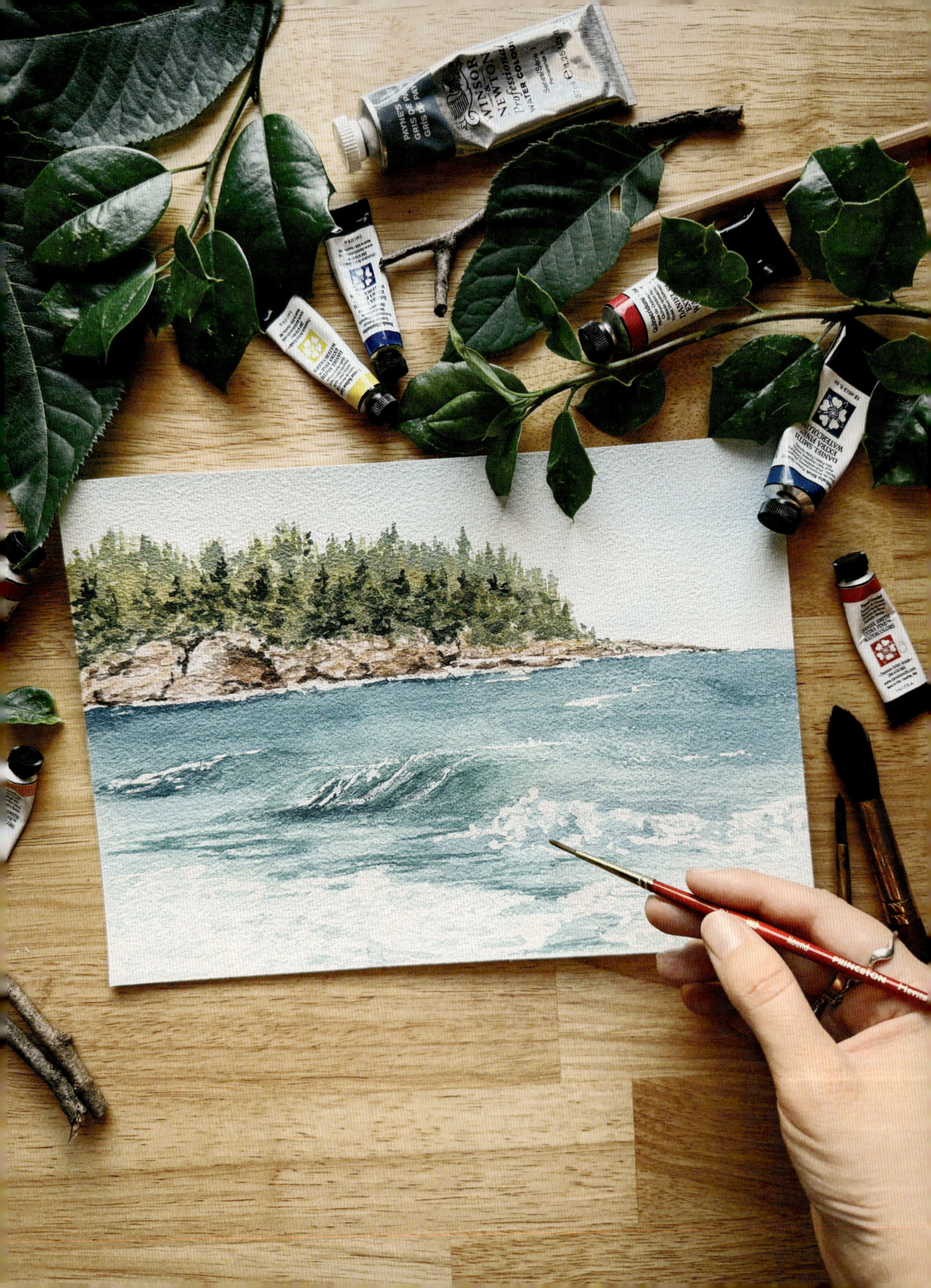

listening at the lake

—Nicholas Sparks

Water is the stuff of life, and witnessing it in all its natural forms is truly a wonder to behold throughout America's most beautiful spots. Whether the waves are crashing the shore, gently lapping over each other, or completely frozen, listening for the rhythm in the water can help make your paintings come to life.

Now, painting water can be tricky—a dance between luminous layers and contrasting strokes, it will often feel unwieldy and uncertain. Just remember this truth about nature: If it doesn't demand perfection from its beauty, why should you?

NORTH CASCADES

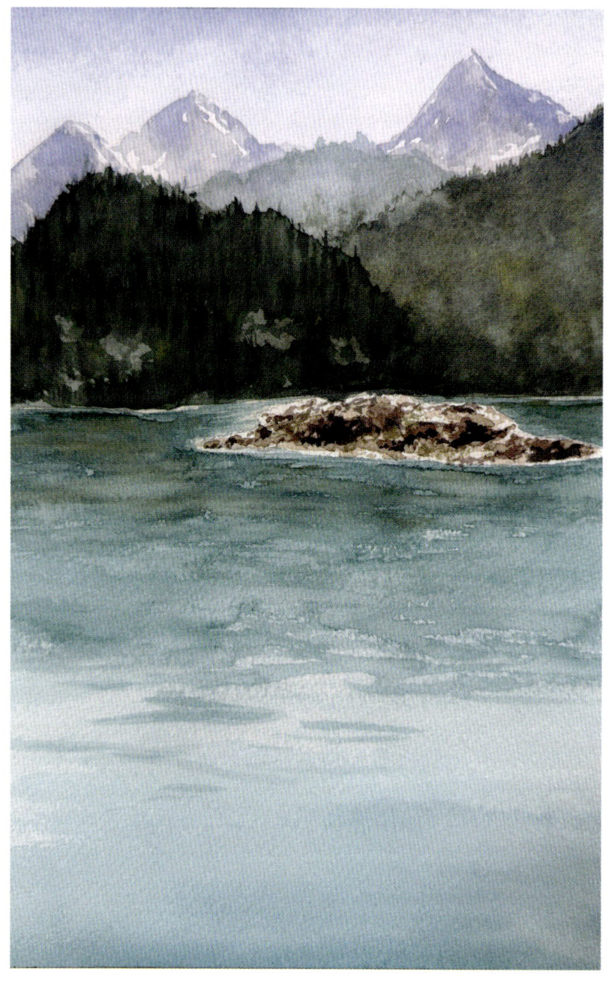

Known for its turquoise hues from glacial flour in the sediment, Diablo Lake in North Cascades National Park is an idyllic paradise surrounded by layers of mountains and trees. With so many textural elements at play, this scene is a wonderful opportunity to practice simplifying the landscape on purpose to elevate the star of the show—in this case, calm blue waters lapping against a glittering sunlit rock.

BRUSHES
Round sizes 2, 6, and 12; Foliage brush

COLOR PALETTE
Phthalo Blue (Green Shade), Hansa Yellow Light, French Ultramarine, New Gamboge, Quinacridone Rose, Payne's Gray, Pyrrol Scarlet

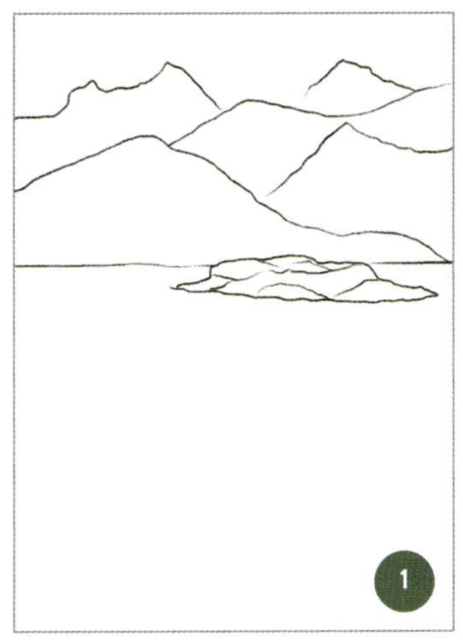

STEP 1: THE SKETCH

Start with a loose pencil sketch of the background mountains (taking up about the top third of the page) and the small island of rocks just in front of the background mountains. Make sure the mountains have a layer of peaks in the back and three overlapping hills in front. The bottom two-thirds of the page should stay clear—it's where the lake will go!

STEP 2: THE UNDERPAINTING

Layer a wash of clean water across the whole page with a size 12 round brush, except for the rock island. With a very watery brush, paint a light value of turquoise (Phthalo Blue + Hansa Yellow Light) in the lake area, dark green (French Ultramarine + New Gamboge) in the front mountain hills, and blue-violet (French Ultramarine + just a hint of Quinacridone Rose) in the sky, fading slightly along the peaks of the background mountains. It's okay if the colors in this wash bleed into each other slightly, but we want all of them to be light and watery, leaving the rock island dry and white. Let this layer dry completely.

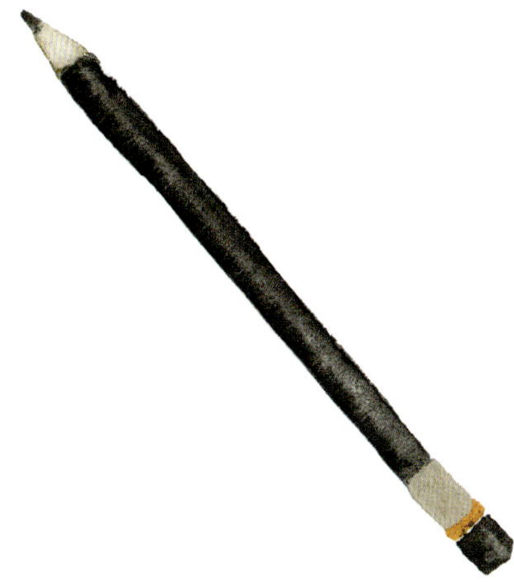

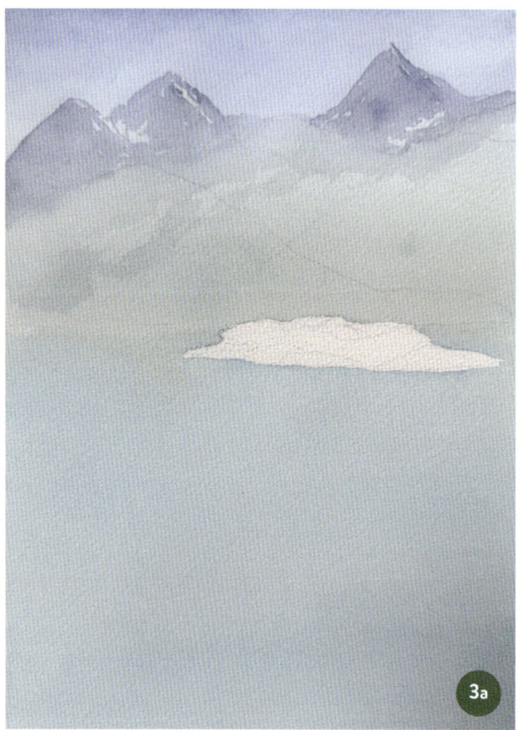

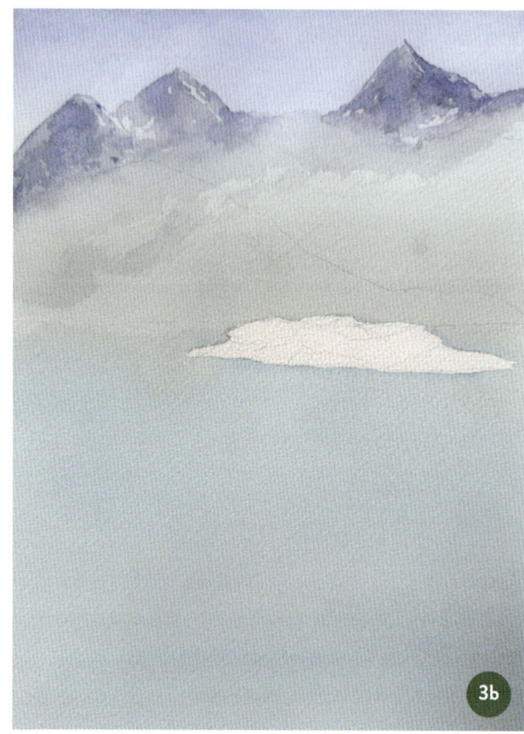

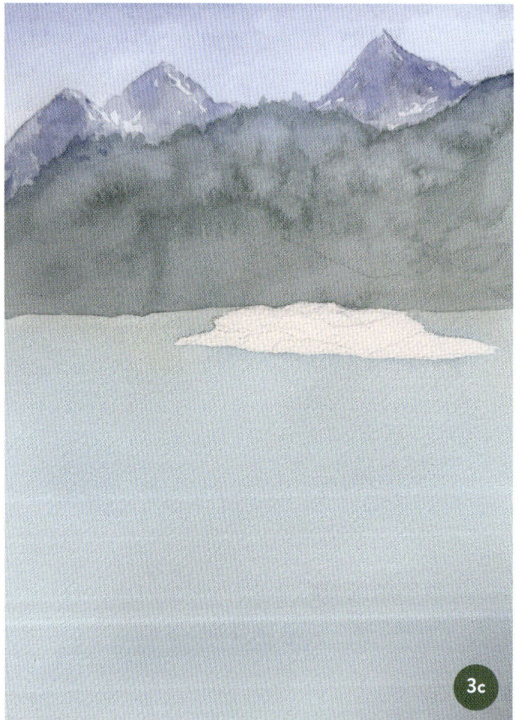

STEP 3: THE MOUNTAINS

With watery Payne's Gray (with maybe a bit of French Ultramarine for some granulation) and a size 6 round brush, paint the background mountains, leaving behind small slivers of dry space along the peaks and the base of the mountains. It doesn't matter where—just that they're there. While that layer is still damp, tap some watery French Ultramarine into a few spots for added texture. It's okay if we get some wonky dried spots! Blot excess moisture off your brush, then feather (page 12) the watery paint down into the next layer to avoid a noticeable dried paint line. Let dry.

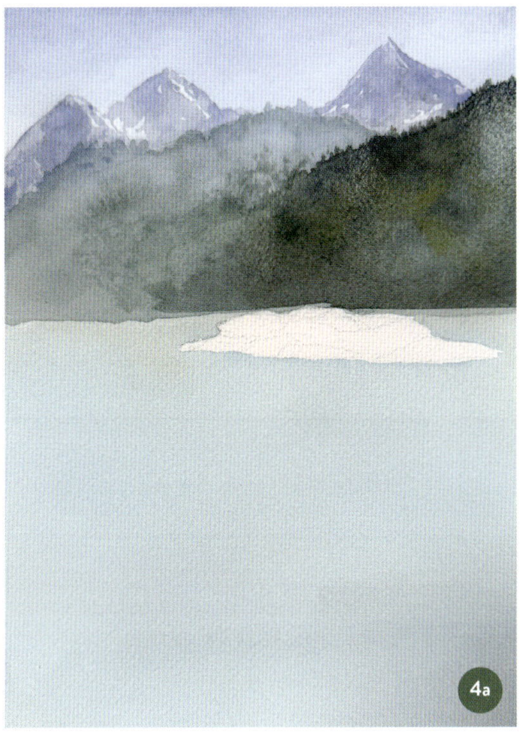

STEP 4: THE TREES

Paint three layers of overlapping trees using the pencil sketch as a guide. Start with a watery dark green mixture (French Ultramarine + New Gamboge), painting the tree layers in one wash with a choppy ridge. (You can use the foliage brush for this or the side of a small paintbrush.) Make sure to paint the tree ridge under the background mountain peaks so they are still clearly visible. Any stray or accidental texture here from dried paint is welcome and will add to the movement. Let dry completely.

Next, use a foliage brush to paint the right-side tree layer. Start with a watery dark green (slightly darker in value than the previous layer, which means more paint), making the ridge clearly defined on the side. As you get closer to the center of the page, use the foliage brush to feather the ridge into the page. While still wet, drop some watery New Gamboge into the layer for added color and movement.

(continued)

Moving to the final tree layer, use an even darker and more vibrant green mixture— add a little Phthalo Blue and/or Hansa Yellow Light to make it a little cooler and less muted. Use the foliage brush to paint a defined tree line along the top ridge, then feather into the previous layer the closer you get to the center of the page. The idea is to make the trees look like they're seamlessly folding into each other while using the darker values to maintain depth between the layers. Leave behind a few craggy dry spots for added rocky texture. While the left side layer is still wet, use a size 2 round brush with New Gamboge, and then Payne's Gray, to paint a few vertical lines in the wet layer, implying larger, more defined tree shapes. Remember: Any stray dried paint lines add texture!

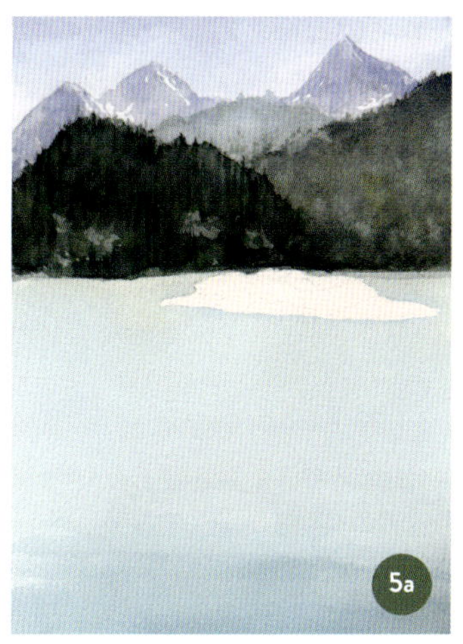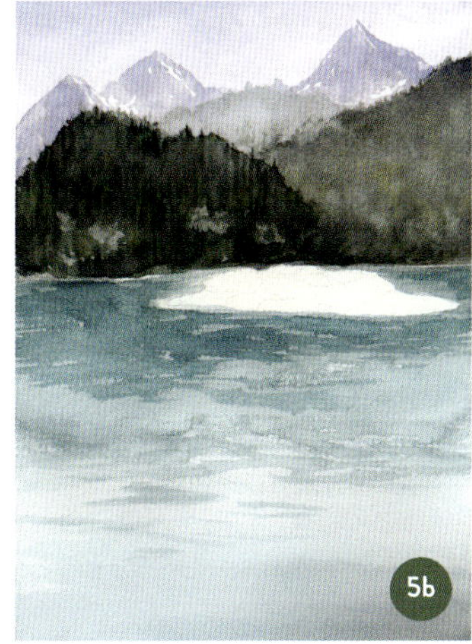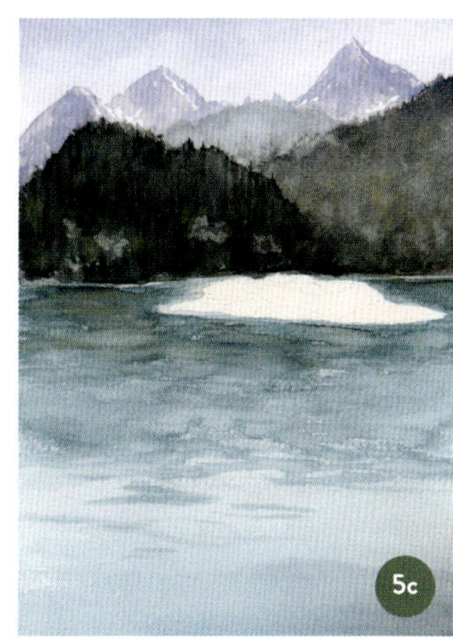

STEP 5: THE LAKE

Mix a watery turquoise (from Step 2), then with a size 12 round brush, start from the bottom of the page and paint upward a few strokes, loosely feathering into the center of the page.

Then, mix a darker-value turquoise, and with a foliage brush, paint a choppy wash just under the tree line, around the dry rocky island, and feathered into the center of the lake. Use short, wispy strokes as you get closer to the center to encourage streaks of dry brush (page 12) marks to mimic sparkles! Then, paint a few choppy zigzag strokes separate from the larger wash, moving down the page to create movement and ripples.

Repeat with a smaller layer of darker tur-quoise, then one more with more yellow in the mix. You can wait for the layers to dry between each new color, or you can paint while the paper is kind of damp or almost dry for an interesting texture. Make sure your strokes are horizontal and loosely zig-zagged each time to maintain the natural water movement.

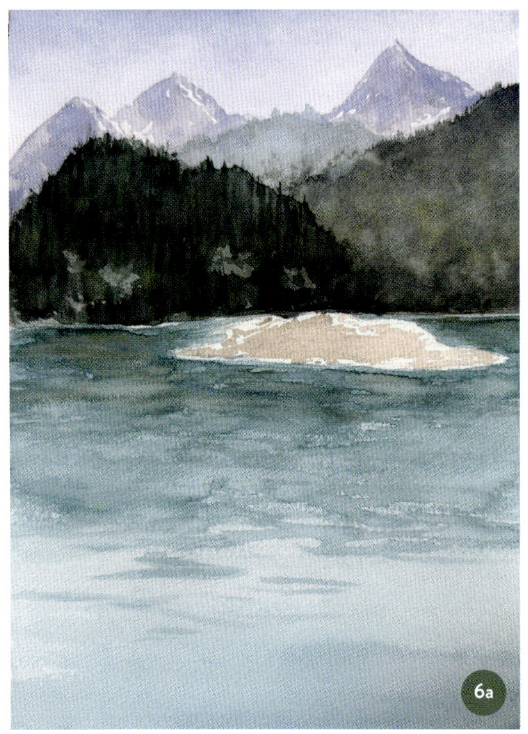

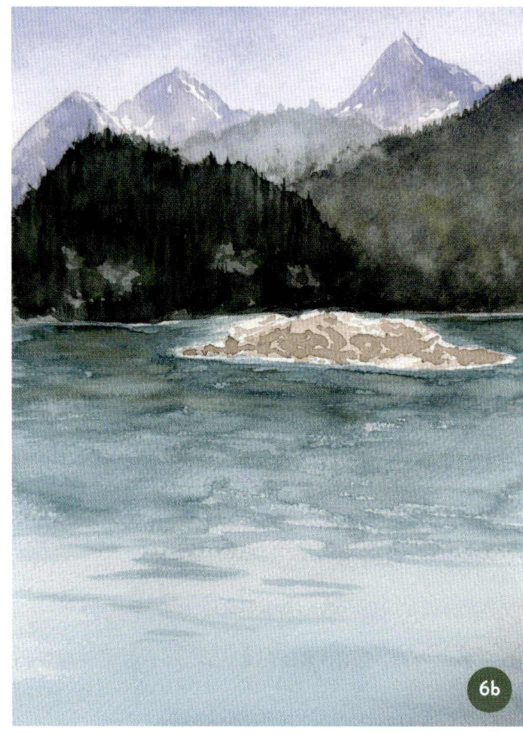

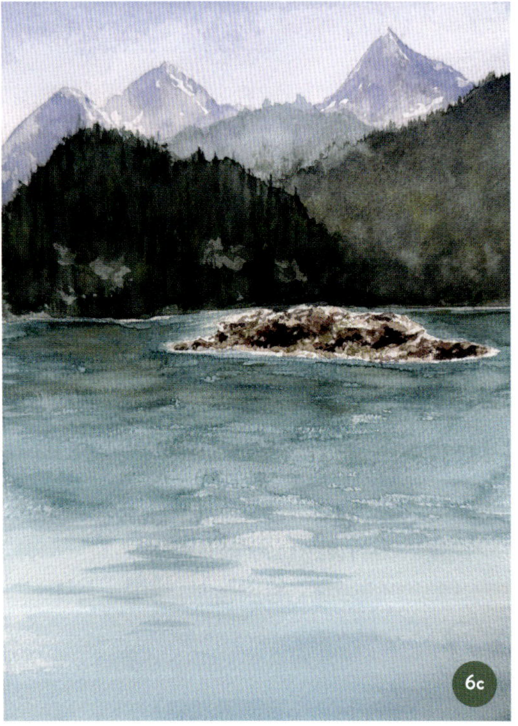

STEP 6: THE ROCKS

Mix a light-value (watery) warm brown (French Ultramarine + Pyrrol Scarlet + New Gamboge), and then use a foliage brush to layer that on the rock island, leaving behind highlights of white space along the top and edges. Let dry, then add darker brown shadows loosely along the bottom and toward the center. Let dry, then add Payne's Gray to the mix to make it even darker, and use a size 2 round brush to add a few more shadows to shape the larger rocks and add contrast.

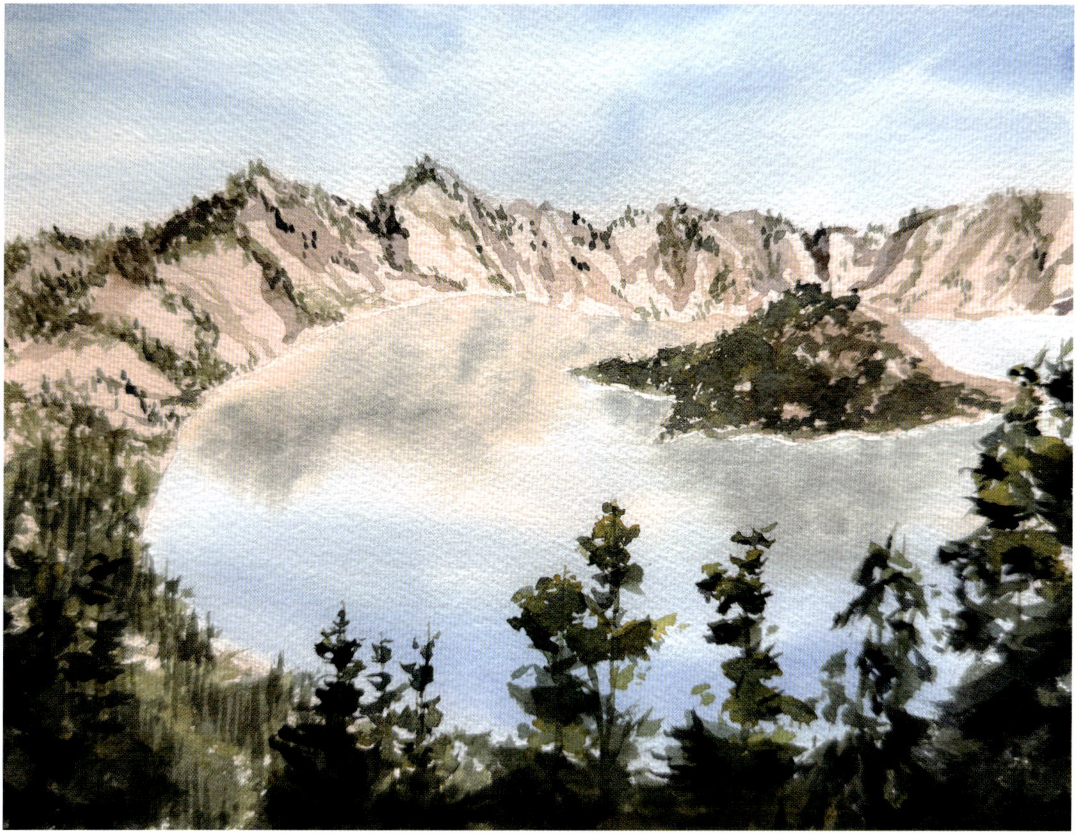

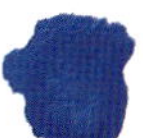

CRATER LAKE

BRUSHES
Round sizes 2, 6, and 12; Foliage brush

COLOR PALETTE
French Ultramarine, Phthalo Blue (Green Shade), Pyrrol Scarlet, New Gamboge

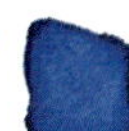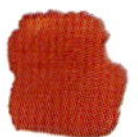

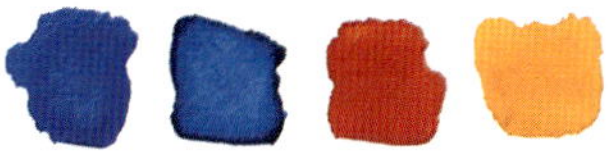

On a clear day, even distant mountain peaks reveal intricate details to the naked eye—and that's exactly what we're practicing with this view of Crater Lake! Frame a clear lake reflection with a crater-shaped mountain range, using mainly size and color value to bring depth and movement to this unique scene.

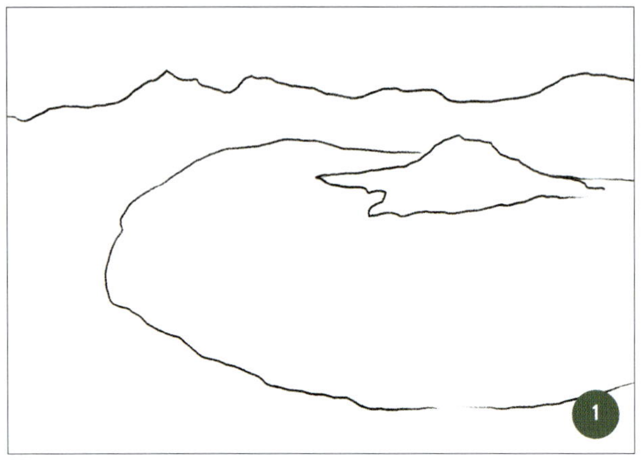

STEP 1: THE SKETCH

Start by sketching the top mountain ridge, the shoreline around the lake, and the small island to the right side. The top ridge should have a few sharp peaks with some smoother sloping lines and move horizontally across the page, about a quarter of the way down from the top. Then, sketch the island as a small hill below the mountain ridge, with a few tapered tendrils of land on either side and in the front. These lines should be loose curves, not precise in any way! Finally, sketch a long C-curve (page 13) for the shoreline, beginning horizontally on the right side of the page moving left, then curving down and around, giving the lake a crater shape.

STEP 2: THE SKY

Mix French Ultramarine and Phthalo Blue for a watery sky blue. Then, layer a wash of clean water across the sky, feathering (page 12) into the mountains just a bit. With a size 6 round brush, paint the sky blue into the watery layer, sometimes using flicks or long strokes to leave behind subtle crisscrossed areas of white space. The goal isn't to paint identifiable clouds so much as to imply a wispy cloud-like texture in the sky. You can also use a thirsty brush (page 11) to lift some of the paint to reveal the white space in long, thin wisps. Let dry completely.

STEP 3: THE UNDERPAINTING + REFLECTION

Mix a watery brown (French Ultramarine + Pyrrol Scarlet + New Gamboge), and then paint the mountain and the island with the mixture with a size 12 round brush. Alternate between spreading the paint and painting with clean water for an even lighter value and watery layer.

Let dry, then paint what will be the reflection of the mountain in the lake. Start with a layer of clean water, then paint a loose sky blue along the bottom edge, leaving behind bits of white space for the wispy clouds. While still wet, use a size 2 round brush to paint the watery mountain reflection, starting with light brown, then adding darker green (French Ultramarine + New Gamboge). This is a wet wash, so the paint will bleed a bit—this is one reason why using a smaller brush will be helpful.

While the layer is still wet, rinse the small brush, blot the excess water on a towel, then paint horizontal strokes directly into the reflection, to imply subtle horizontal wave movement in the reflection. Remember: This is a blurry reflection and only one piece of the puzzle, so it's okay if it looks a little wonky or washed out! Let dry completely.

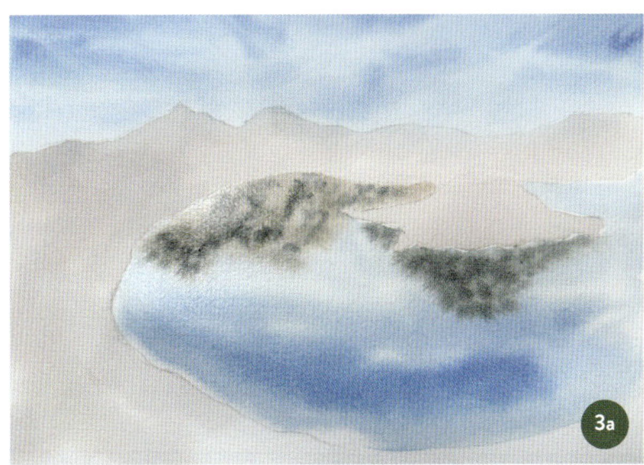

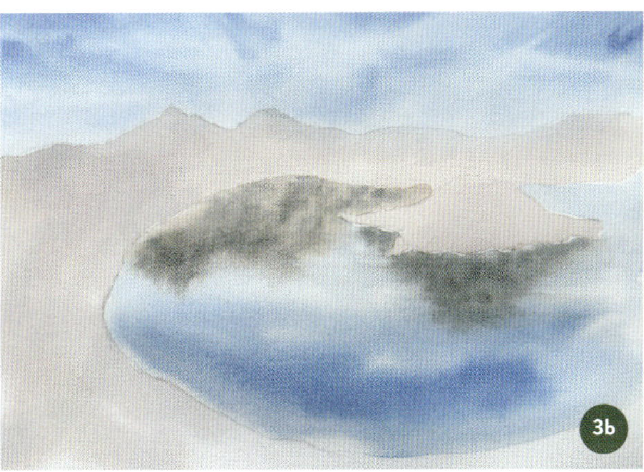

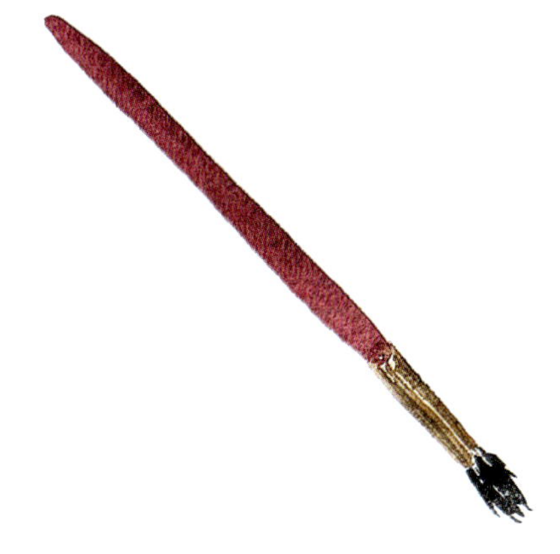

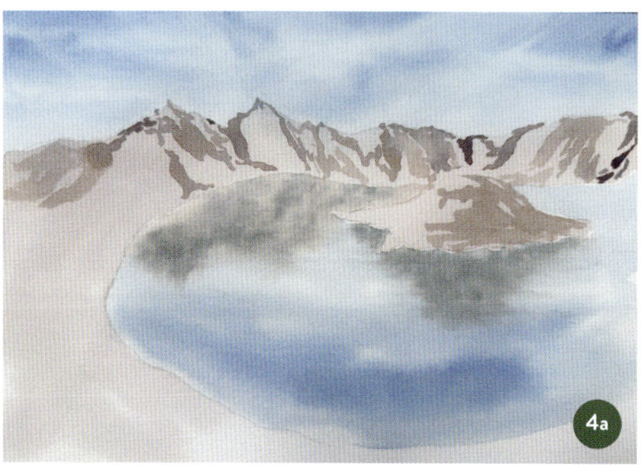

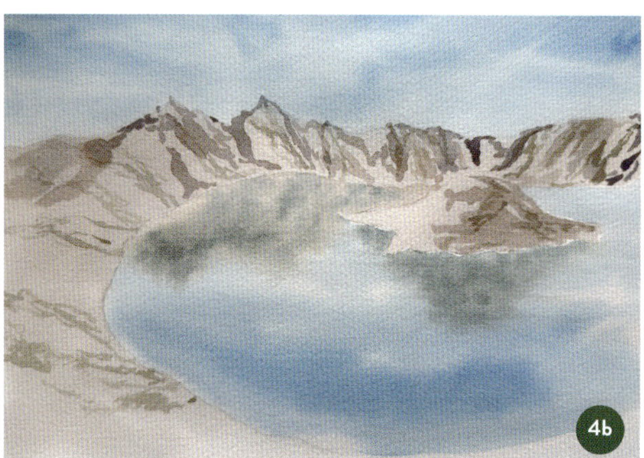

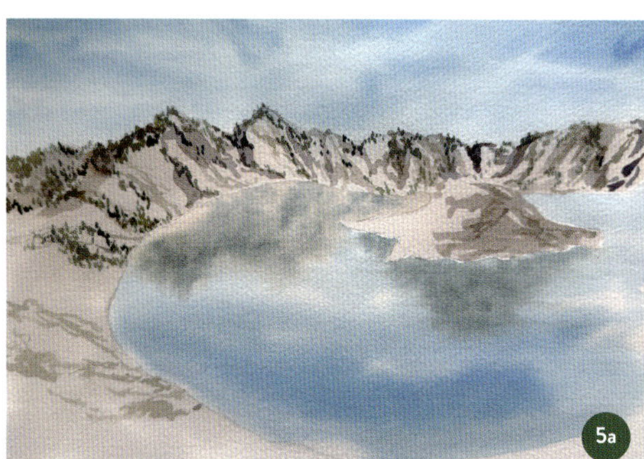

STEP 4: THE MOUNTAIN

Mix a more medium-value brown (still a bit watery), and then paint loose, slanted shadows across the top of the mountain and to the side of the island, leaving behind plenty of the lighter layer. Let dry, then repeat with smaller shadows this time, sometimes layering on top of the previous shadow lines, sometimes venturing to other parts of the mountain. As you curve around to the left side, make the lines more horizontal rather than vertical to give the crater shape more definition. These lines are supposed to look a bit chaotic and loose—a shaky, uncertain hand is a good thing here!

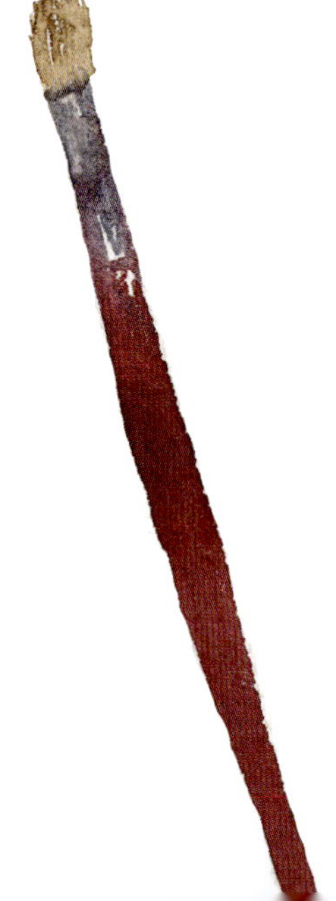

STEP 5: THE TREES

Mix a dark green (French Ultramarine + New Gamboge), and paint tiny tree textures along the back of the mountain using just the tip of a size 2 round brush. Try to maintain a loose zigzag movement with the clusters of trees, sometimes cascading down the mountain, sometimes moving along the ridgeline. The idea is that there is no uniformity or symmetry, just natural movement.

Next, use the same dark green mix with a foliage brush to tap a foliage texture along the bottom and to the side of the mountain. The foliage texture should be larger in the front (near the bottom of the page) and gradually get smaller toward the back. Use foliage texture on top of the previously painted clusters of trees in some areas to make them look fuller. Repeat with a slightly darker-value green (add a bit more French Ultramarine), leaving behind flickers of the previous light layer as you go. Use a foliage brush to add greenery to the left side of the island, leaving behind bits of the lighter layers as highlights on the right side.

(continued)

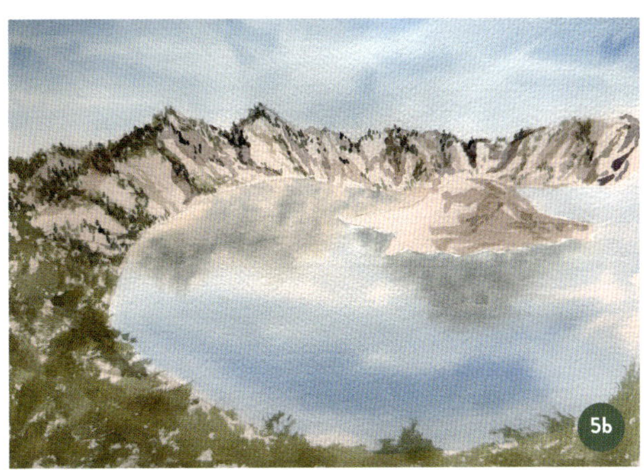

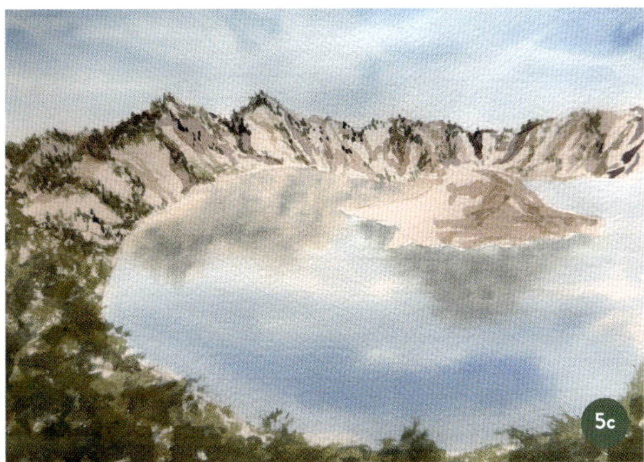

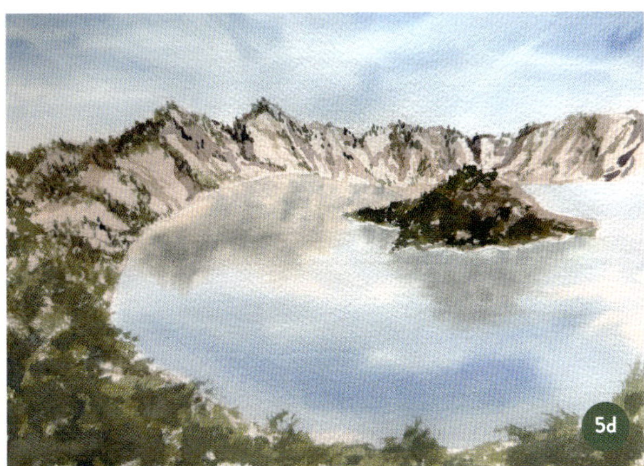

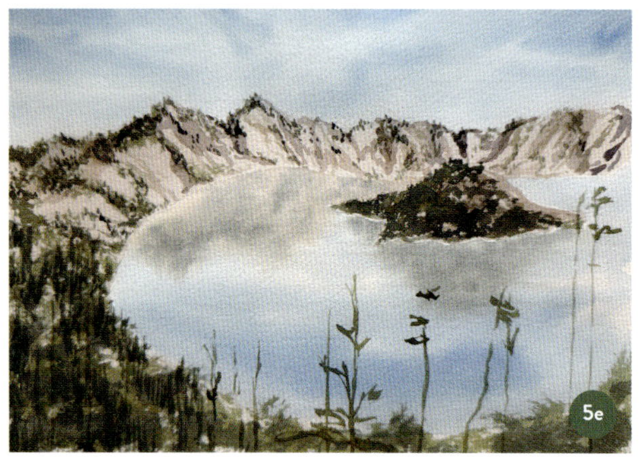

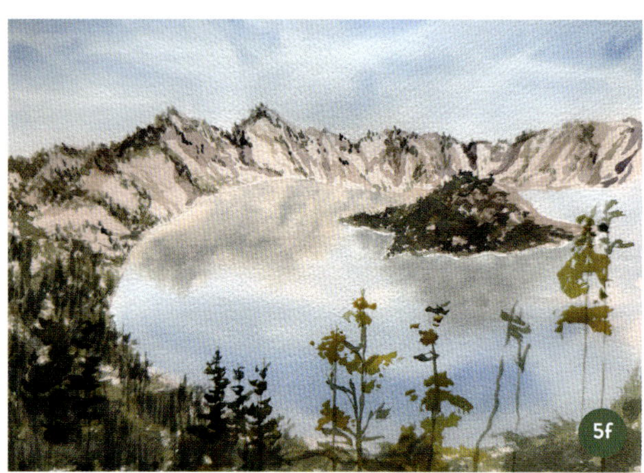

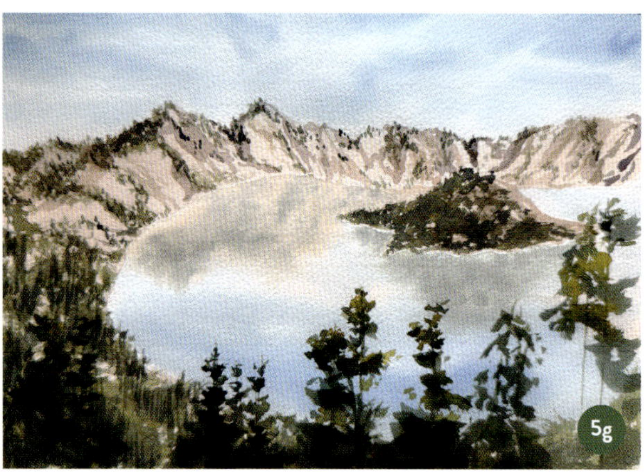

Next, use a size 2 round brush to paint the trunks of a few trees along the front and to the right, gradually growing shorter and more clustered together as the mountain curves up on the left side of the page. Add clusters of vertical lines especially along the bottom left to imply trees that are closer to the front (larger) but still farther away than the largest trees in the foreground.

Paint the foreground trees using random marks and strokes (see "scumbling" [page 14]), starting with lighter, more yellow-green layers, then adding darker values to add more shape. You can use a foliage brush or a size 2 round brush, but make sure each tree looks at least slightly different from the one next to it—either in direction of the needles, the height of the tree trunk, the pattern of the foliage, or some combination of all three.

Continue with the foliage layers, adding darker-value shadows under the lighter strokes. Make sure to leave behind wisps of the lighter layers—the contrast between the highlights and the shadows will create a satisfying depth to the foreground trees.

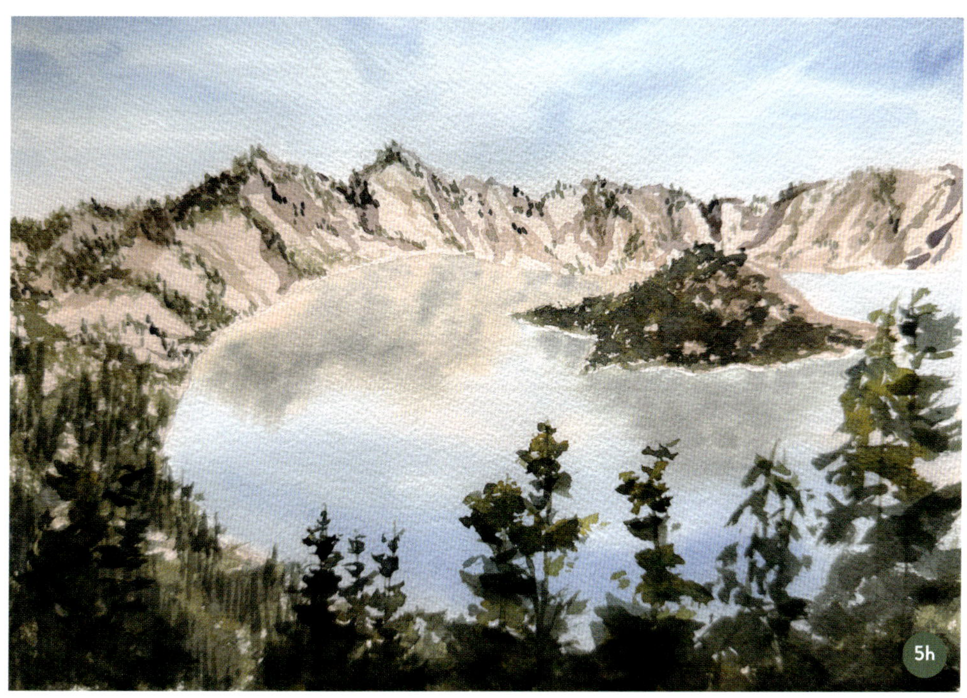

5h

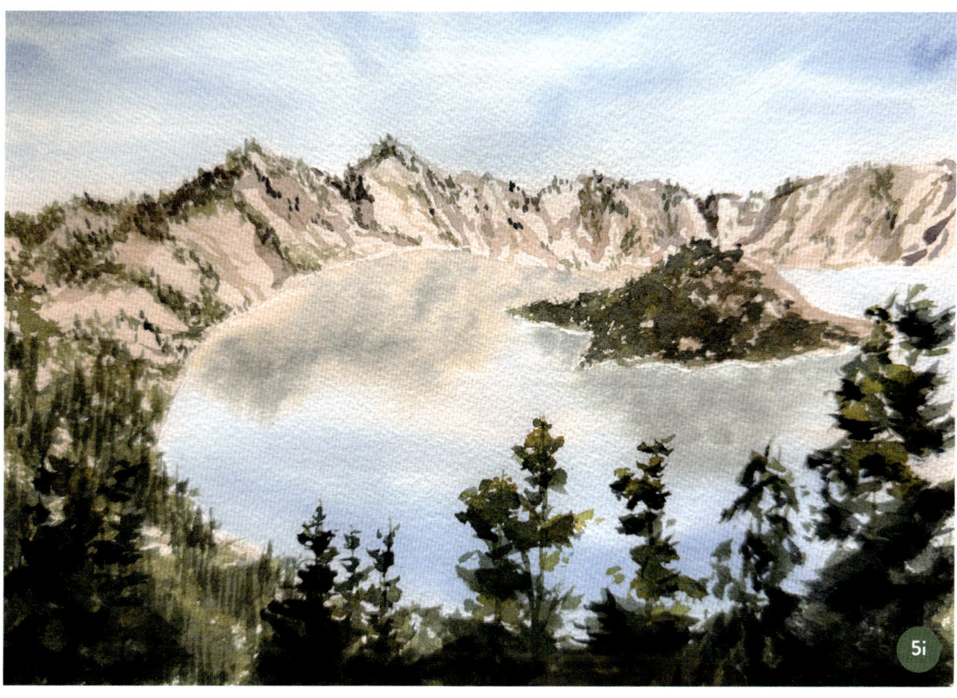

5i

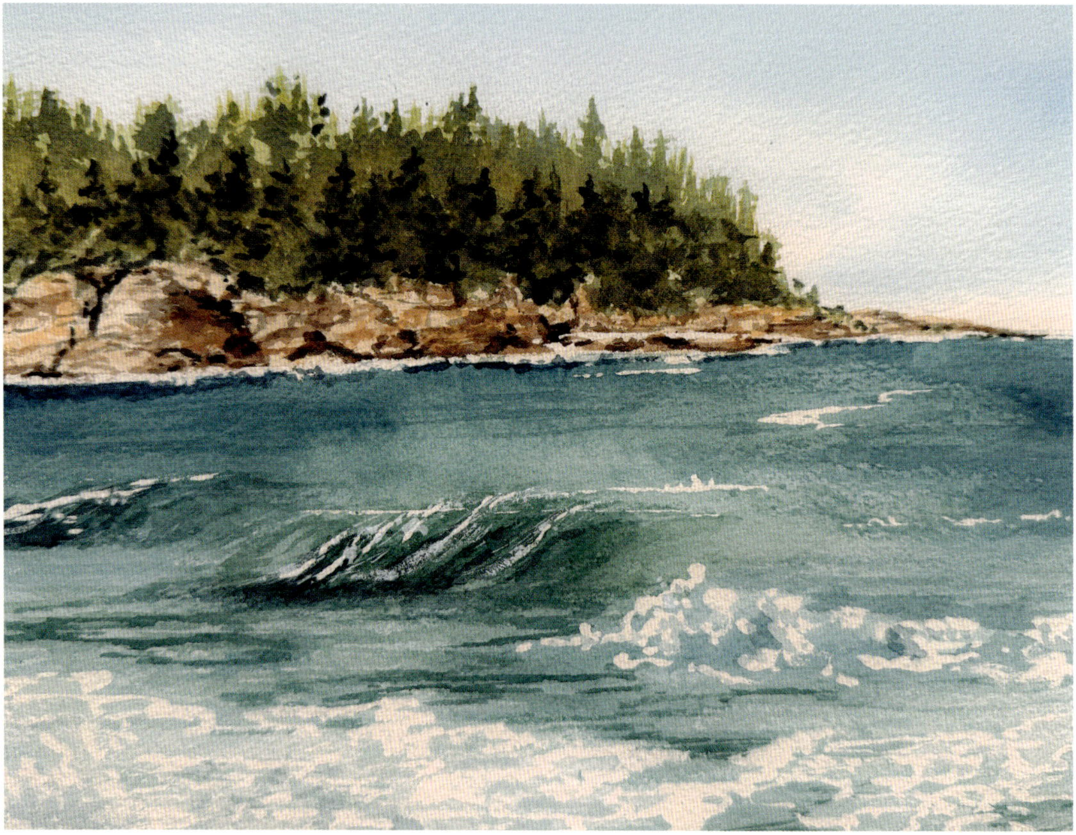

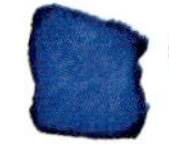

ACADIA

BRUSHES
Round sizes 2 and 12; Foliage brush;
Masking fluid brush

COLOR PALETTE
Phthalo Blue (Green Shade), French
Ultramarine, New Gamboge, Pyrrol Scarlet,
Hansa Yellow Light, Payne's Gray,
white gouache

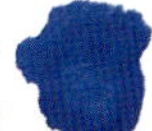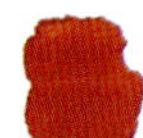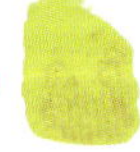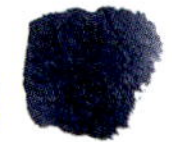

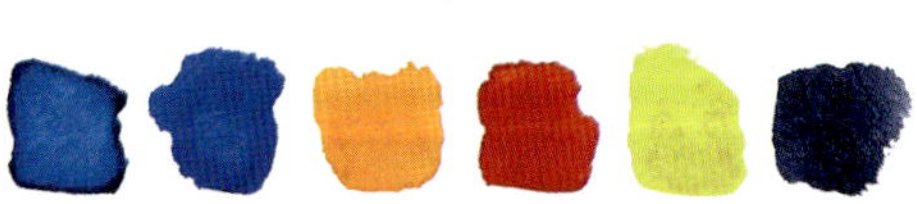

You can almost taste adventure in the windy sea air when surrounded by Acadia's rocky landscape. This choppy northeastern ocean, surrounded by thick forests and rocky shores, sets the stage for many storied adventures. Here we'll practice layering different textures and marks together.

Note: This project uses masking fluid.

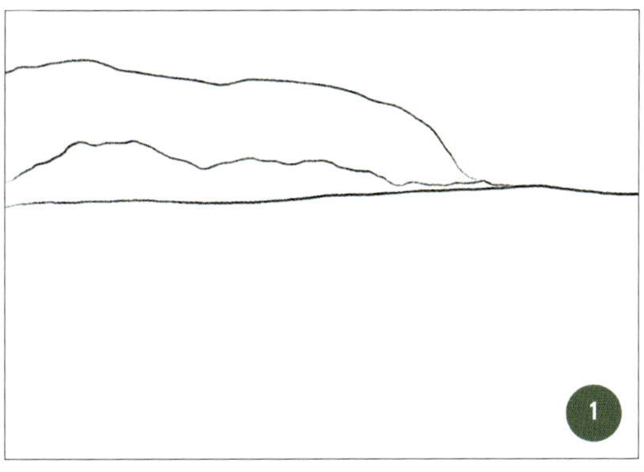

STEP 1: THE SKETCH

Sketch a loose horizontal line along the top third of the page, separating the water from the landscape. Just above the line, sketch an area for the rocky shore across the page, larger on the left side and tapering toward the right edge. Then, sketch an area for trees above the rocks just beneath the top edge of the page and sloping downward.

Use your masking fluid brush prepped with soap and masking fluid (page 15) to paint the bottom of the page to mask areas for seafoam. Use a mix of soft zigzag motions and blobby lines to create a natural wave movement, with the waves closer-knit toward the bottom of the page, growing much sparser and smaller moving up the page. Add a few small dots and lines along the shore. To create movement for an optional rolling wave in the center of the water, paint several elongated S-curves (page 13) close together and tapering off to the left side (to imply a distance perspective). Let dry for 30 minutes or until tacky.

Note: It's helpful to look at the finished reference photo for this step, as we're masking the white space before painting. If masking fluid is too scary, you can also add all the foamy movement with white gouache after you've painted everything else. (Using white gouache is not cheating—just different!)

STEP 2: THE SKY

Mix Phthalo Blue and French Ultramarine with a lot of water to create a light-value sky blue. With a size 12 round brush, wet the sky area and part of the tree area with clean water, then add the watery sky blue. It's okay if the blue bleeds into the trees— we'll cover that up pretty easily—but make sure the blue doesn't touch the rocky area. Let dry.

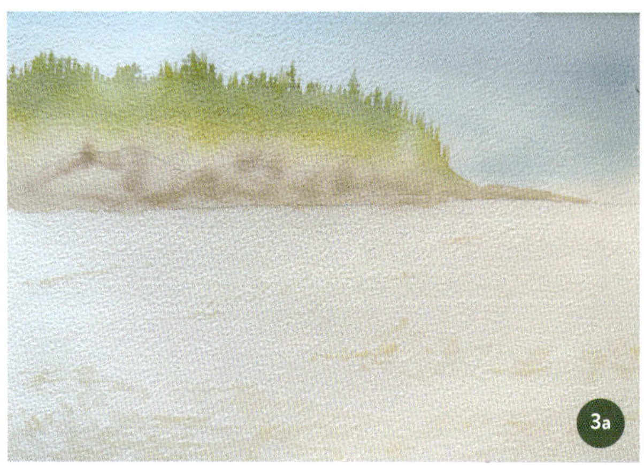

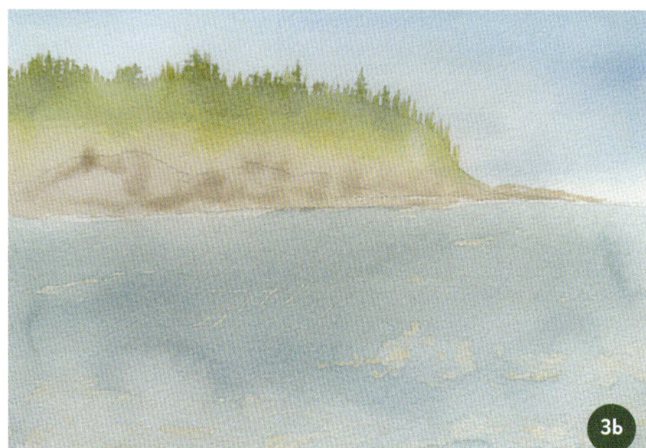

STEP 3: THE UNDERPAINTING

Next, let's paint the wet-on-wet (page 10) underlayers for the scene before building more detail. With a size 12 round brush, layer a wash of clean water over the landscape area. Then, use a size 2 round brush with a warm yellow-green mix (French Ultramarine + New Gamboge) to paint a loose underlayer in the watery tree area. While still wet, add the tree tops into the green underlayer using small vertical strokes of the size 2 brush and the yellow-green paint. Keep the green paint away from the rocky area by pushing it away with a clean brush as much as possible. Then, tap a watery warm brown mix (French Ultramarine + Pyrrol Scarlet + New Gamboge) into the still-wet rocky area, leaving behind plenty of white space. (It's okay if the brown and the green bleed a little or if the brown escapes the sketch of the rocky area for now.)

Let dry, then mix a watery turquoise (Phthalo Blue + a bit of Hansa Yellow Light). Layer a wash of clean water over the ocean area, then paint the light-value turquoise across the watery area.

STEP 4: THE TREES

Mix a medium-value yellow-green (could use the same mix from Step 3, with more paint and less water in the mixture), maybe adding a bit more French Ultramarine to make it a bit greener. Use a foliage brush and loosely tap all around to paint the trees, leaving behind some spots of the lighter underlayer. Then paint in a few darker tree tops as well. While still wet, you can use the foliage brush for a few taps of just New Gamboge for an interesting mix of color in the layer. Let dry, then add a bit of Payne's Gray to the green mix to make it even darker, and paint a line of more identifiable evergreen trees in front, either using a smaller foliage brush or a size 2 round brush.

Then, add even more Payne's Gray to make the green darker still, and paint a few contrasting marks on the front trees, leaving behind plenty of the previous layers while adding depth with the dark-value marks. The idea here is to give some of the trees more detail, while others look like they're all blending together in a distant cluster, starting with lighter layers in the back and growing darker toward the front. It's okay if the bottoms of the trees brush up against the rocky area! Add a few odd taps of green along the tapered shore as well. Let dry.

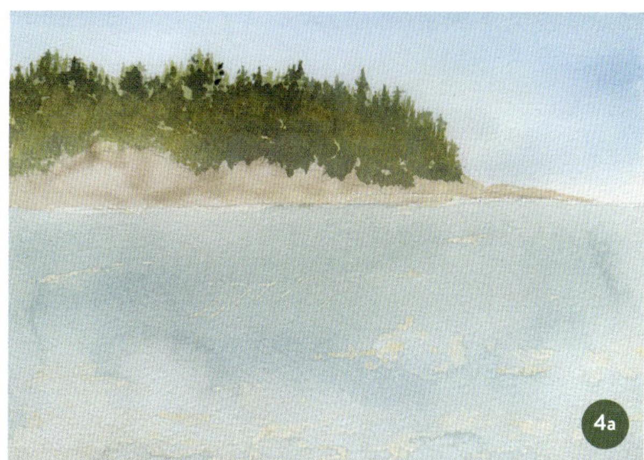

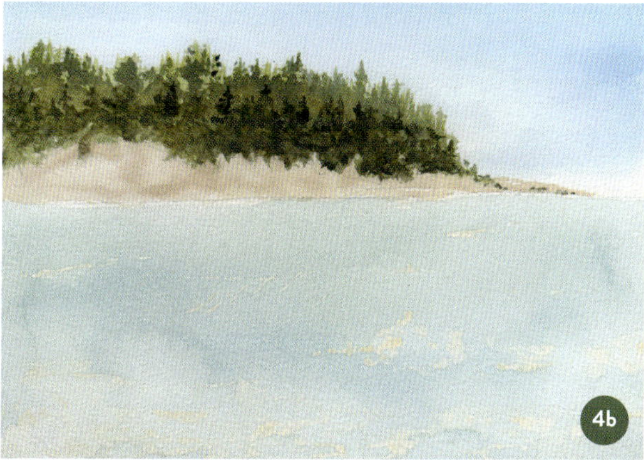

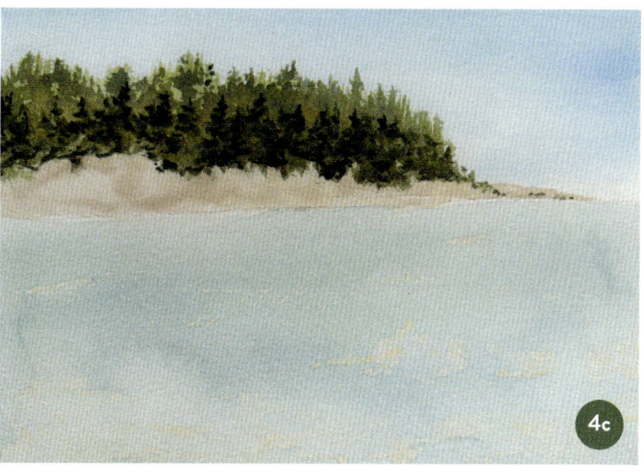

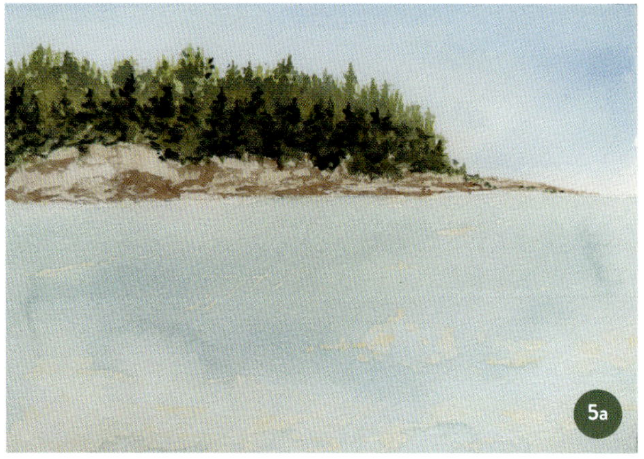

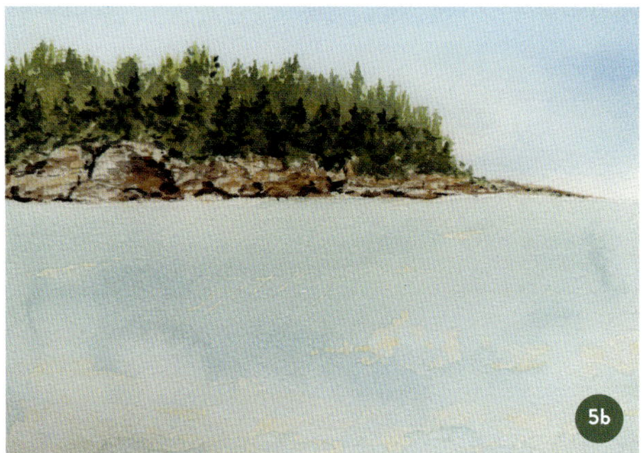

STEP 5: THE ROCKS

With a size 2 round brush and a medium-value brown mix (French Ultramarine + Pyrrol Scarlet + New Gamboge), use the wet-on-dry technique (page 12) to loosely brush paint over the rocky area to create some dry brush (page 12) texture and shadows along the bottom of the rocky area and in some areas on the top. Add a bit of Payne's Gray to the brown mix to darken the value, then repeat, this time adding darker shadows around some of the areas. While not painting individual rocks necessarily, adding a few intentional dark shadows along one side of some areas will subtly imply a more structured shape without losing the distance perspective.

Repeat with adding a slightly darker-value brown to the same spots once dry in order to sharpen the contrast even more in some areas. Remember: Less is more when it comes to adding dark values to provide structure and movement. The darker the value, the less paint you actually need.

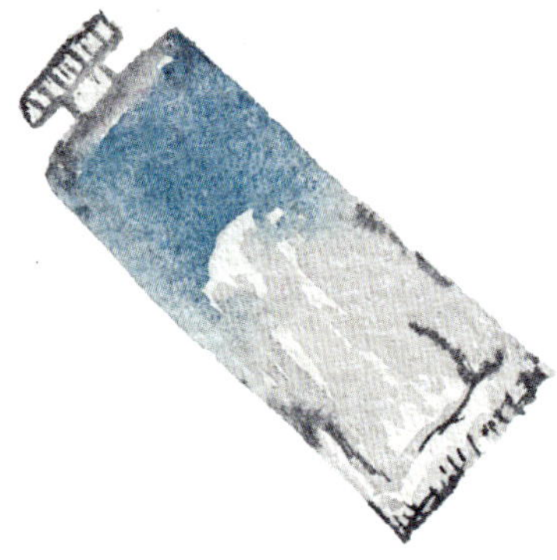

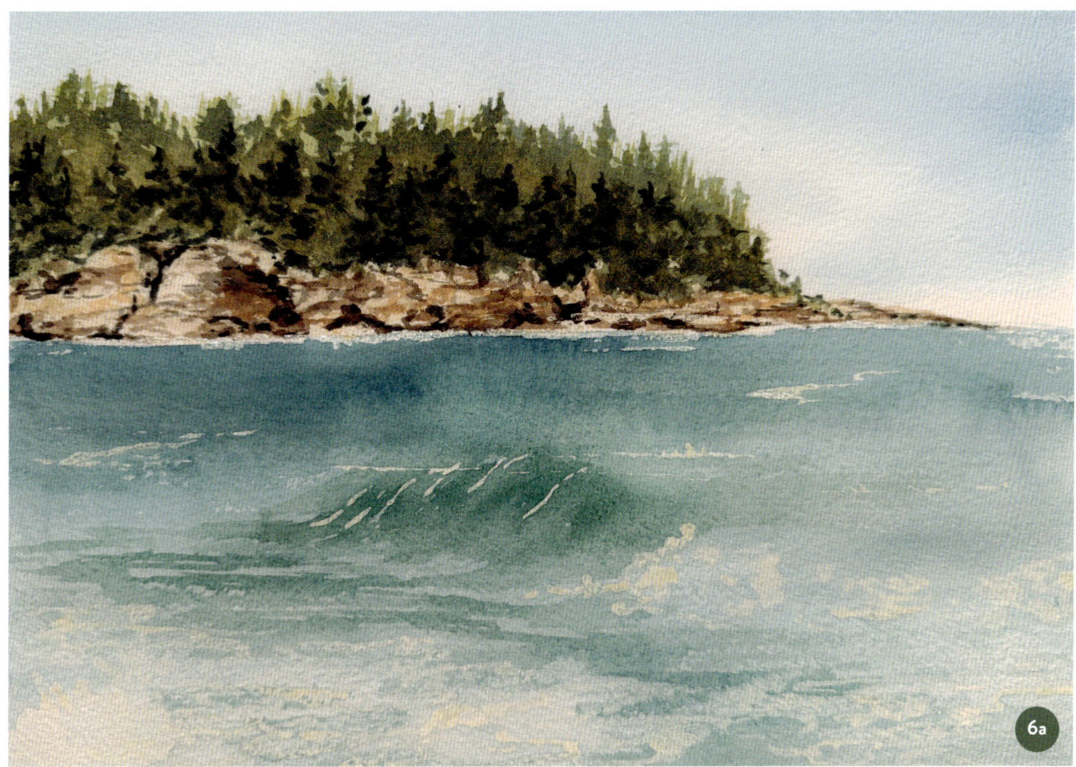

STEP 6: THE WATER

While we have one large water area, the water is moving differently across three main sub-areas. We have the bottom portion, where it's mainly seafoam in loose zigzags. Then a rolling wave or two in the middle area, and finally, distant and more scattered movement toward the back by the landscape. As you begin painting these sub-areas as a cohesive waterscape, remember that the idea isn't accuracy or perfection—it's to capture the wildness of the water using imperfect movement and even random strokes of paint, building layers of value and using size to imply distance (small in the back, large in the front).

(continued)

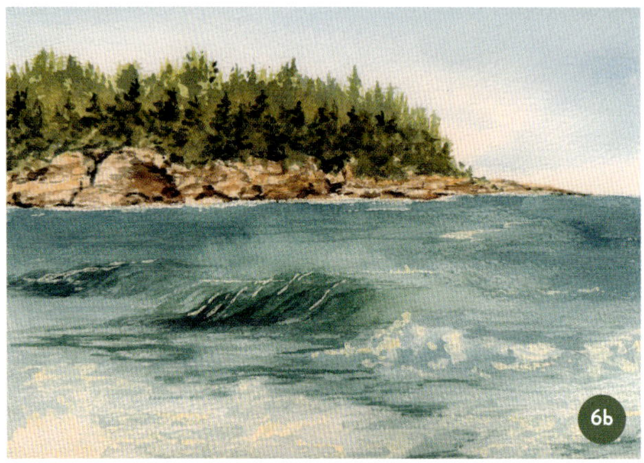

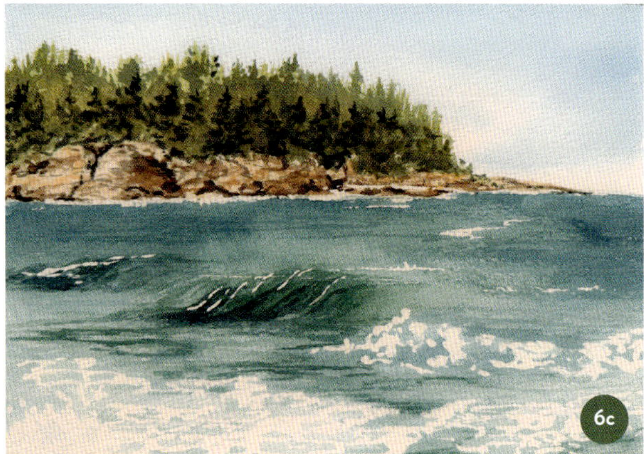

Start with a size 12 round brush to paint a medium-value layer of turquoise (Phthalo Blue + a bit of Hansa Yellow Light) on the water, darker and bluer toward the back, lighter (watery) and greener toward the front. Let dry, then use a size 2 round brush and green-leaning turquoise (a bit more yellow) to paint loose zigzag wave texture just above the masked sea-foam area. Make a darker-value turquoise mix, then repeat, leaving behind some of the lighter layers. Add a few wet-on-dry (page 12) S-curves (page 13) and blobby zigzags to the rolling wave areas (if you chose to paint any).

To add more detail and texture to the distant water toward the back, use light-value (watery) turquoise starting from the right side and flicking inward, creating a very subtle horizontal dry-brush texture (to mimic distant waves). Add long, skinny, and loose light-value zigzag shapes just beneath the rocky area for subtler wave lines in the distance.

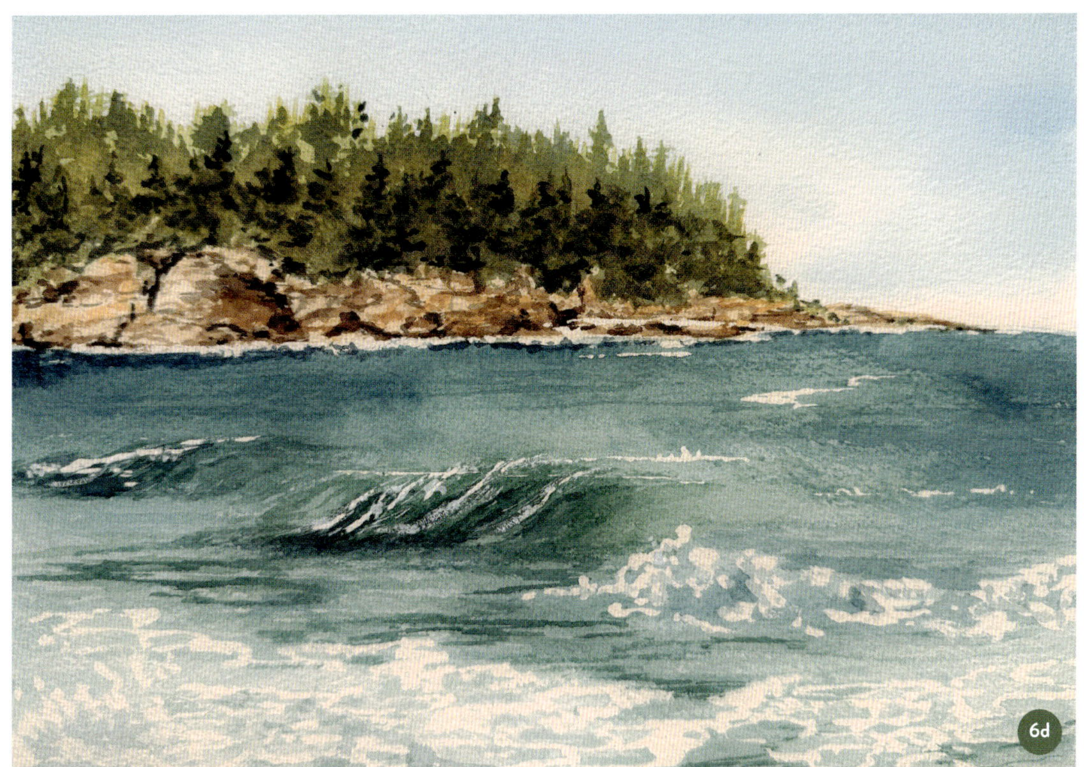

Let dry, then remove the masking fluid by gently rubbing it away with your finger or an eraser (page 15). Mix a watery turquoise, and with a size 2 round brush, paint a few loose zigzag motions around the seafoam area, just to add a bit of shadow and depth between the waves. Not too much here!

We still want most of this to be white space. Use white gouache in quick flicks of dry brush texture to add any seafoam spray along the waves or to tighten up areas where the masking fluid didn't do what you hoped.

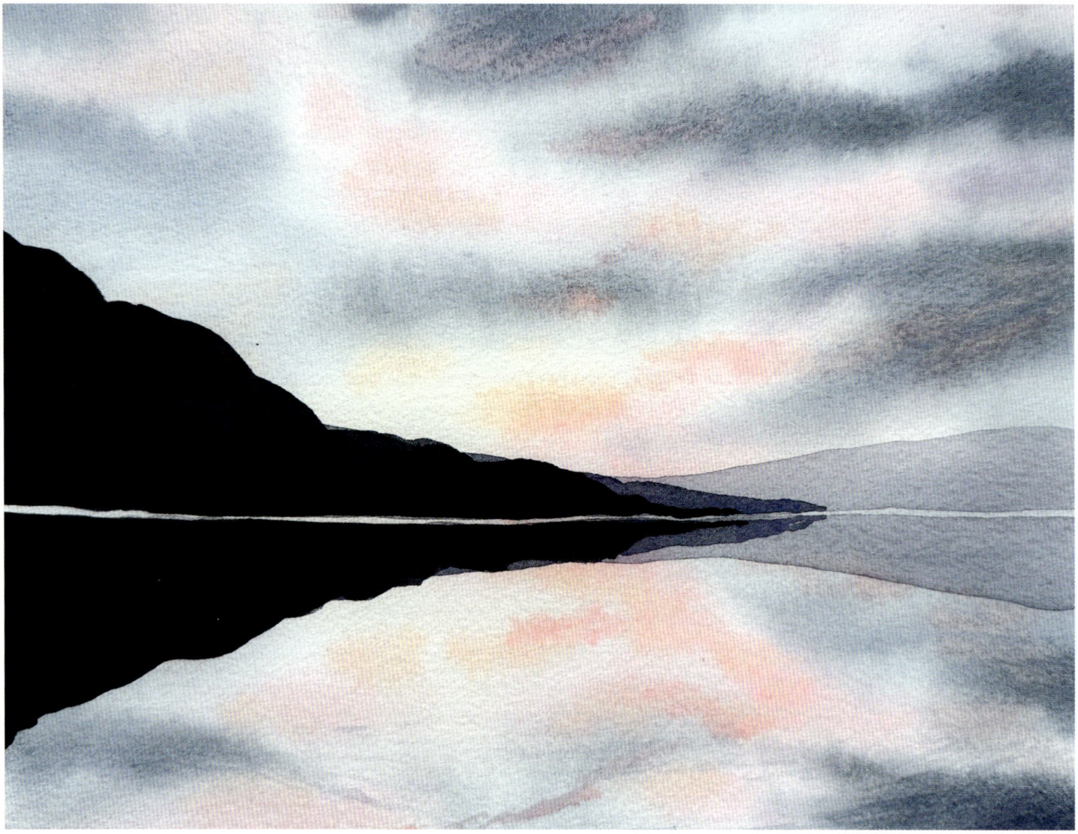

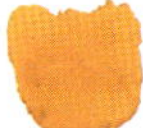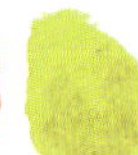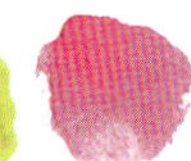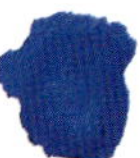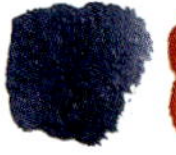

DEATH VALLEY

BRUSHES
Round sizes 2, 6, and 12

COLOR PALETTE
New Gamboge, Hansa Yellow Light, Opera Pink, French Ultramarine, Payne's Gray, Pyrrol Scarlet

While normally a dry desert, Death Valley sometimes receives enough precipitation to amass a small lake called Badwater Basin—turning a crackling salt flat into a mind-bending reflection pool. Let's paint a simple but stunning sunset reflection with a few dark mountain layers to contrast against the luminous lake and sky.

STEP 1: THE SKY AND THE LAKE

Paint the sky and the sky's reflection in the lake at the same time. Using a size 12 round brush, start with a layer of clean water across the whole page, then envision a horizontal line (or sketch one in) about a third of the way up the page, separating the lake from the sky. With a size 6 round brush, tap a watery yellow mix (New Gamboge + Hansa Yellow Light) just to the left of center, both above and below the separating line. Create a watery mix of Opera Pink and a bit of New Gamboge, and paint loose, wispy strokes of the pinks in the sky and in the reflection. Let dry completely, then rewet with clean water. Mix French Ultramarine and Payne's Gray with some water, and paint around the yellow and pink areas, leaving some blurry white space between the blue and the clouds. We're painting the colorful clouds first, then painting the sky around them to enhance the glowing effect by leaving behind blurry borders of white space. Use a thirsty brush (page 11) to lift any paint that bleeds into the clouds too much.

Let the paper dry just a bit longer, but before it dries all the way, paint a few more small wisps with the yellow and pink mixes for added cloudy texture in the sky and the reflection. Let dry completely.

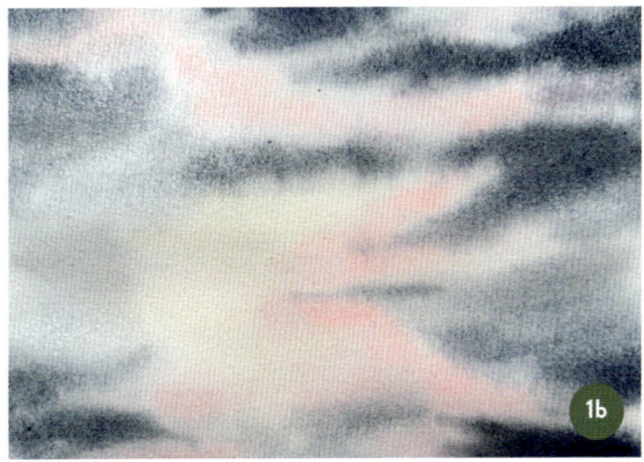

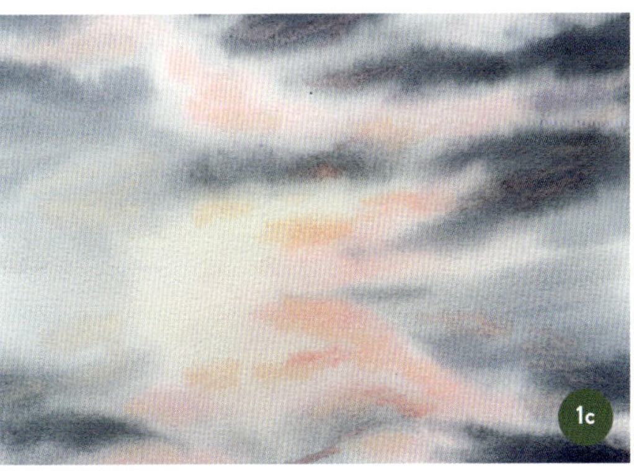

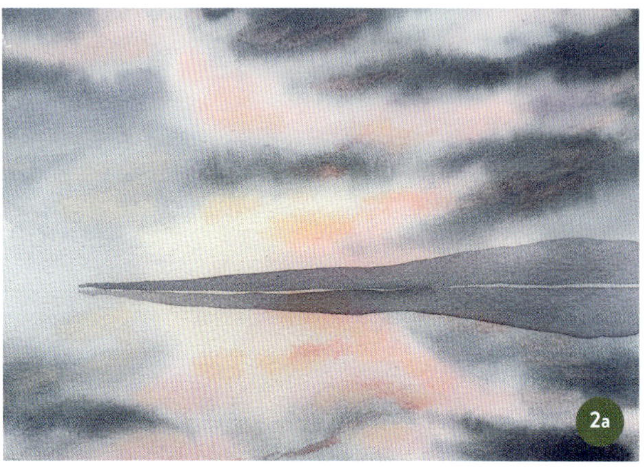

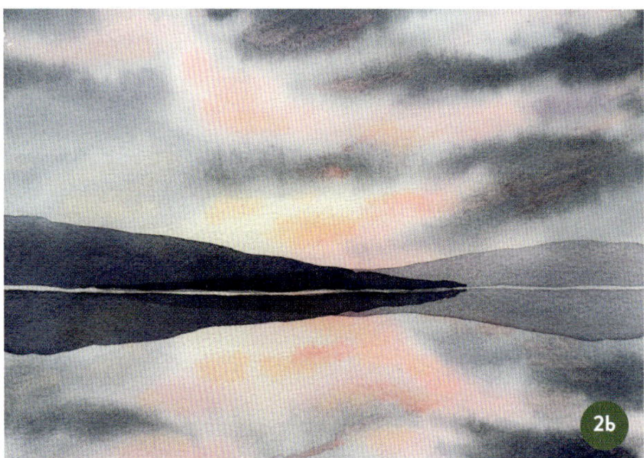

STEP 2: THE MOUNTAINS

Mix Payne's Gray with just a bit of Pyrrol Scarlet to create a muted blue violet, then add water to make it light value. Using a size 6 round brush, paint the background mountain layer and its reflection coming out from the right side of the page and tapering down, leaving a thin line of negative space (page 15) between them. Let dry completely, then add a bit more Payne's Gray to the mix and paint the next mountain layer, this time starting from the left side. Let dry completely, then paint the final mountain layer with more Payne's Gray in the mix, starting the mountain higher on the left side, tapering off just behind the previous layer.

STEP 3: THE DETAILS

Finally, use a size 2 round brush with quite watery Payne's Gray, and paint a few loose zigzag marks and rocky shapes in the lake, implying a cracking desert ground beneath the shallow lake water.

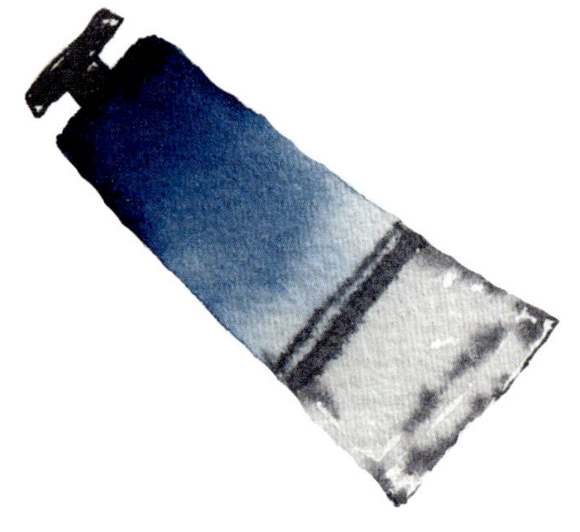

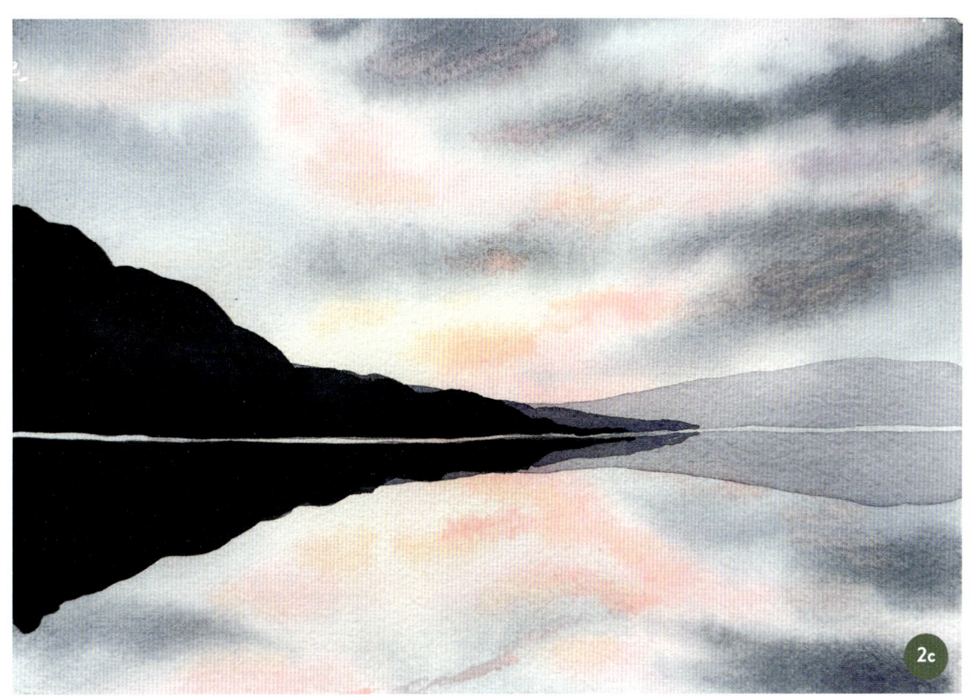

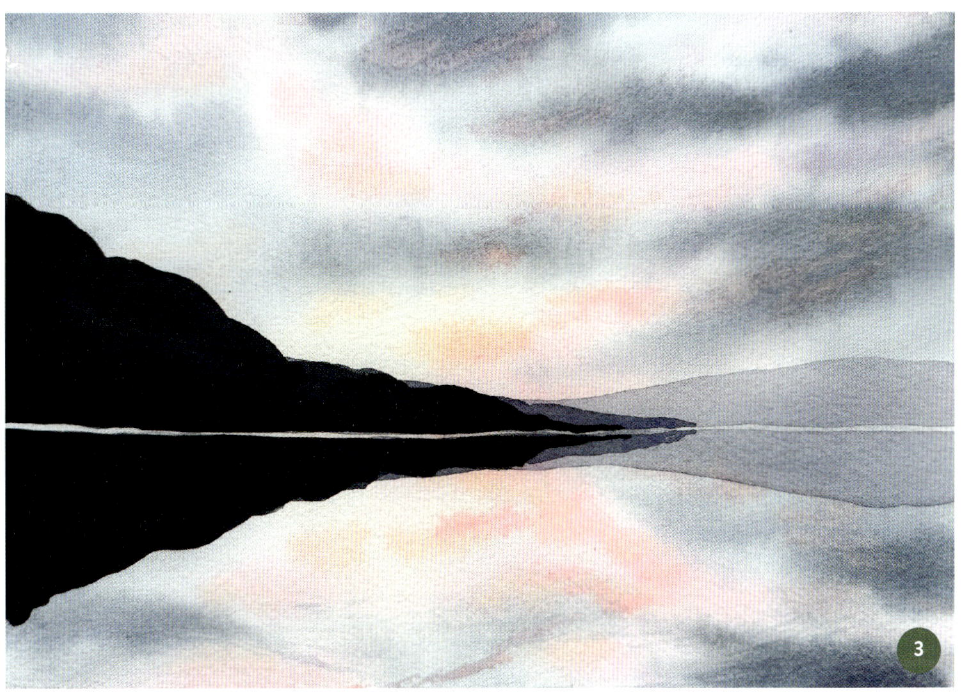

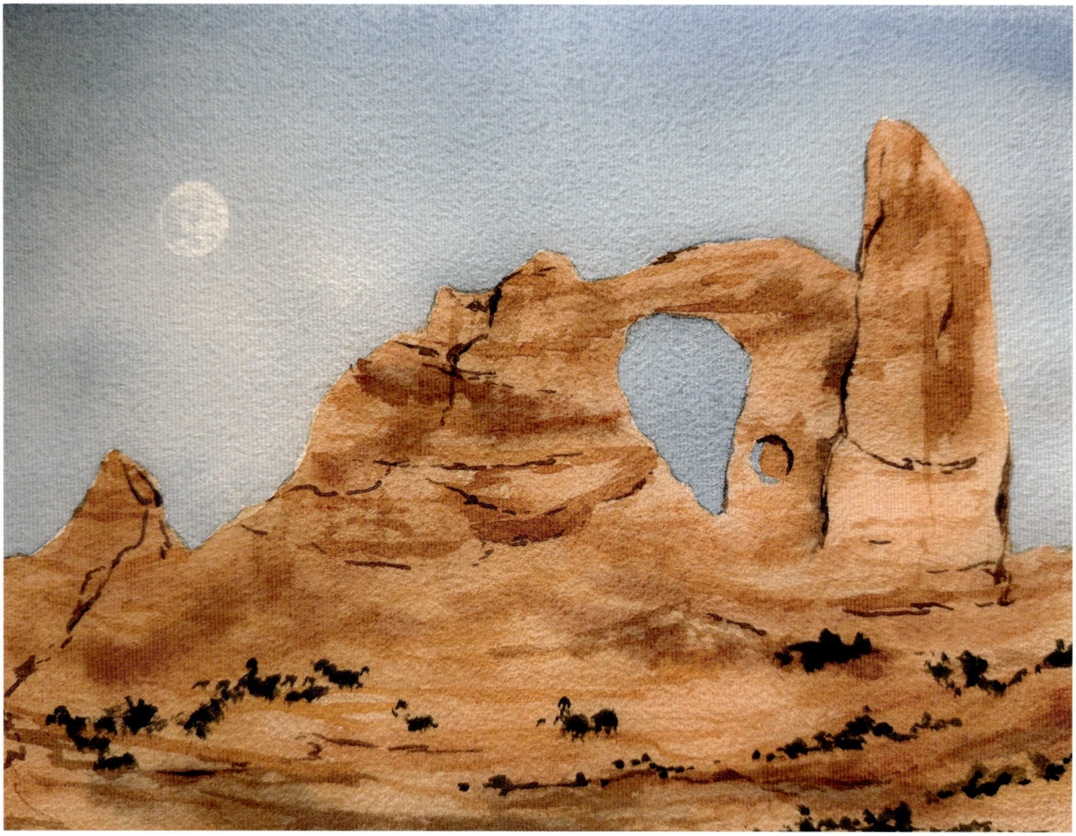

ARCHES

BRUSHES
Round sizes 2 and 12; Foliage brush

COLOR PALETTE
French Ultramarine, Quinacridone Rose,
New Gamboge, Pyrrol Scarlet, white
gouache, Payne's Gray

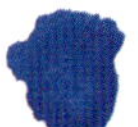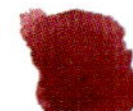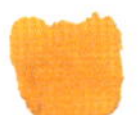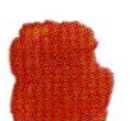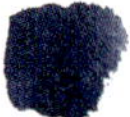

Arches National Park is home
to some of the most delightful
rock formations, inspiring even
the most serious humans to let
their imaginations run wild with
pretend play in the desert. With
its castle-like column and giant
window, building up the slow layers
of Turret Arch will be a whimsical
foray into your imagination.

STEP 1: THE SKETCH

Start by sketching the turret: a long, vertical rocky formation jutting up a little bit away from the right side of the page. Then sketch a sloping-down C-curve (page 13), starting midway through the left edge of the turret and moving outward. Sketch a large window and a small window under the C-curve to shape the arch. Behind the arch, sketch a rocky mountain ridge moving in a jagged curve toward the center left of the page. Sketch a few lines on the other side of the turret and along the bottom of the page for the ground.

STEP 2: THE SKY

This scene will be just before twilight, so the sky is just slightly more blue than violet. Mix a watery French Ultramarine with just a hint of Quinacridone Rose. Layer a wash of clean water across the sky with a size 12 round brush, leaving the rock formations dry. Paint the sky a watery blue-violet, as well as the large window in the arch and a sliver of a C-curve on the smaller window. Let dry completely.

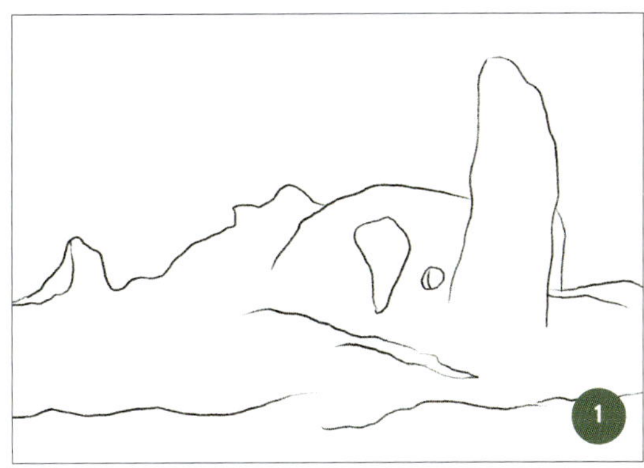

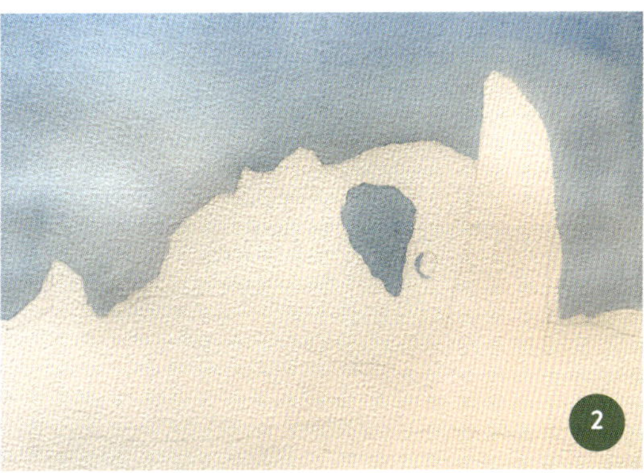

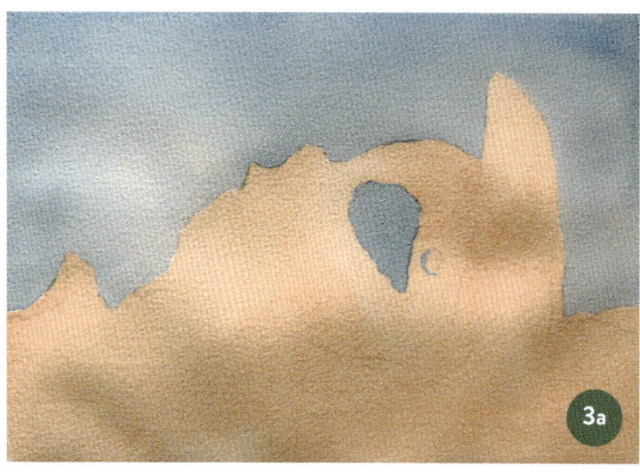
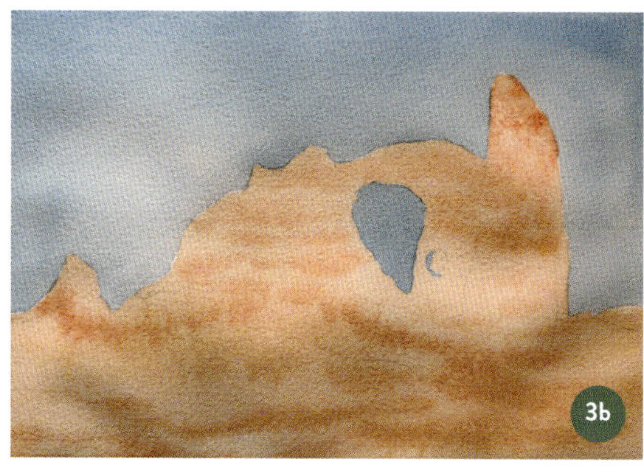

STEP 3: THE ARCH

Mix a watery orange-brown (New Gamboge + Pyrrol Scarlet + French Ultramarine—with more Pyrrol Scarlet than the others). Paint the arch and the ground beneath it. While this layer is still wet, use a size 2 round brush with slightly darker-value orange-brown (add more paint), and layer a few blend-y horizontal stripes across the ground and the arch. Mix an even darker brown (with a bit more French Ultramarine to make it more of a warm maroon), and repeat in a few spots. It's okay if some of the arch is dried by now—having a mix of blend-y stripes plus more defined-but-jagged paint lines adds texture!

Let dry, then use a size 2 round brush with watery mixes of orange brown and maroon to paint wet-on-dry (page 12) jagged stripes (both vertical and horizontal, always using a kind of shaky, zigzag movement) across the arch and the ground. Remember that in real life, these rock formations were formed over thousands of years ago kind of at random—it's okay for your strokes to look and feel kind of random too! Use varying pressure on your brush to alter the thickness sometimes, and lightly brush a mostly dry brush across the page for some rougher texture. Let dry, then use a watery orange brown to paint across the whole arch again, slightly darkening it (to indicate the time of day when the sun is setting), and to loosen some of the stripes, making them look more weathered. (You could also paint over the formation with just clean water to loosen the paint a bit, if you don't want to add more color.)

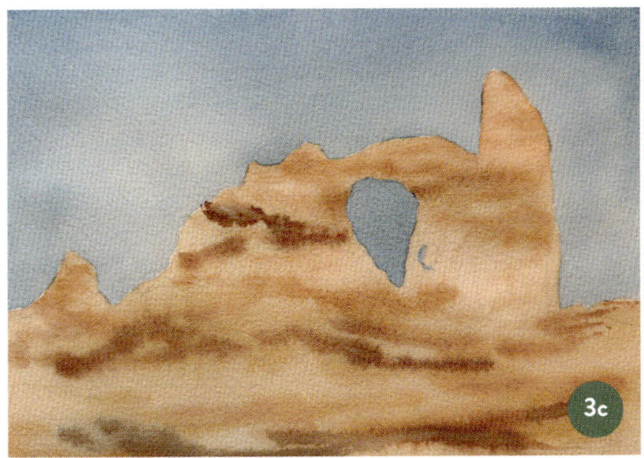

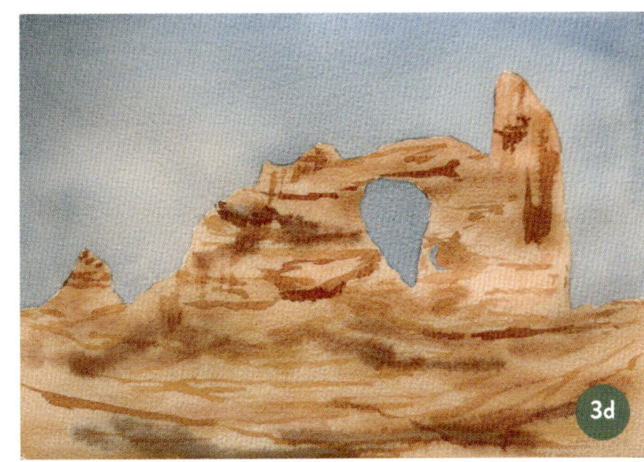

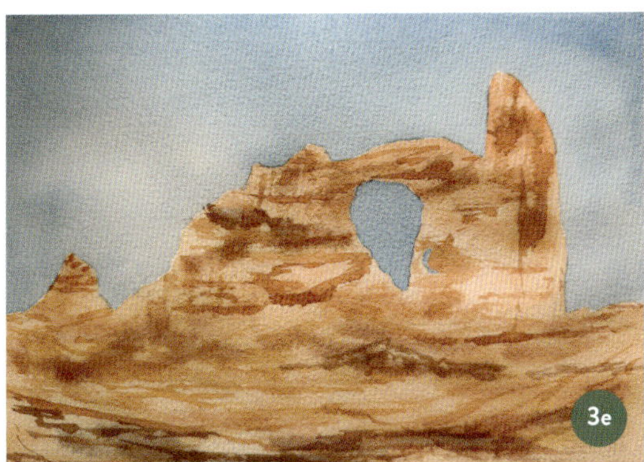

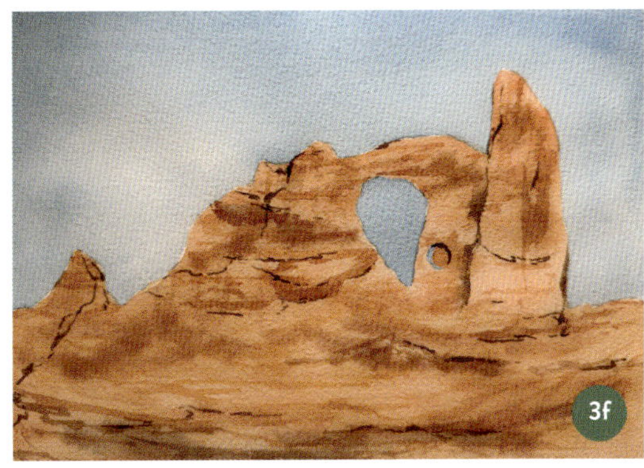

Let dry completely, then mix a darker-value brown. With a size 2 round brush, add a few thin shadows along some of the crevices and edges of the formations to separate them and also add depth to any specific cracks. Specifically, add a small brown C-curve along the opposite edge of the small window to indicate an indent in the rock.

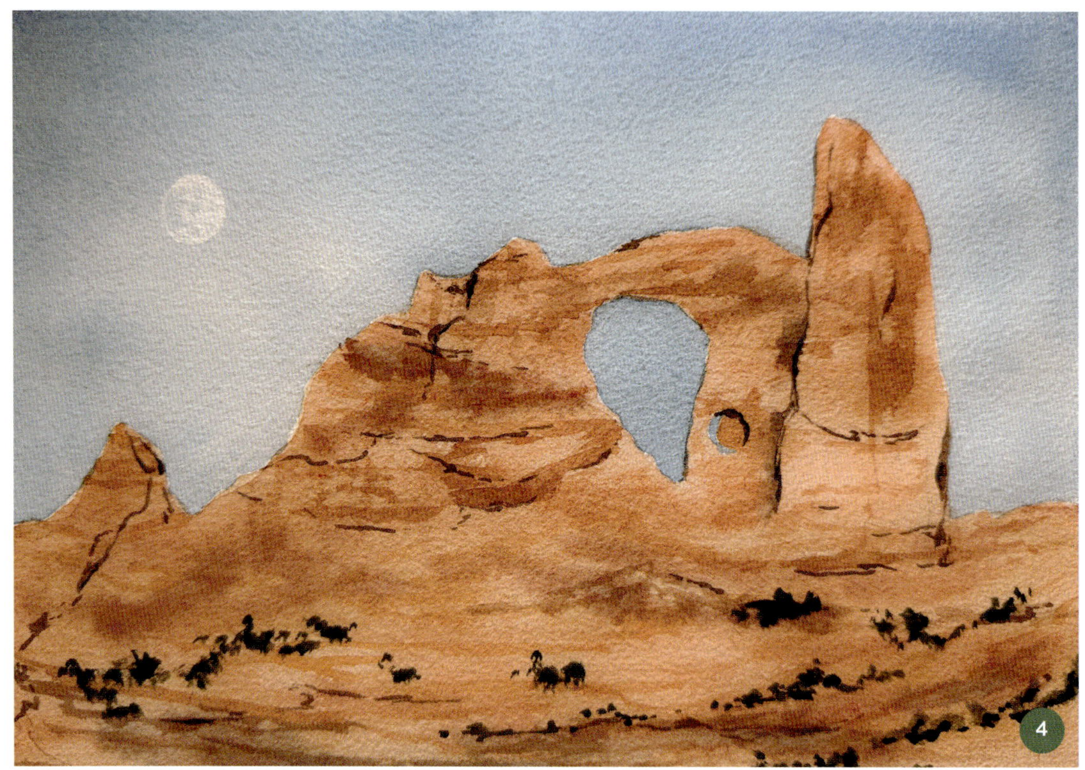

STEP 4: FINAL DETAILS

Use white gouache to paint a small moon in the top left of the sky. Start with a circle, then paint a few watery blobs along the right edge, gradually tapering off, leaving behind bits of the blue sky underneath. Finally, mix a dark green (Payne's Gray + New Gamboge), and use a foliage brush to paint a few lines of scattered desert brush along the ground.

ZION

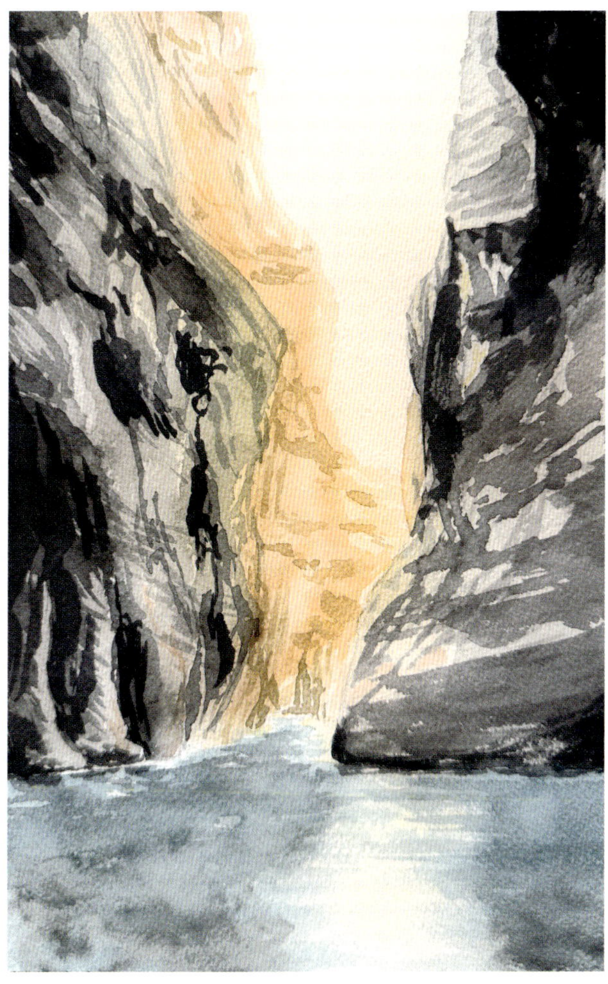

Hiking the Zion Narrows is like receiving a giant hug from the mountains themselves, and painting them can be much the same! Let's paint these narrow rock faces one luminous layer at a time, slowly building up texture and value, to craft a scene that's almost as mind-bending as the real thing.

BRUSHES

Round sizes 2, 6, and 12; Foliage brush

COLOR PALETTE

New Gamboge, Payne's Gray, Phthalo Blue (Green Shade), Hansa Yellow Light, Pyrrol Scarlet, French Ultramarine

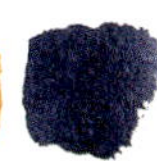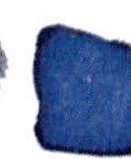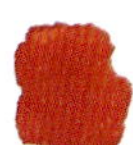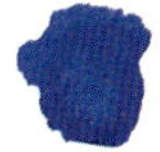

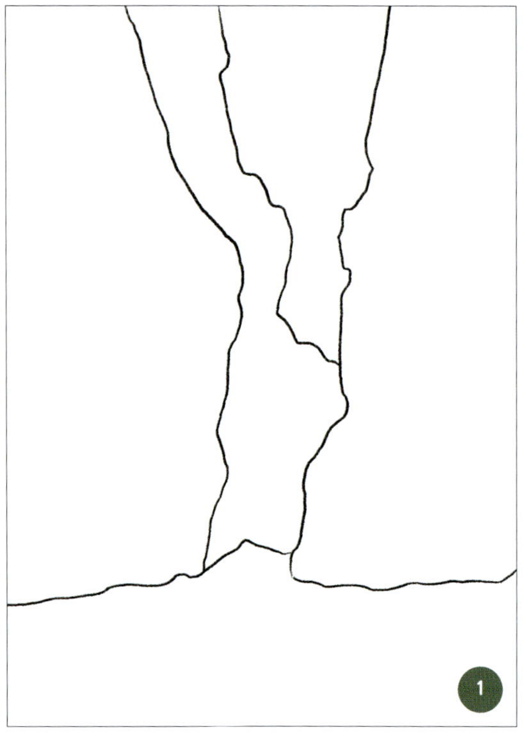

STEP 1: THE SKETCH

Start with three jagged vertical lines and one jagged horizontal line to separate the rock faces from the sky and the creek. The horizontal line should sit about a fourth of the way up from the bottom of the page, with two vertical lines beginning about midway through the horizontal line, each framing a loose column through the center of the page, and then jutting outward toward their respective sides. Add a third vertical line coming out of the right rock face in a fork, dividing the center. The sections, from the left to right, should be: outer rock face, inner rock face, sky, outer rock face. Finally, add a few jagged vertical lines to the two outer rock faces to reference where you might want to add cracks and shadows during painting.

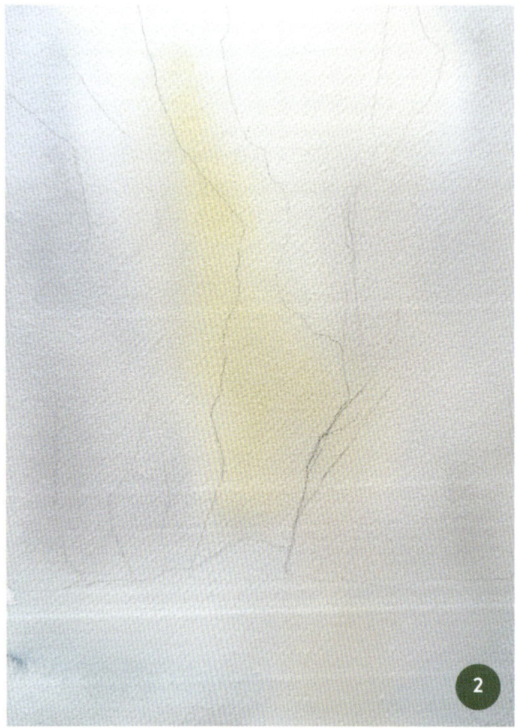

STEP 2: THE UNDERPAINTING

Create three separate watery mixes for this first wash: New Gamboge, Payne's Gray, and Turquoise (Phthalo Blue + a bit of Hansa Yellow Light). Use a size 12 round brush to layer a wash of clean water across the entire page. Add watery strokes of each color to their respective sections: New Gamboge for the inner rock face (slightly darker-value on the rock face, then lighter in the sky); Payne's Gray for the outer rock faces; and turquoise for the creek with a sliver of New Gamboge running down the center right of the water for a highlight. It's okay if the paint bleeds between the reference lines, but it's important that this layer is very light in value (which translates to quite watery and pale). Let dry completely.

STEP 3: THE INNER ROCK FACE

Next, let's add some texture to the inner rock face. This wall is most directly in the sunlight, which means we're using warm colors (to contrast with the cool neutrals of the outer rock faces, which are largely in shadow). Mix a watery warm brown (New Gamboge + Pyrrol Scarlet + French Ultramarine, but with more yellow and red than blue). Then, use a foliage brush or a smaller round brush (either size 2 or 6) to paint a luminous wash across the inner rock face while carving out random dry marks, which will act as highlights along the edge closest to the sky. Use lots of water, or alternate between using paint and water to create a blend-y texture.

Let dry completely, and then make the brown mix slightly darker in value (add more paint), but still watery. Use a size 2 round brush or a foliage brush to add loose horizontal and vertical stripes across the inner rock face, leaving behind plenty of the lighter layers beneath.

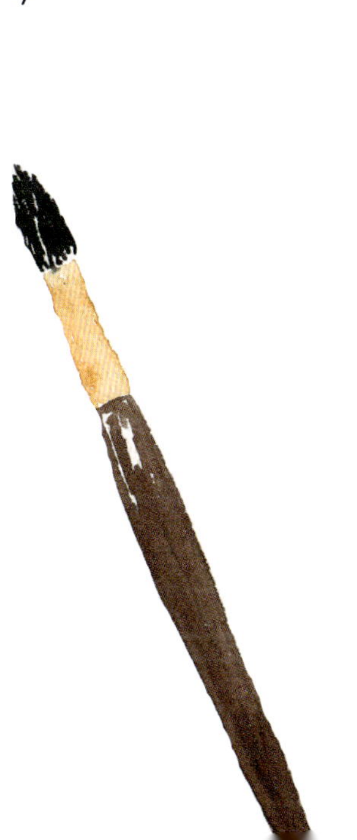

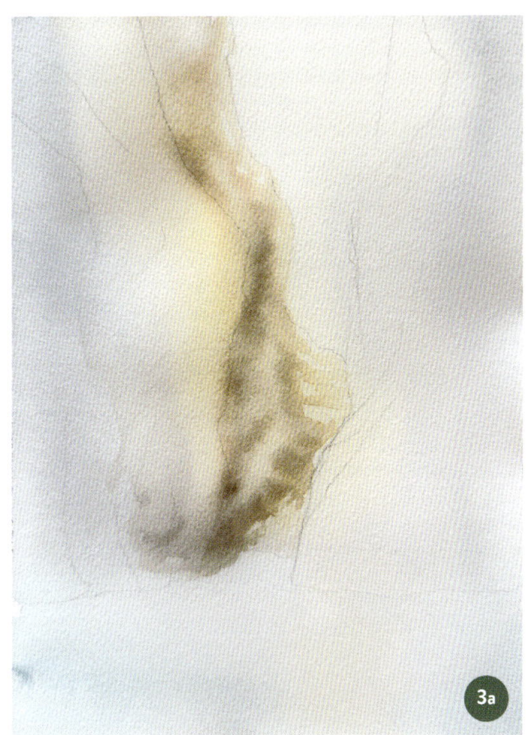

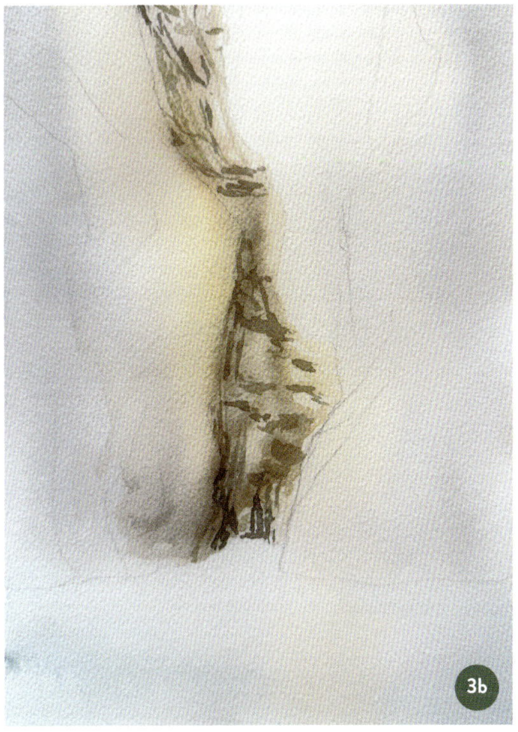

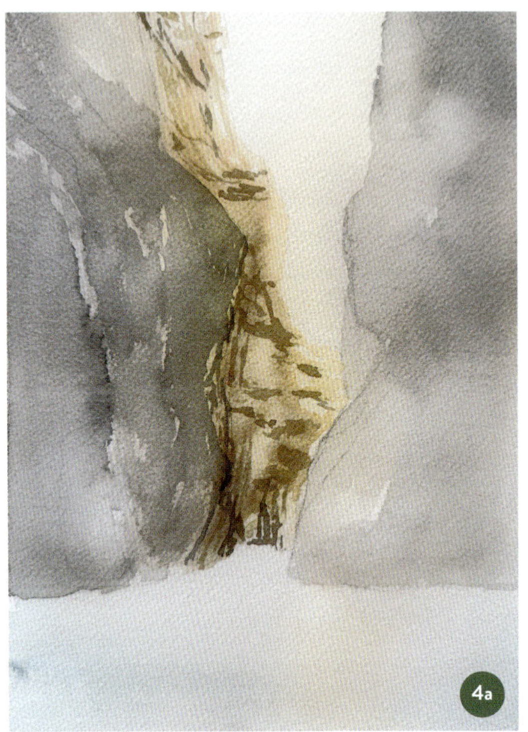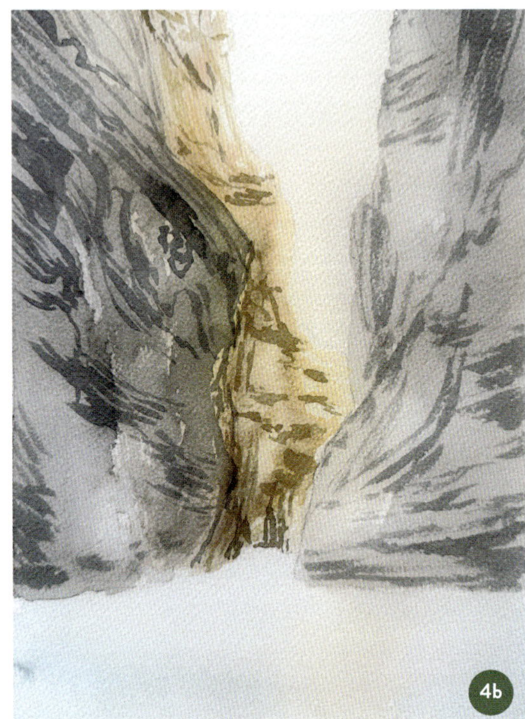

STEP 4: THE OUTER ROCK FACES

Create a watery, neutral gray mix (Payne's Gray + some of the brown mix), then paint a textured wash across both outer rock faces, leaving behind plenty of random dry spots and rough edges. (A foliage brush is great for this.) Tap water in some places to push away the paint, making the wash varied in value and in texture. Let dry, then add a bit more Payne's Gray to the mix (making it slightly darker in value), and paint more rocky stripes in all configurations (vertical, horizontal, sideways)—the goal isn't precision here, so it's okay if you feel a bit uncertain. Rocks are supposed to look wonky! Add a handful of S-curves (page 13) and whorls for more variation (and to play!). Let dry.

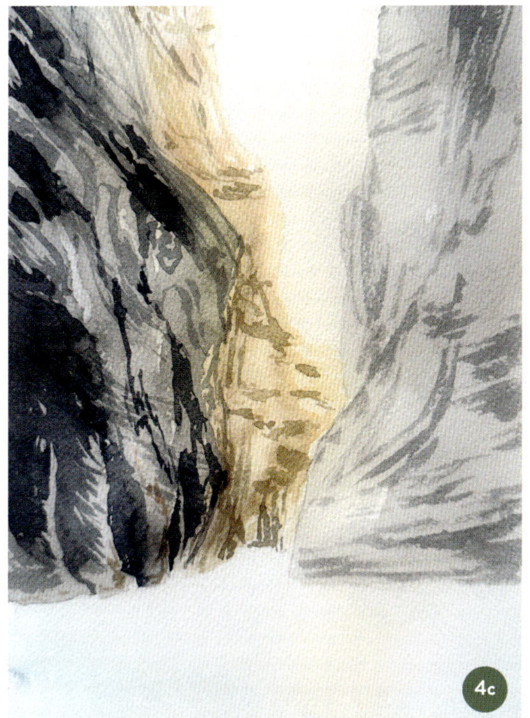

4c

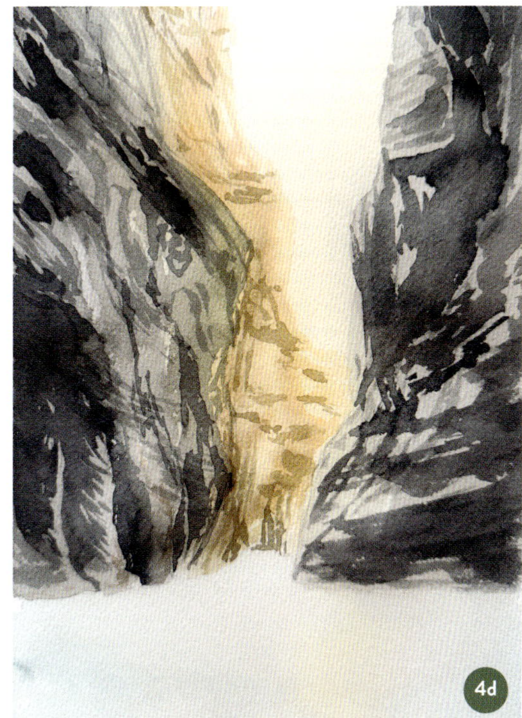

4d

Mix in even more Payne's Gray, making a medium-value gray, then repeat on the left outer rock face with slightly larger painted surface areas along the edge of the paper especially (which is where the rock is the most in shadow). Use the reference lines from the sketch to leave behind some smaller areas of dry spots along the right side, implying crevices or indents in some places on the rock face. Repeat with the right rock face, with the shadows more along the right edge and the highlights more toward the center. Remember: The darker we go in value, the less paint we actually need to deepen the shadows. The most important thing here is to identify where the light source is (the center sky) and add highlights and shadows accordingly.

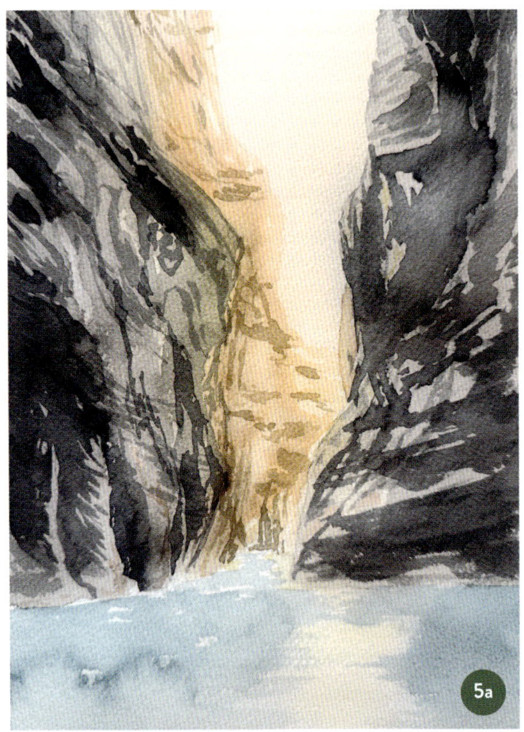

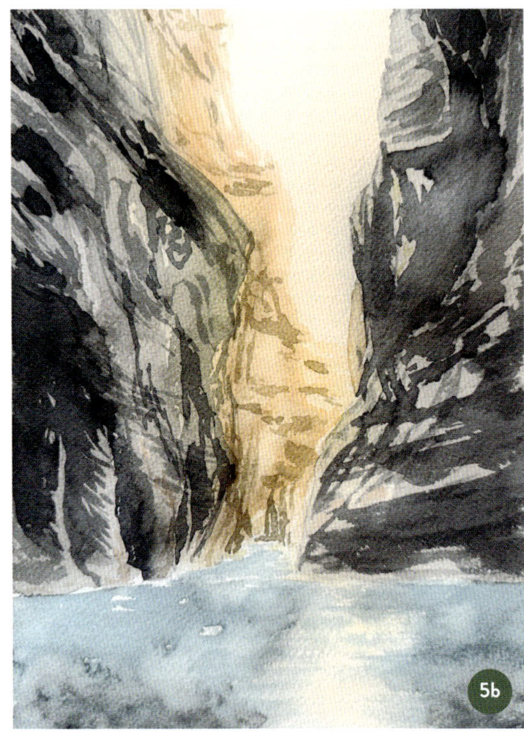

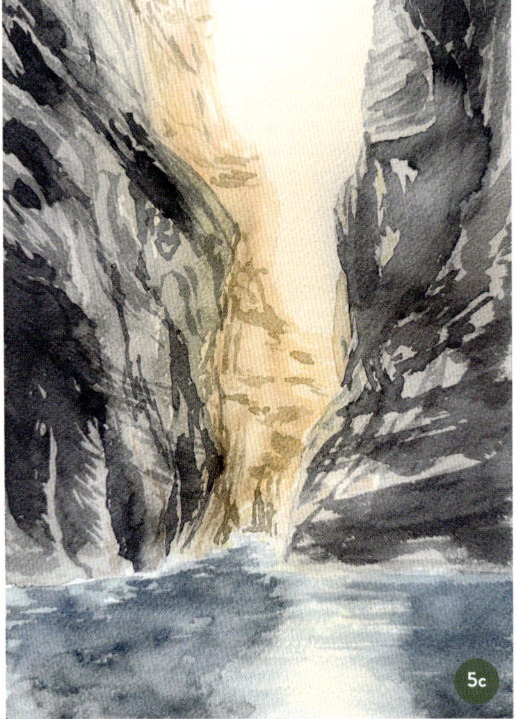

STEP 5: THE CREEK + FINAL DETAILS

Paint another layer of watery turquoise (Phthalo Blue + a bit of Hansa Yellow Light) along the creek area, leaving behind occasional slivers of light space and carving out a jagged area along the center right where the yellow highlights are. Make the creek taper upward a bit, going in between the rock faces to add more depth. You could stop here with the water, or you could add a bit of Payne's Gray to the mix and add one more watery layer to the creek—this time adding just a few horizontal stripes and dry brush (page 12) textures across the yellow highlight area, implying a more wavelike movement. Finally, use a slightly darker Payne's Gray (not all the way dark, but darker than the previous layers) to add even more depth to the shadows on the outer rock faces.

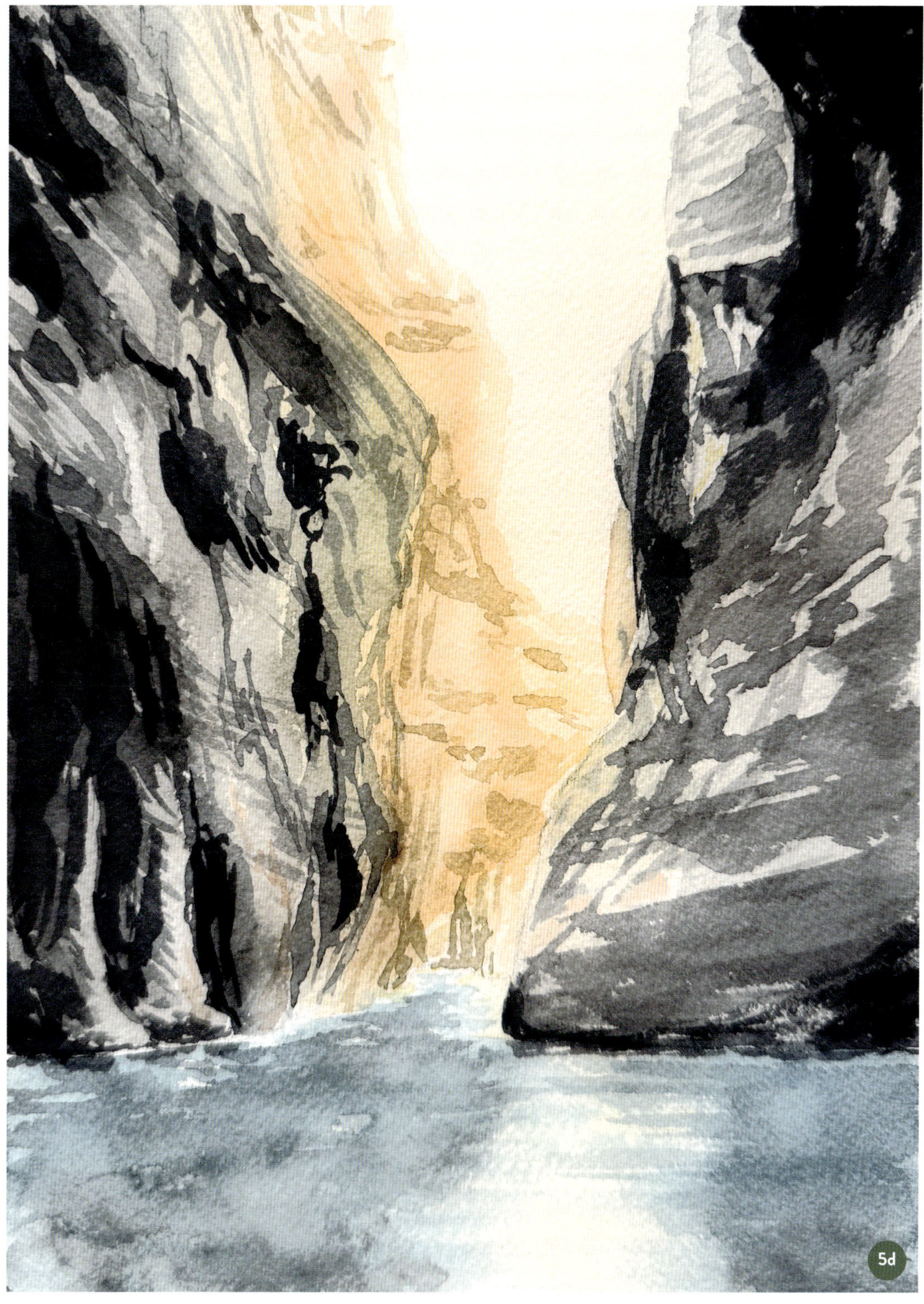

5d

BIG BEND

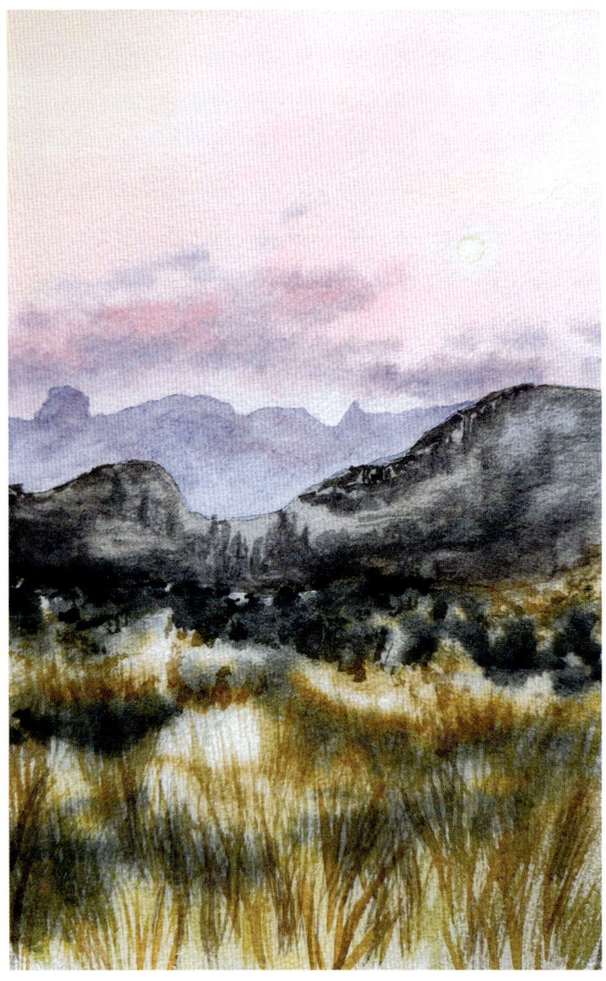

The magic of Big Bend National Park lies in the endless possibility of wide-open spaces—and that's exactly what this scene captures. Let's use shifting light and glimmering textures to bring this desert to life.

BRUSHES
Round sizes 2, 6, and 12; Foliage brush

COLOR PALETTE
New Gamboge, Opera Pink, French Ultramarine, Quinacridone Rose, Payne's Gray, Pyrrol Scarlet

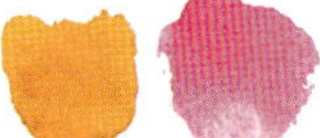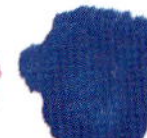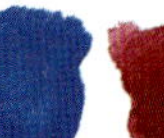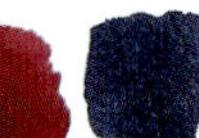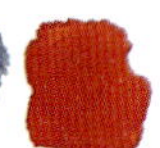

STEP 1: THE SKETCH

Sketch four overlapping horizontal lines to denote the sky, two layers of mountains, and two areas of plains beneath the mountains. The two mountain ridges should have a few dips and slopes, but they should be more rounded or squared as opposed to sharp points. Then, the two lines for the landscape should be relatively close together near the center left, sloping outward as you move toward the right. (These will help capture distance.) Finally, sketch a small circle in the center right of the sky.

STEP 2: THE SKY

Layer a wash of clean water across the sky area with a size 12 round brush (it can brush into the background mountain layer). Mix a light-value (watery) New Gamboge, and drop some into the sky. Let dry, then rewet with clean water, and drop in a watery mix of Opera Pink and New Gamboge (to make a coral color), leaving behind a swirling blend of yellow, orange, and pink. Carefully paint around the circle (which is the sun), leaving it the light yellow from the layer before.

(continued)

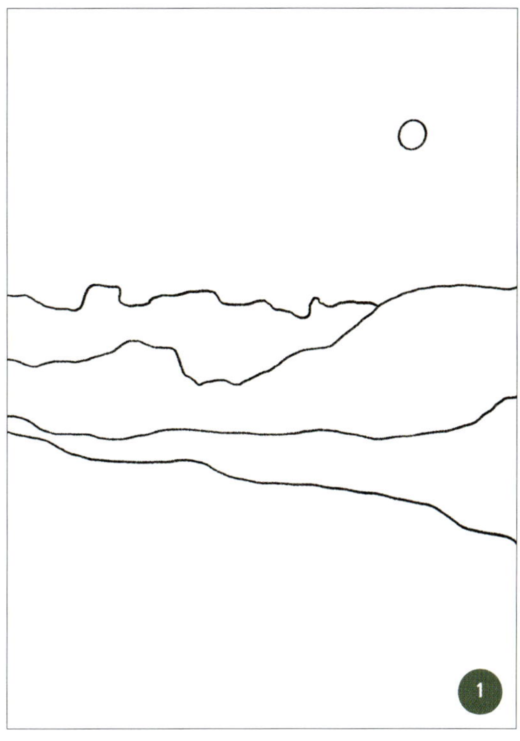

Create a medium-value (a little watery) violet mix with French Ultramarine and a bit of Quinacridone Rose. Then, while the sky is still wet, use a relatively dry size 6 round brush (Painting on Dry Paper [page 12]) to paint a cloud along the bottom of the sky. Paint in loose, wispy strokes, using as little water in the paint and on your brush as possible so the cloud is still blurry but doesn't blend away too much. Add a little more Quinacridone Rose to the mix, and paint the top of the clouds so there's a glimmery mix of violet and pink. Then, use a size 2 round brush to paint the sun a light-value New Gamboge with a little bit of white space around the edges. Let dry completely.

STEP 3: THE MOUNTAINS

Paint the background mountain layer a shadowy violet, with very little detail. Start with a watery gray violet mix (French Ultramarine + Quinacridone Rose + Payne's Gray), then tap bits of French Ultramarine and Quinacridone Rose into the wet wash for subtle color variation. Let dry, then create a watery yellow brown mix (New Gamboge + a bit of Pyrrol Scarlet and French Ultramarine) and paint the second mountain layer. While that's drying, mix a darker brown by adding more Pyrrol Scarlet and French Ultramarine to the

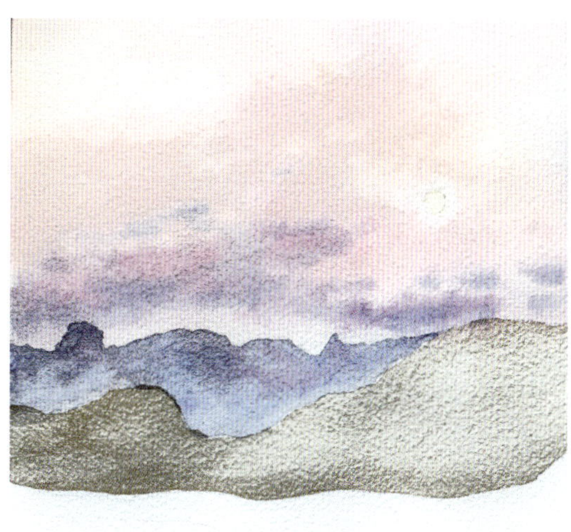

yellow brown mix, and then paint horizontal and vertical lines across the middle mountain layer while it's still damp, leaving behind bits of the yellow layer. Let dry, then mix a dark green (New Gamboge + Payne's Gray), and paint some crossing horizontal and vertical green marks to the mountain layer. This is still relatively in the background, so we want it to look a little shrouded and hazy while still implying some rocky texture. Let dry completely.

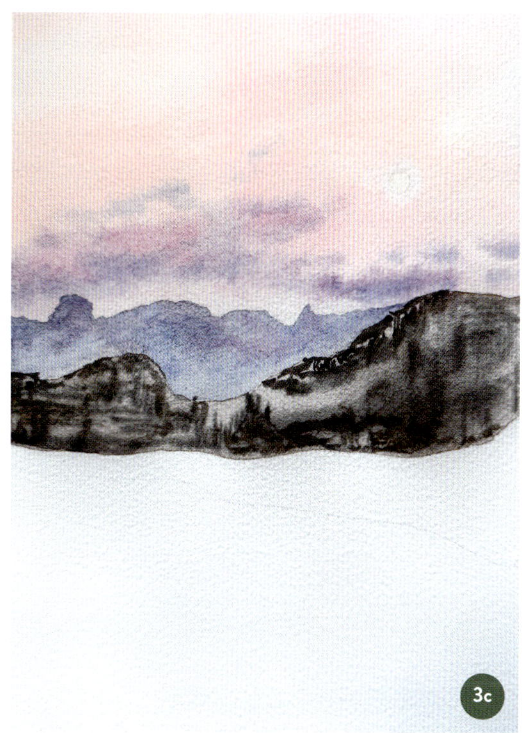

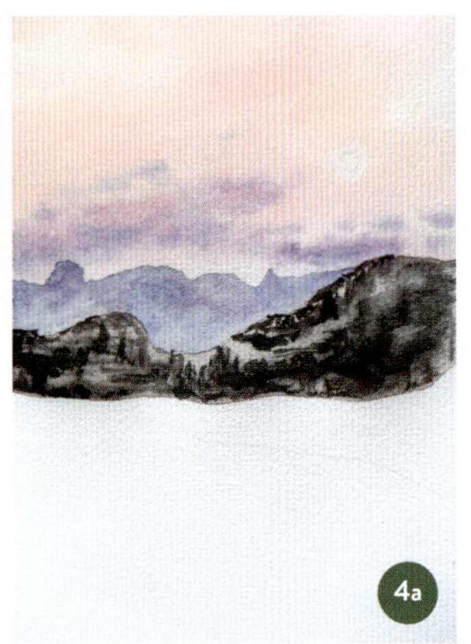

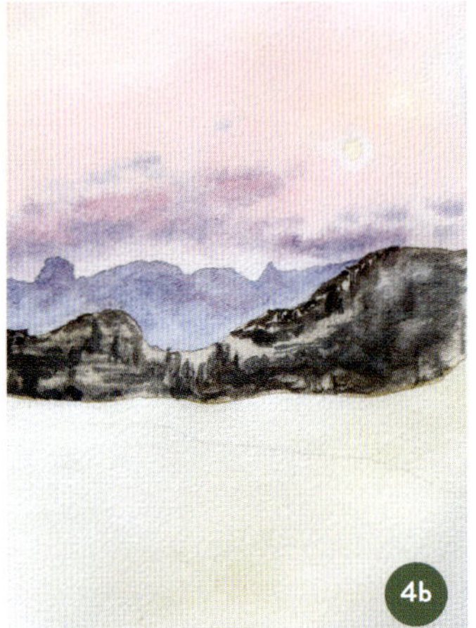

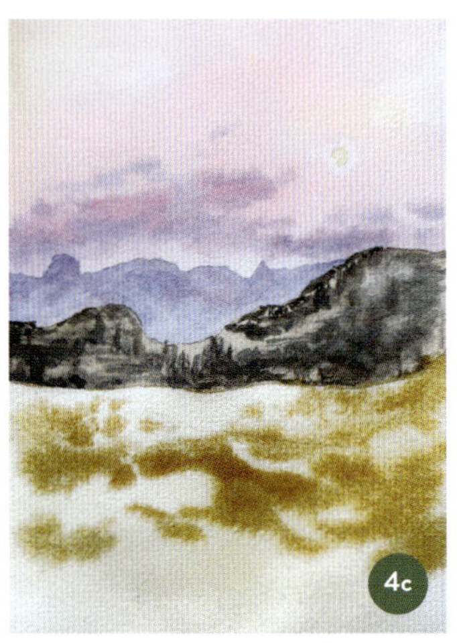

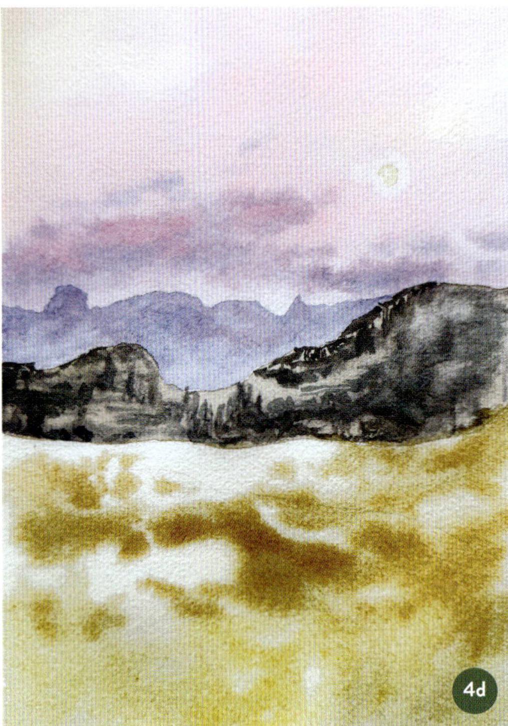

STEP 4: THE LANDSCAPE

Layer a wash of clean water across the rest of the page, then tap in watery New Gamboge, using the wet-on-wet technique (page 10) to get a luminous texture. Mix more yellow brown, then use a size 6 round brush to tap the darker-value color in loose strokes across the landscape, leaving behind some areas of light space. Accuracy is not important here—random zigzag strokes with choppy marks works, especially if you keep the smaller marks toward the back to maintain a distance effect (because smaller marks in the back denote distance). Repeat with a mix of slightly brighter green (French Ultramarine + New Gamboge), making sure to leave behind slivers of white space throughout, using those loose zigzag strokes to imply movement in the plains.

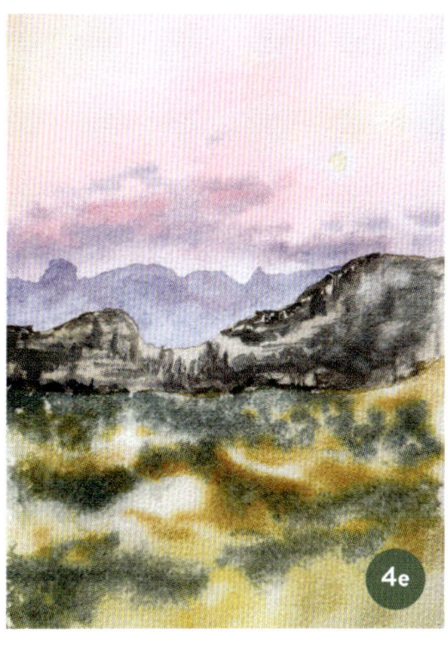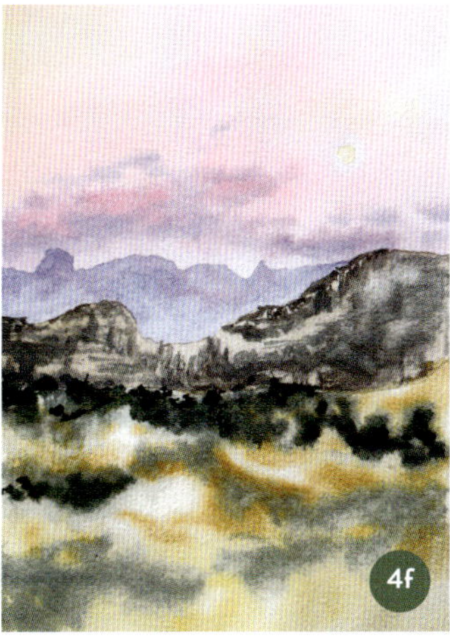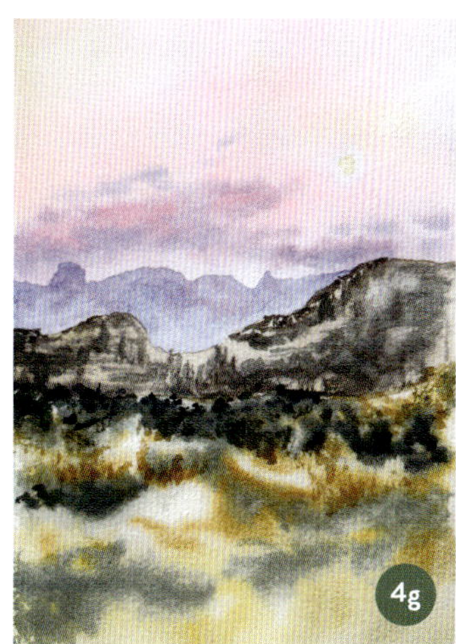

Add Payne's Gray to the green mix, then use a size 2 round brush to tap a few darker marks toward the back (where the top landscape sketch line was). Let dry completely, then repeat with the yellow-brown mix. These marks should be small and in the distance, implying desert brush near the distant mountain range.

Next, use a foliage brush or a size 2 round brush to start painting grass (starting with the bottom of the blade with a quick flick upward to get thin, sharp lines) with the yellow-brown mix.

(continued)

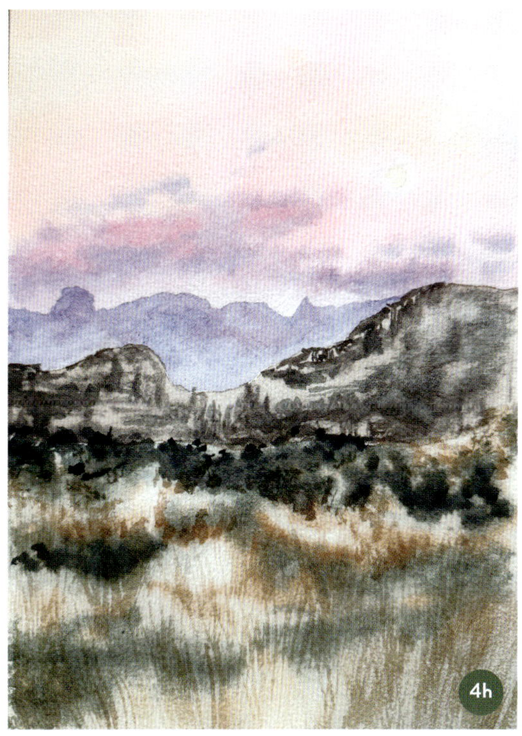

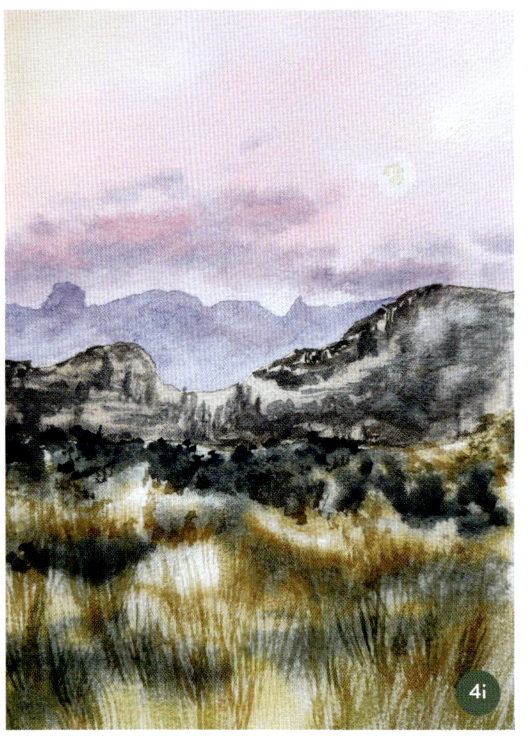

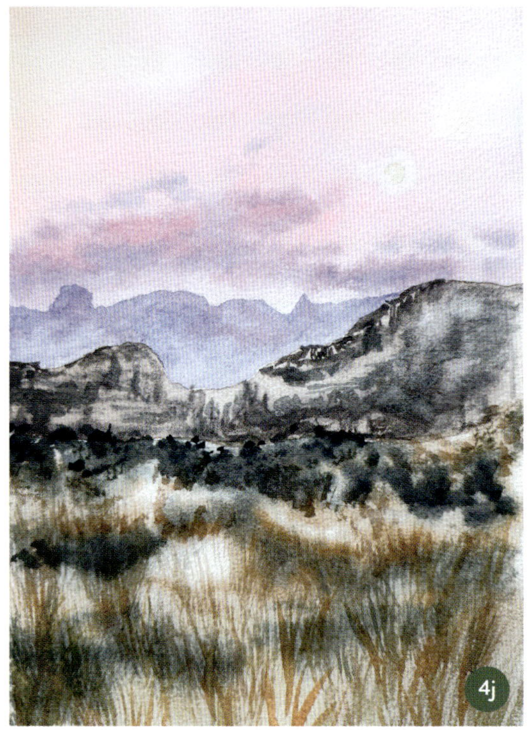

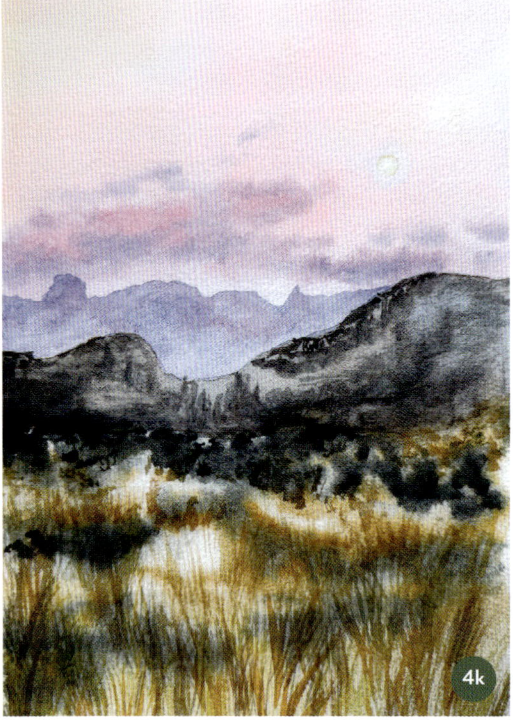

Make sure the stalks toward the back (near the mountains) are smaller, growing larger as you get to the front (the bottom edge of the page). Slowly add darker-value yellow strokes, then some watery green strokes. The idea is to make the plain have a lot of movement between the luminous underlayers and the grass swaying in various directions.

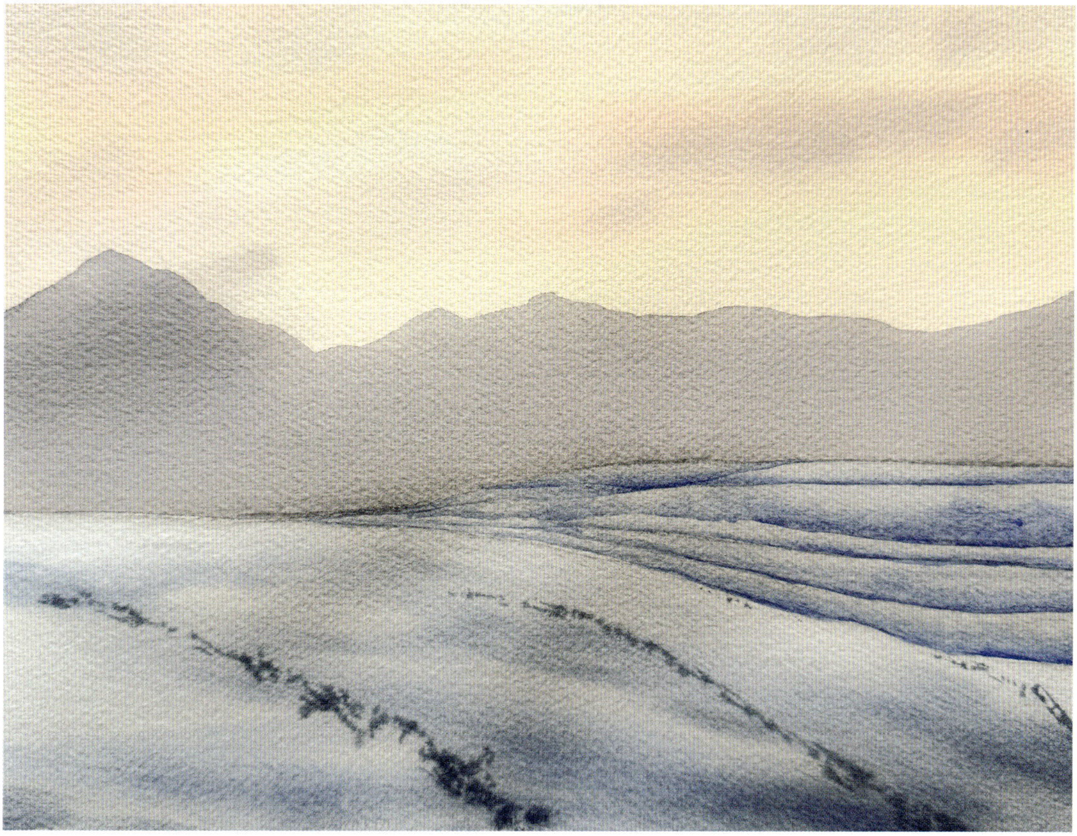

WHITE SANDS

BRUSHES
Round sizes 2, 6, and 12; Foliage brush

COLOR PALETTE
Hansa Yellow Light, New Gamboge, Opera Pink, Quinacridone Rose, French Ultramarine, Payne's Gray

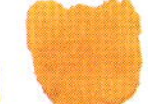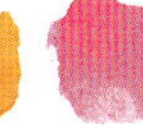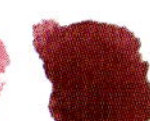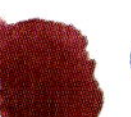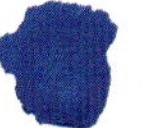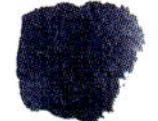

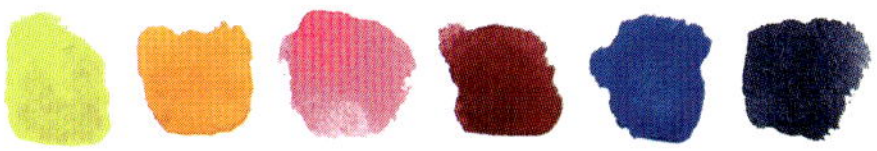

Amidst the push and pull of dying light and evening shadows, the shimmering layers of White Sands National Park look as smooth and calm as fallen snow. Luminous layers and contrasting colors will help you paint this surprisingly serene desert scene.

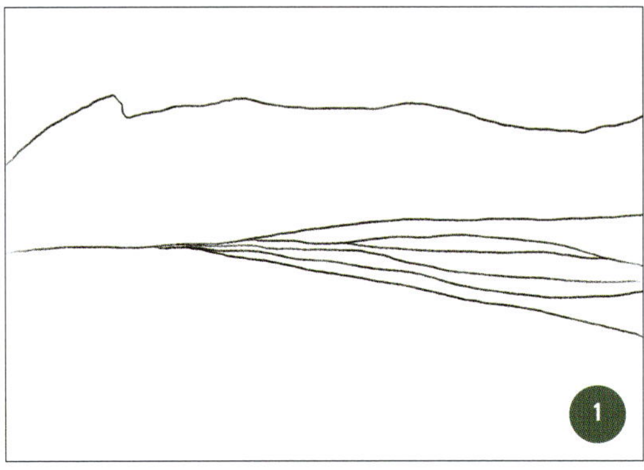

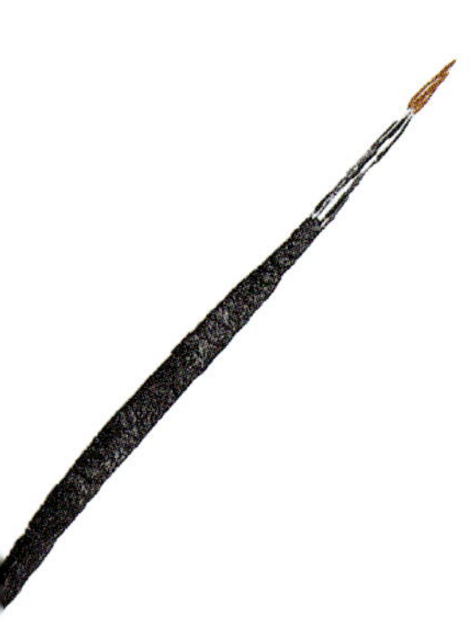

STEP 1: THE SKETCH

Sketch the far mountain ridge along the top third of the page, creating at least one triangle-like peak along the left side, then move to the right side in a mix of jagged and smooth slopes. Just beneath the center of the page, sketch a relatively horizontal line to separate the mountain from the sands. Then, from the left side of the horizontal line, slope downward to the right, creating a large foreground sand dune in the left corner. Within the smaller section now separated to the top right, separate into several smaller slivers using sloping lines, all starting from the top left corner. These sections will look more natural if they're not all the same size—more variation typically means a more natural effect.

STEP 2: THE SKY

Create watery mixes of Hansa Yellow Light and New Gamboge (together and separate). Also, use your creativity to create violet and pink mixes with Opera Pink, Quinacridone Rose, and French Ultramarine. Layer a wash of clean water across the sky with a size 12 round brush, then start with small strokes of watery yellow mixes across the sky. Then, use a size 6 round brush (a smaller brush limits the water) to paint small wisps of the violet and pink mixes. Ultimately, we want a subtle, pale sky with luminous glimmers of yellow, orange, violet, and pink—using the wet-on-wet technique (page 10) will help the watercolor mostly do this all on its own! Let dry completely.

STEP 3: THE MOUNTAIN

Mix a shadowy blue-violet (French Ultra-marine + Quinacridone Rose + Payne's Gray), then add lots of water to a size 12 round brush before painting with the blue-violet mix. In this light, the background mountain should look a relatively flat shade of blue violet, like a silhouette.

STEP 4: THE SAND

Layer a very light-value (watery) wash of French Ultramarine across the sands. Let dry, then start painting the slivers of background sand layers, one at a time. Use a size 2 round brush to wet a sliver with clean water, then pick up a small amount of French Ultramarine, and tap it along the bottom of the sliver. This will allow the paint to subtly blend upward, leaving the bottom a medium-value blue and gradually lightened as it goes up. If the paint blends upward too fast and too dark, use a thirsty brush (page 11) to lift paint from the top of the sliver, revealing the light layer beneath. Repeat with all the slivers of sand, making sure to dry each layer before moving onto the next.

(continued)

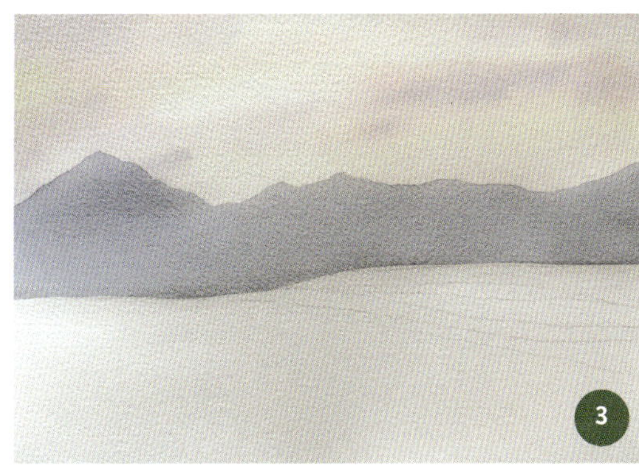

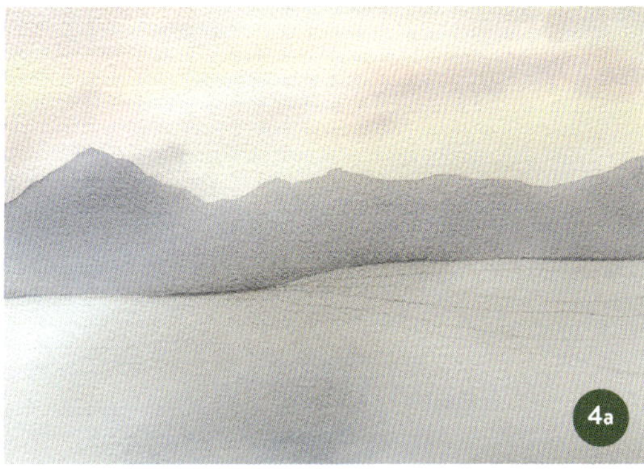

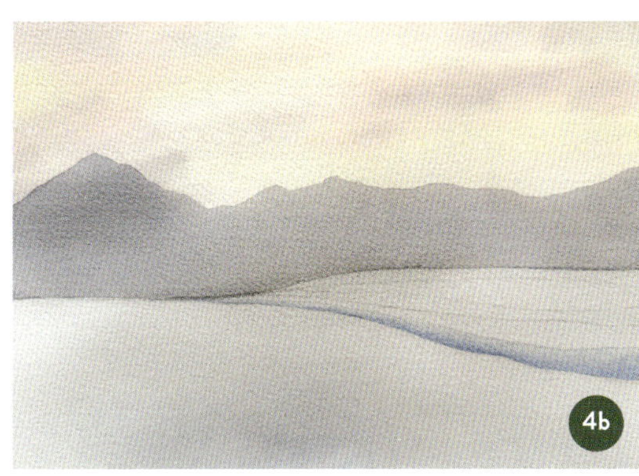

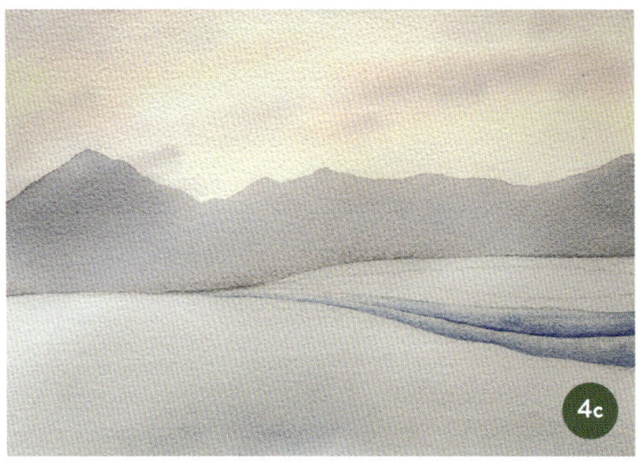

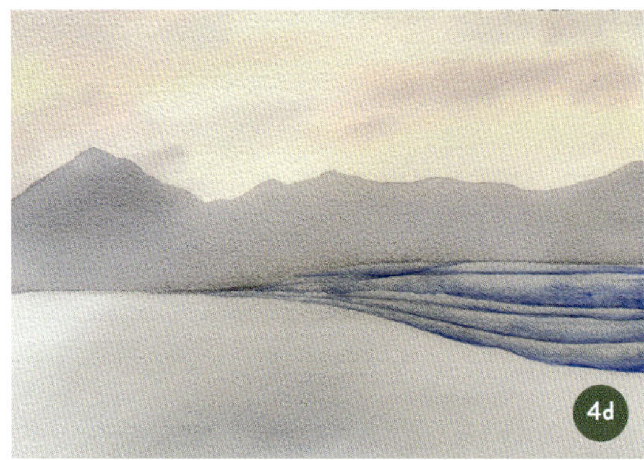

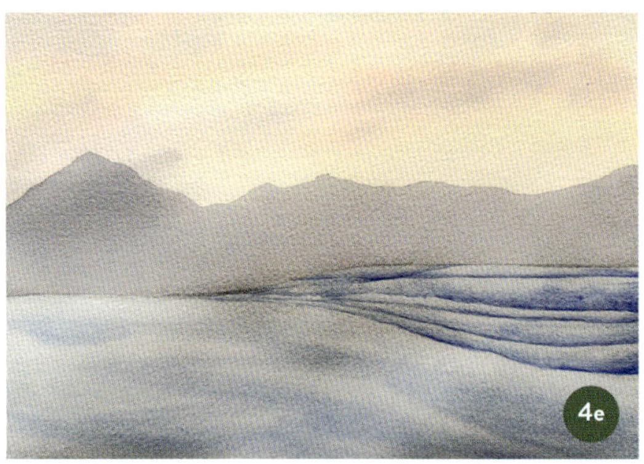

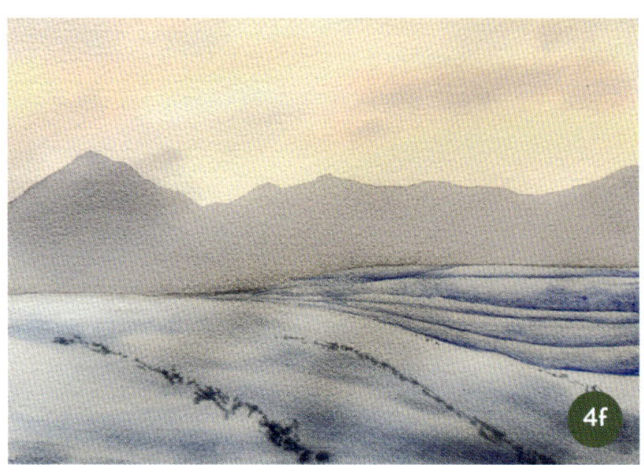

Then, layer a wash of clean water across the foreground sand, and use a size 6 round brush to paint medium-value (still watery, but with more color) French Ultramarine strokes in loosely zigzag shapes, leaving behind strokes of light space and creating shifting shadows on the sand. Let dry for a bit, but before it's all the way dry, use a foliage brush with medium-value Payne's Gray to paint a few blurry and shadowy footsteps in the sand, starting from the bottom and sloping upward. These don't have to be footstep-shaped—small little marks with the foliage brush will be enough to imply a shuffling movement. Make the marks smaller the farther into the distance you go. You could also do this on dry paper if the damp paper isn't quite working.

GRAND CANYON

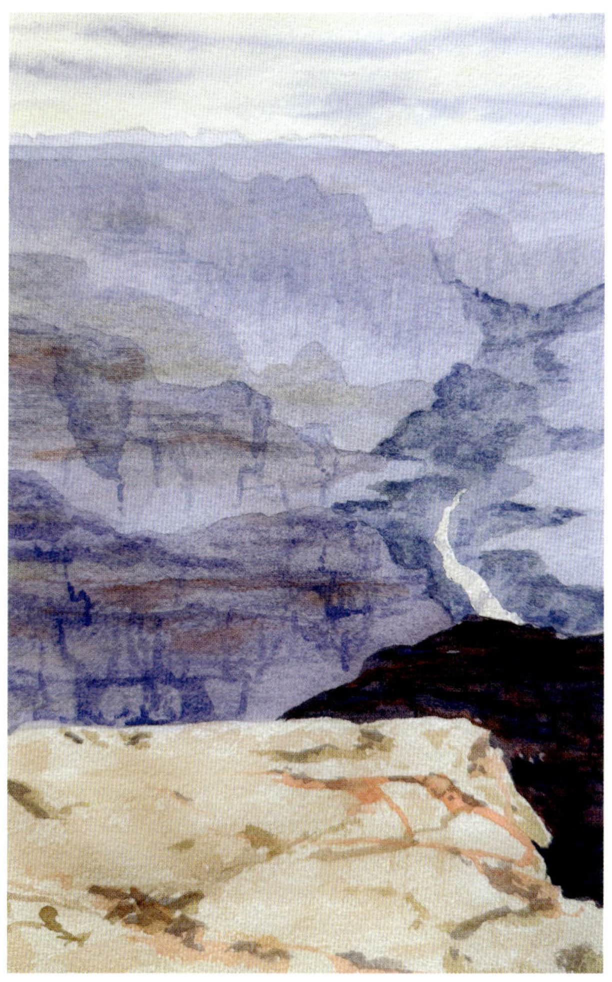

Perhaps one of the most famous landmarks worldwide, the Grand Canyon's steep ridges and maze of gorges are as dizzying as they are breathtaking. In this twilight scene, let's use hazy washes and subtle textures to capture an unforgettable overlook, seemingly into the depths of the earth itself.

BRUSHES

Round sizes 2, 6, and 12; Masking fluid brush

COLOR PALETTE

New Gamboge, Hansa Yellow Light, French Ultramarine, Quinacridone Rose, Pyrrol Scarlet, Payne's Gray

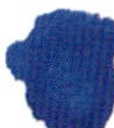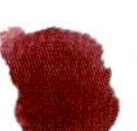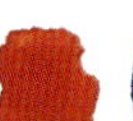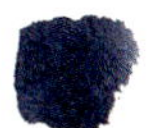

Note: This project uses masking fluid.

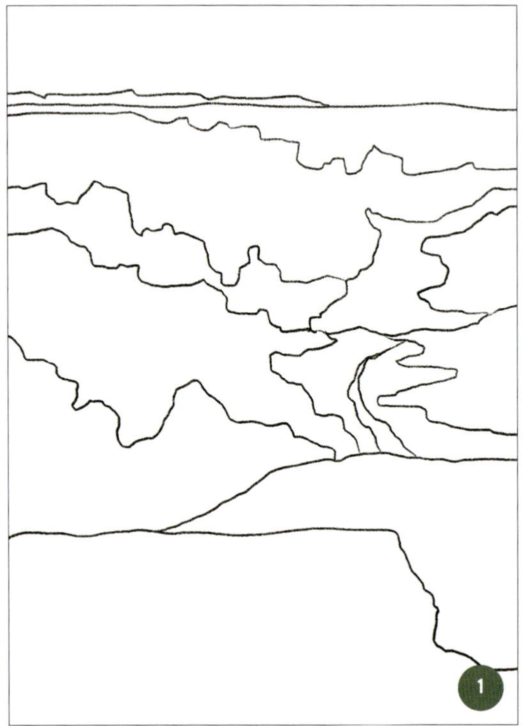

STEP 1: THE SKETCH

Create a sketch for reference, separating a small sky area with a relatively horizontal line (taking up maybe an eighth toward the top of the page), a large canyon area (multiple layers moving horizontally and down across the page, with more geometric and blocky hills and valleys), and a large, flat rock taking up about a fourth of the bottom of the page. Nestled into the canyon layers, on the right of the page, sketch in a more vertically oriented gorge with a small river tapering upward, making sure the edges of the gorge are similarly blocky and loosely jagged. Sketch another line separating the flat foreground area into two, so there's a rocky platform with another just under it to the right. Sketch a small, distant canyon ridge above the horizon line as well. Finally, use your masking fluid brush prepped with soap and masking fluid (page 15) to paint across the river, reserving that space. Let dry for 30 minutes or until tacky.

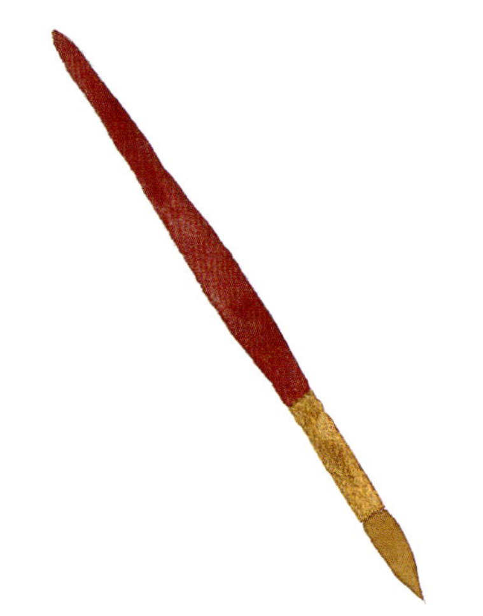

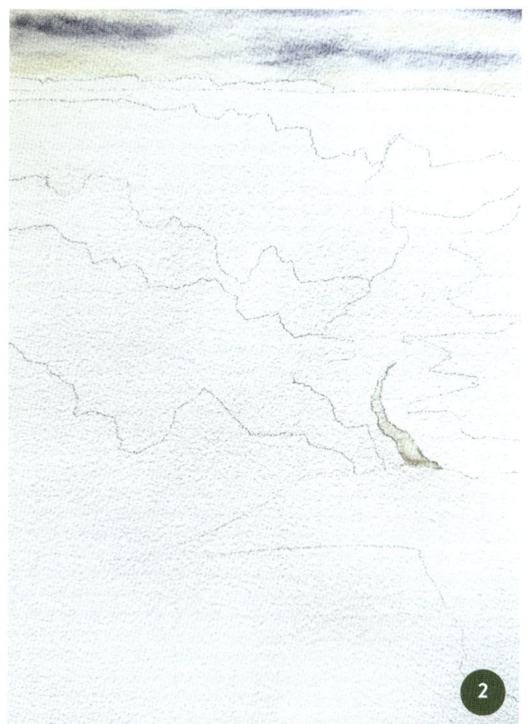

STEP 2: THE SKY

Layer a wash of clean water across the sky. Then, create a yellow mix (New Gamboge + Hansa Yellow Light) and a blue-violet mix (French Ultramarine + a bit of Quinacridone Rose), and use a size 6 round brush to paint loose horizontal stripes in both colors. Start with the violet, then add the yellow. Let dry completely.

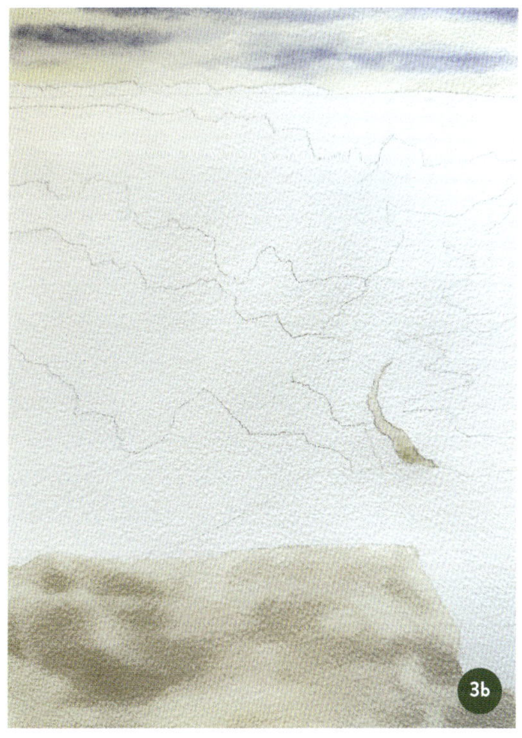

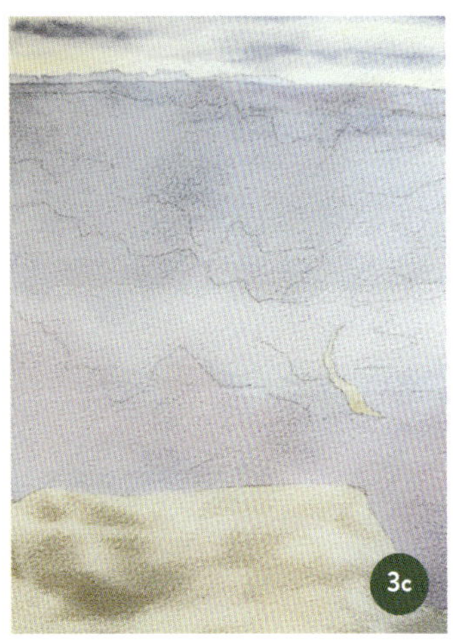 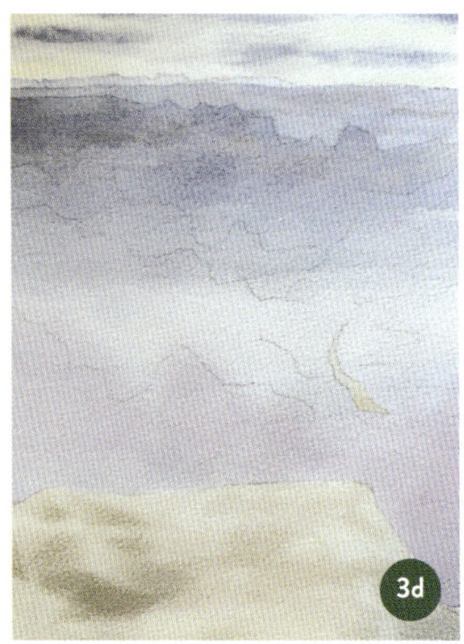 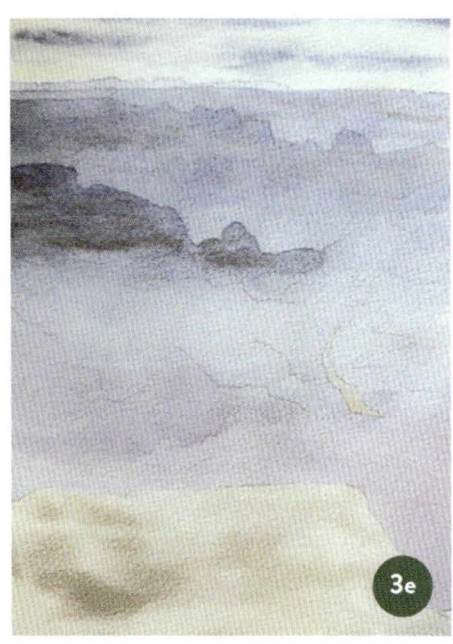

STEP 3: THE MOUNTAINS, PART ONE

First, paint a watery wash of the yellow mix across the foreground flat rock. While it's still wet, tap in some watery brown strokes (New Gamboge + Pyrrol Scarlet + French Ultramarine) to create a shadowy and luminous wash on the foreground rock. While this scene is at twilight, this rock will retain the most direct sunlight, so preserve the light layer here.

Let dry completely, then paint the rest of the canyon area a light-value wash of blue-violet and red-violet (more red-violet toward the foreground). To get a luminous wash, start with a layer of clean water first, then use a size 12 round brush to tap in the color, using various mixes of French Ultramarine and Quinacridone Rose. Let dry, then repeat on dry paper with slightly darker-value (but still quite watery) blue-violet (add just a bit of Payne's Gray), and paint everything below the farthest canyon ridge along the horizon, leaving that ridge the lightest value. Stop just above the river and feather (page 12) into the dry layers below to avoid obvious dried paint lines. While still wet, use a size 2 round brush to paint very subtle horizontal lines across the far canyons, either in the blue-violet or red-violet mixes. Let dry completely, then repeat, using the next highest canyon line as a reference point, leaving the layer above the lighter value.

While still wet, use a size 2 round brush to add some yellow-brown hints as well. The idea here is as we're moving down the canyon, we're subtly denoting the individual canyon layers and glimmers of color in the shifting light—while still being kind to ourselves regarding accuracy because the canyon is in shadow during twilight, so it's okay if it's a bit muddled. Repeat with the next mountain layer down, leaving the gorge clear.

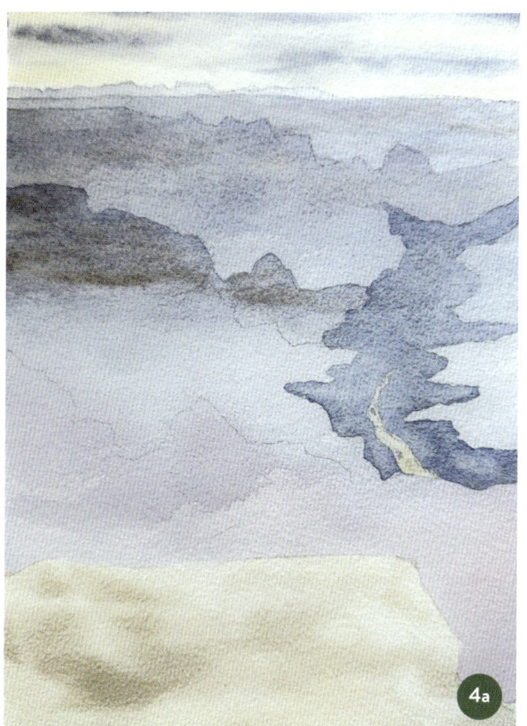

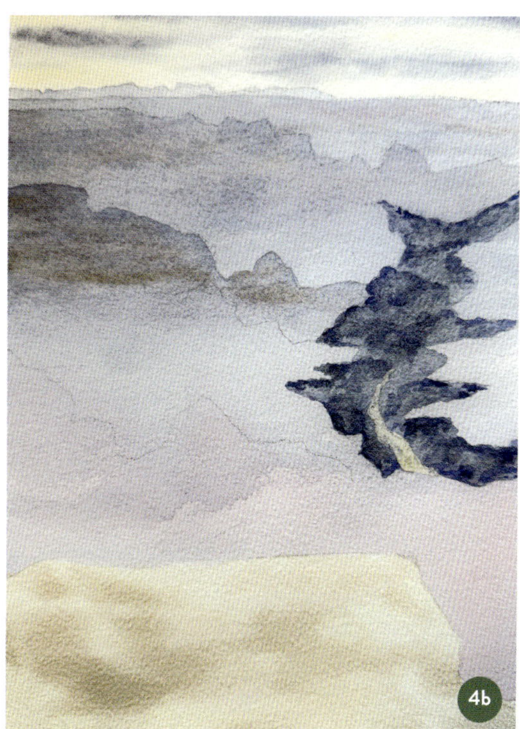

STEP 4: THE GORGE

Create a slightly darker blue-violet mix (more of a medium value, still watery but not as much as prior layers). Paint the gorge with the darker blue-violet. It's deeper and steeper than the rest of the canyon, so we want this to look slightly darker and bluer. Let dry, then use a size 2 round brush to paint small flicks of blue-violet dry brush (page 12) marks along the edges of the gorge, moving down toward the river, creating the illusion of depth and dimension. Repeat with some light-value Payne's Gray dry brush marks for added color movement. Let dry completely, then remove the masking fluid by gently rubbing it away with your finger or an eraser (page 15). With a size 6 round brush, paint a few scattered marks along the river with a light-value (watery) blue-violet mix for subtle texture. Make sure the river as a whole is much, much lighter than the canyon.

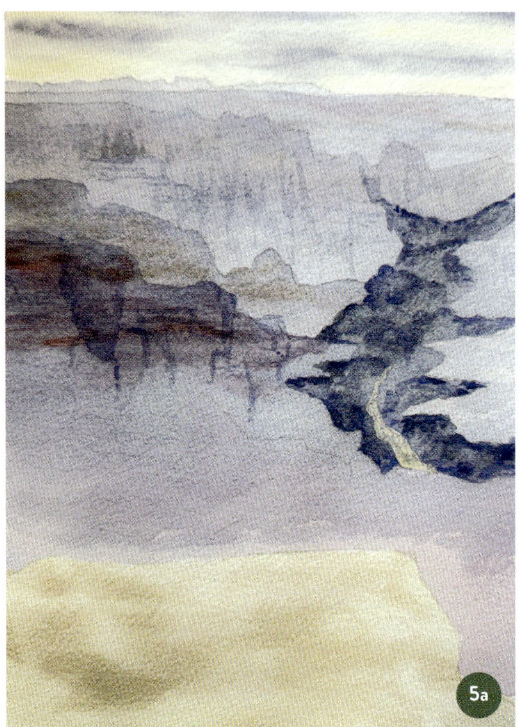
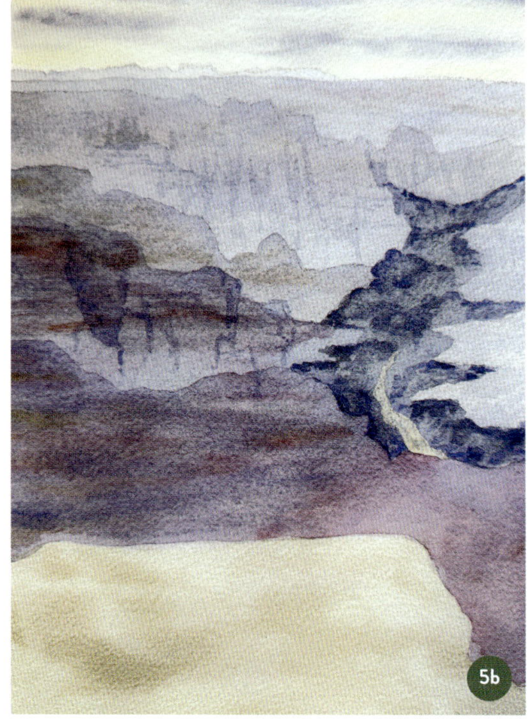

STEP 5: THE MOUNTAINS, PART TWO

Paint the next mountain layer, this time adding wet-on-wet (page 10) horizontal strokes of brownish red (Pyrrol Scarlet + a bit of French Ultramarine) into the wet blue-violet layer. Let dry, then use a size 2 round brush with watery blue-violet paint to add a few jagged vertical lines to this layer for added depth and detail. You can optionally add some light, jagged vertical texture to the background layers as well to blend the layers a bit more smoothly. Repeat one last time with slightly darker-value paint. The end result should look like the canyon layers kind of all blend together while also still maintaining a subtle distinction from one another.

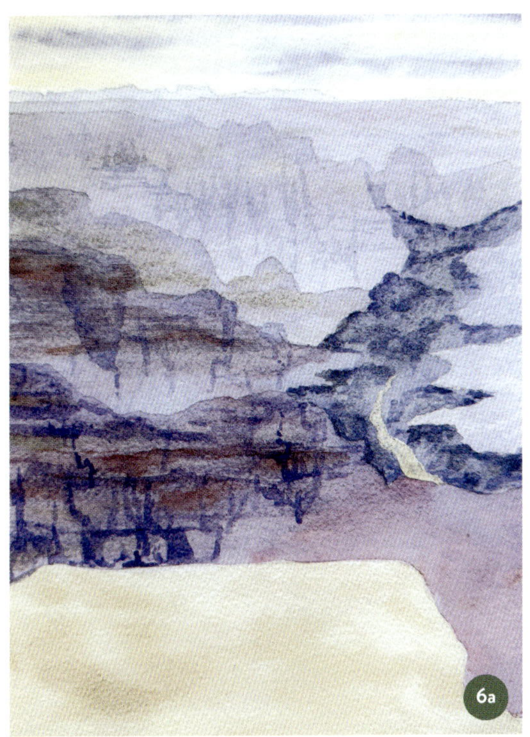

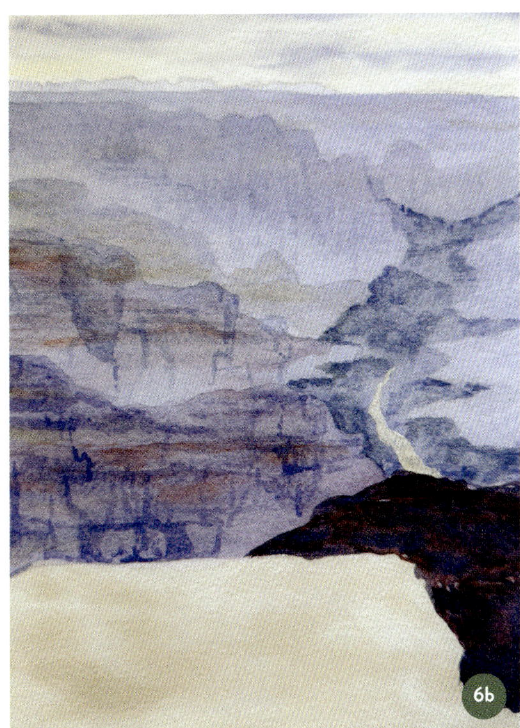

STEP 6: THE FOREGROUND ROCKS

Paint the sub-foreground rock off to the right side a dark-value blue-violet with streaks of Pyrrol Scarlet. This rock is very much in a twilight shadow, but it's close, so we want to see some variation. Let dry, then use a size 2 round brush to paint more detailed horizontal and vertical lines, bringing out more of a rocky texture. Finally, create watery orange (Pyrrol Scarlet + New Gamboge) and brown mixes (add French Ultramarine to the orange mix), and paint a few scattered marks across the foreground flat rock. Make the brown a tad darker (with some Payne's Gray), and slightly darken a few of the shadows.

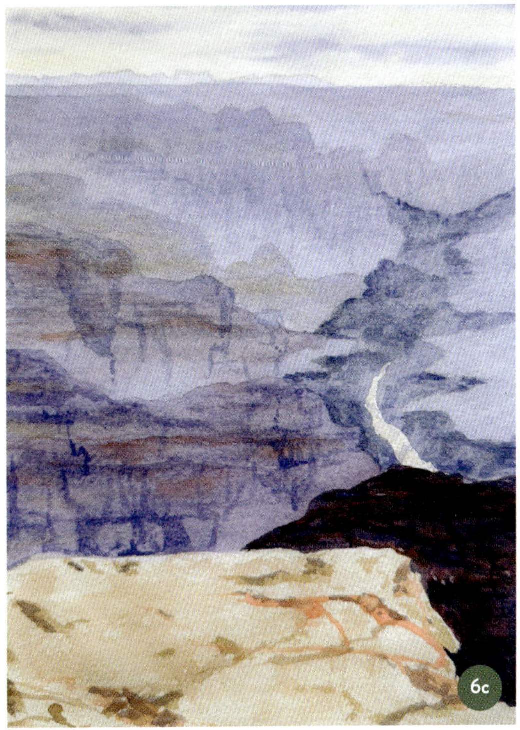

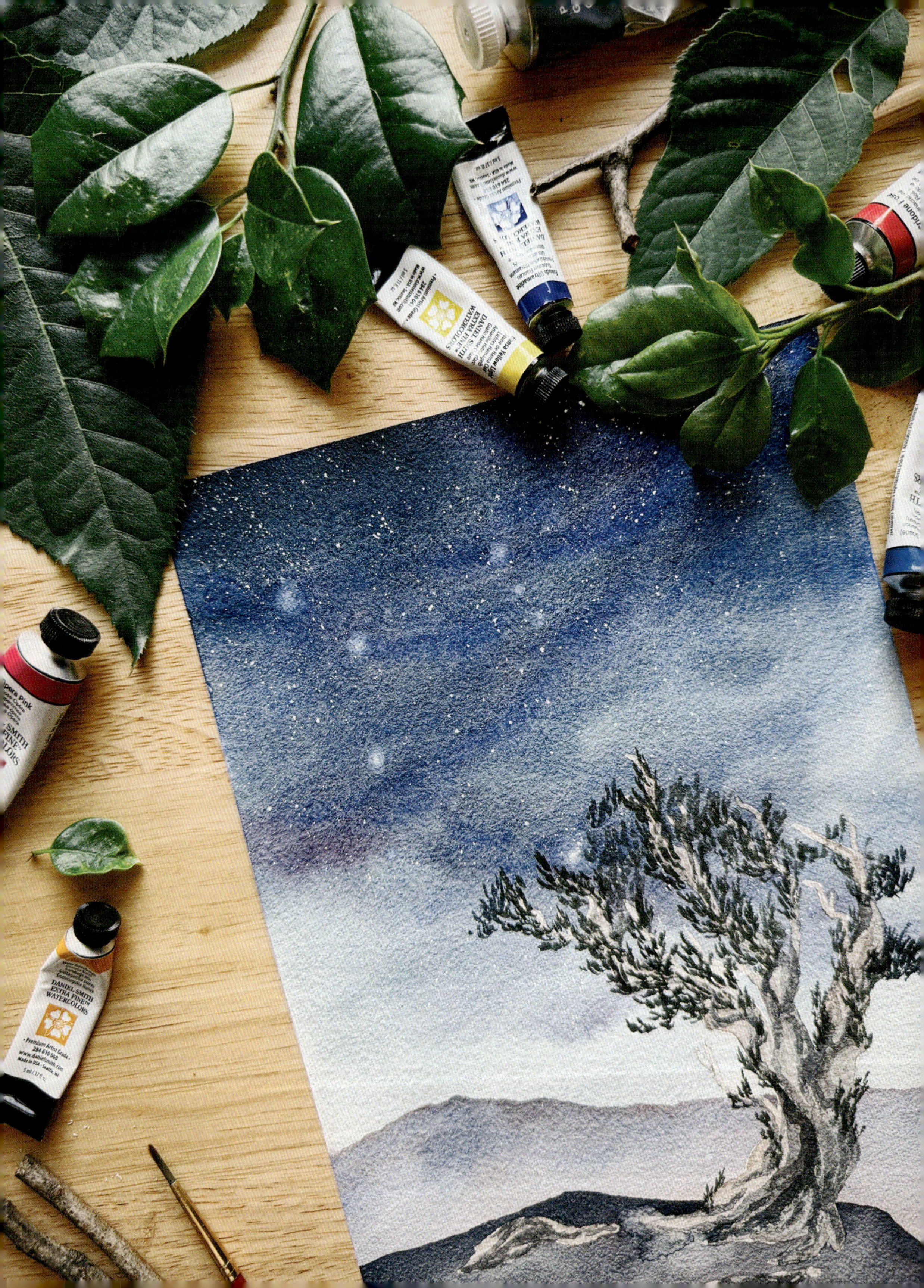

floating through the forest

"*The clearest way into the universe is through a forest wilderness.*"

—John Muir

Seen one tree, seen them all, said literally no one who has looked closely at an actual tree, because my goodness—there are some wonky ones out there! This chapter explores all different kinds of trees in America's national parks, from the most ancient and the most plentiful to trees that *aren't even trees* anymore.

My best advice to aspiring watercolor tree painters is to remember, again, just how wild looking trees are in real life! They're sharp and brambly and misshapen—and that's exactly what makes them so inspiring to behold. Happy little trees are allowed to also be *wonky little trees*, so let go of that need for exactness and embrace all the imperfection your brush has to offer.

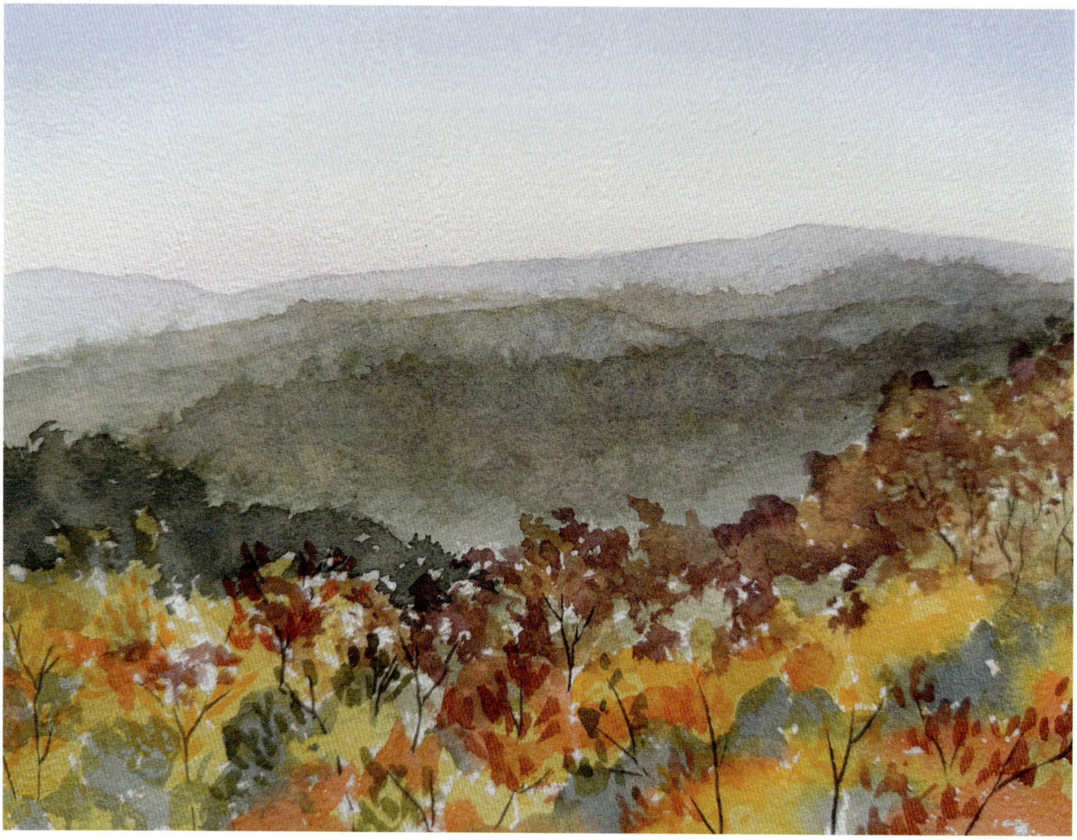

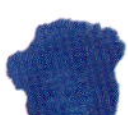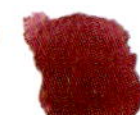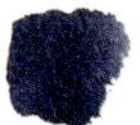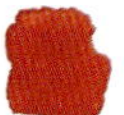

SHENANDOAH

BRUSHES
Round sizes 2 and 12; Foliage brush

COLOR PALETTE
French Ultramarine, Quinacridone Rose,
New Gamboge, Payne's Gray, Pyrrol Scarlet

Infinite rolling hills as far as the eye can see are what makes Shenandoah National Park so iconic, and through careful layers and intentional play with values and color, we can absolutely capture that magic with watercolor. Let's give a "just barely autumn" evening in Shenandoah a try, weaving brilliant oranges and yellows with lingering greens for a fall rainbow worthy of any storybook setting.

STEP 1: THE SKETCH

Sketch the overlapping mountain layers, starting about a third of the way down from the top of the page. Each layer should be gently sloping, with smooth curves to imply rolling hills. Vary each line a bit for a more natural look, and end with the final line starting about midway on the right side of the page, sloping downward. (This is the foreground tree layer.)

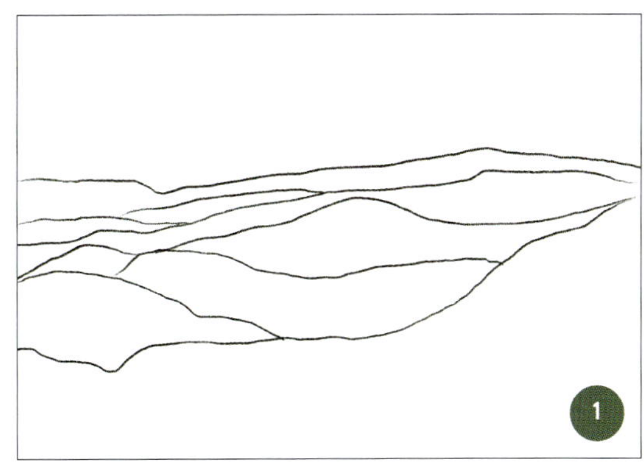

STEP 2: THE SKY

Next, we'll paint the sky a pale twilight gradient. Create watery mixes of violet (French Ultramarine + Quinacridone Rose), New Gamboge, and French Ultramarine. Layer a wash of clean water across the sky with a size 12 round brush, just above the first mountain layer. Then, layer a few long strokes of each color, starting with violet along the bottom. Rinse, then add New Gamboge in the middle. Rinse again, then add French Ultramarine along the top edge. Lots of water here—we want just a hint of color. Let dry completely.

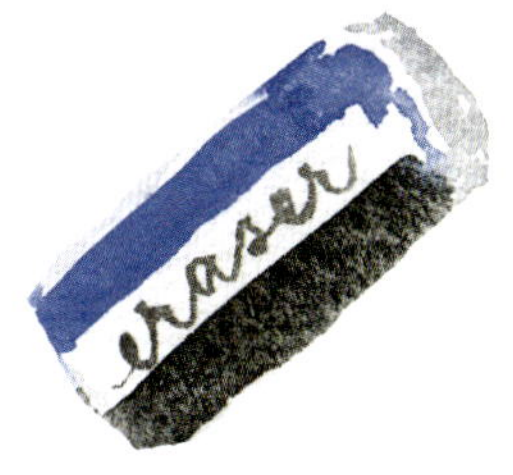

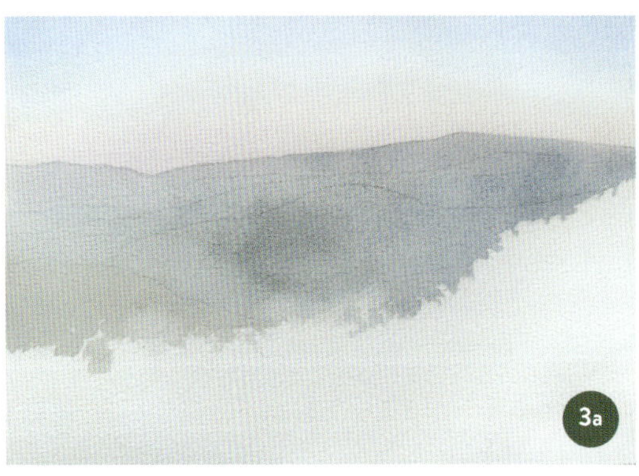

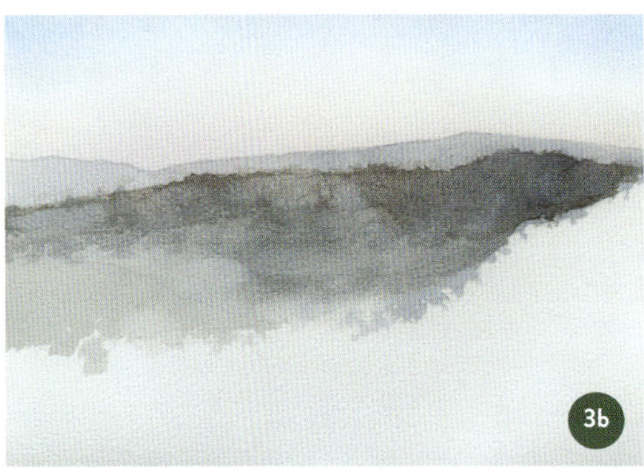

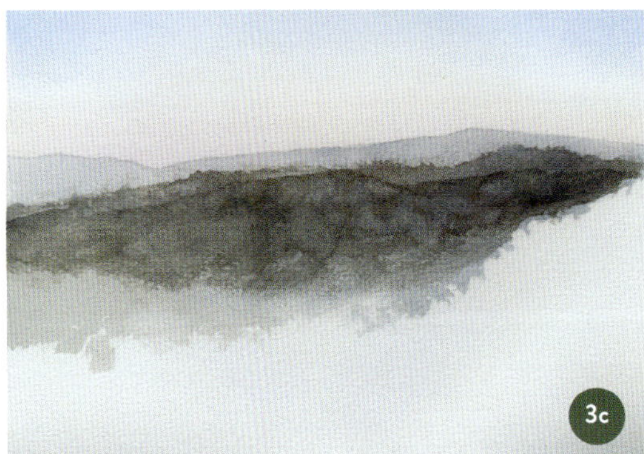

STEP 3: THE BACKGROUND TREES

Paint a shadowy underlayer across the background tree layers with a watery mix of French Ultramarine and Payne's Gray, then add just a bit of New Gamboge to the mix to make a dark green as you move toward the foreground. Use a foliage brush (either for the whole thing, or just the edge) to carve out a foliage texture between the background tree layers and the foreground tree layer. Let dry.

Next, paint the background tree layers one at a time, front to back, drying each layer in between. This is the beginning of autumn, which means some of the leaves are turning while some are still green—from a distance, those colors blend together for a kind of hazy, muted mix of colors. To create the illusion of flickers of colors kind of blended together, start with one wash of color (perhaps a watery, muted yellow-green + New Gamboge + a hint of French Ultramarine), then use a smaller brush to tap a few other colors into the wet wash (Pyrrol Scarlet, New Gamboge). Use a foliage brush to tap along the top edge and create a textured tree line. Let dry, then repeat, growing slightly more vibrant and green (more paint) with each layer, still keeping them fairly light value and watery.

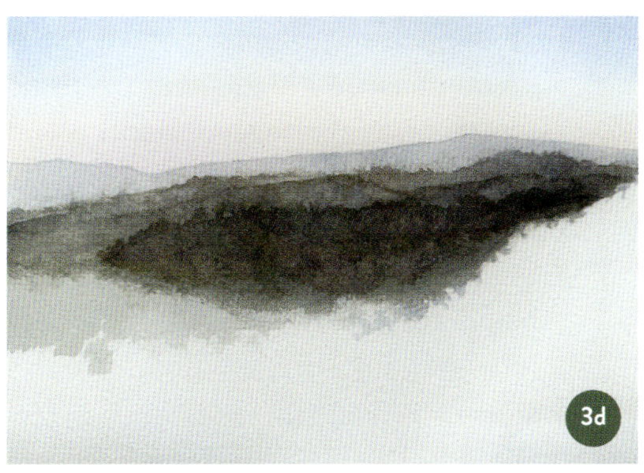

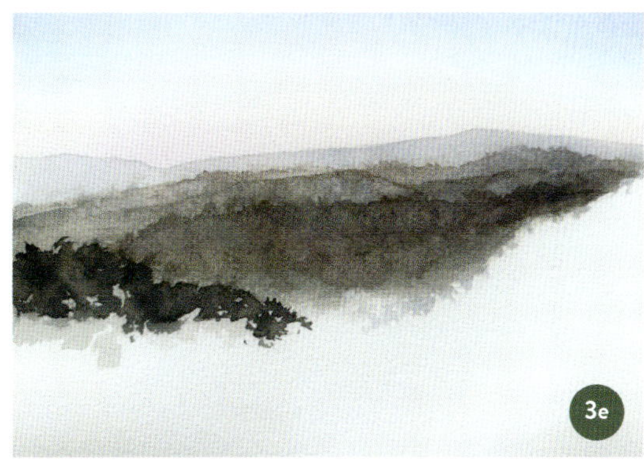

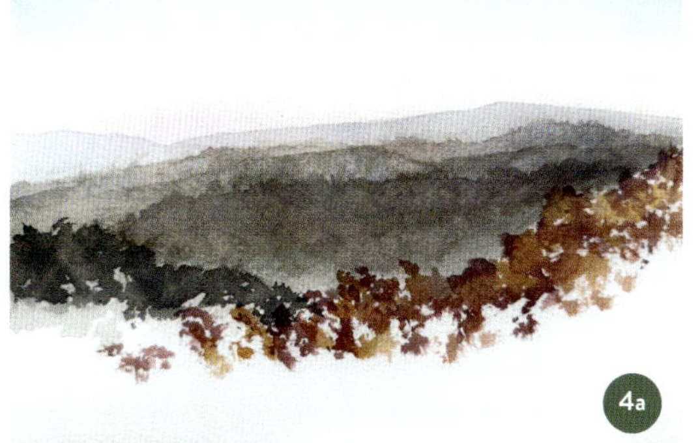

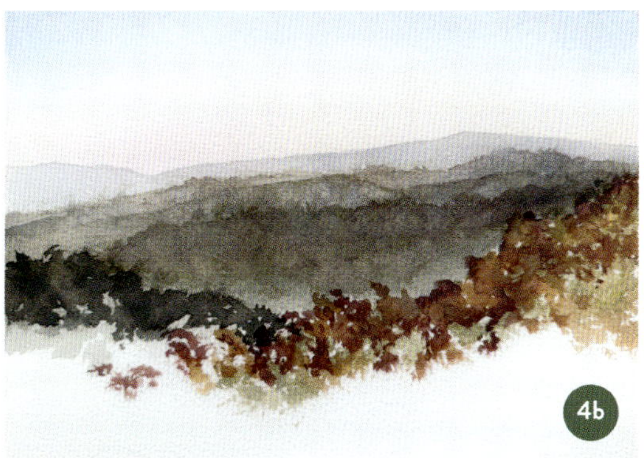

When you get to the final background layer, just behind the foreground, mix a darker green (French Ultramarine + a hint of New Gamboge), and use the foliage brush to make it ultra textured, leaving behind flickers of the lighter layer beneath. While the green is still wet, add a couple taps of New Gamboge for subtle color variation. Let dry completely.

STEP 4: THE FOREGROUND TREES

Create autumnal mixes (various combinations of Pyrrol Scarlet, New Gamboge, and a bit of French Ultramarine to make any mix more maroon), and paint the foreground trees by tapping with a foliage brush. Pay attention to the size of the marks—smaller in the back, larger in the front—and shape the foliage together in sloping curves rather than straight lines. We also want the trees in the back to be more muted, while the trees in the front will be more vibrant. Add some hints of yellow-green.

(continued)

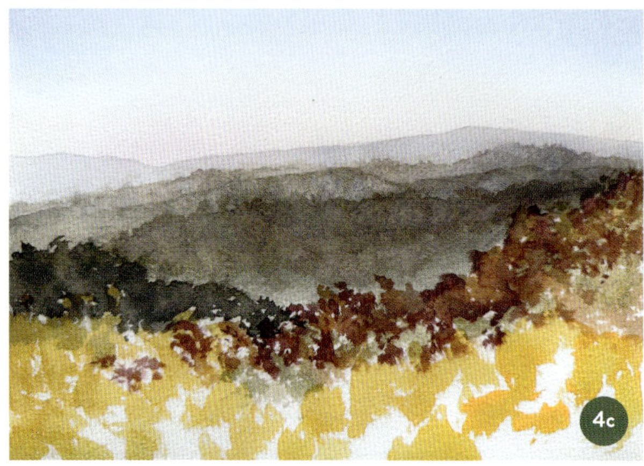

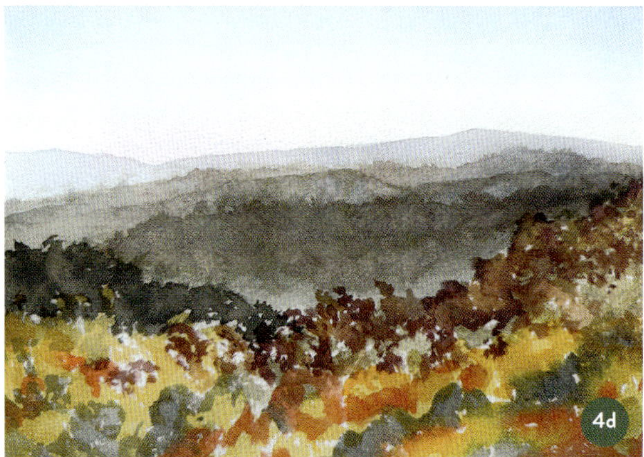

Then, use a foliage brush with medium-value New Gamboge paint to create larger foliage marks along the bottom of the page. (Remember that the largest marks are toward the front.) Use New Gamboge to paint some of the lighter flickers left behind in any background layers. While still wet, add a few curves of orange and green foliage textures along the bottom of the page, keeping a curved, rather than straight, movement.

Let dry, then mix a dark brown (New Gamboge + Pyrrol Scarlet + French Ultramarine + Payne's Gray). Use a size 2 round brush to paint a few thin trunks and forked branches coming up and between some of the foliage marks (larger in the front, smaller and thinner in the back). Leave a few gaps between the branches to imply overlapping leaves. Branches are easiest to paint when you start at the bottom, then drag your brush upward and gently lift.

Finally, to differentiate the foreground trees from the back even
more, use a size 2 round brush to tap
a few random leaf-life marks in various oranges, yellows, and browns.
(A brush footprint works well for
this [page 13].) We're not trying to
single out individual trees—more
like adding smaller and more defined
textures only in the foreground to
add contrast and draw our eyes
to the main event: the beautiful
autumn trees.

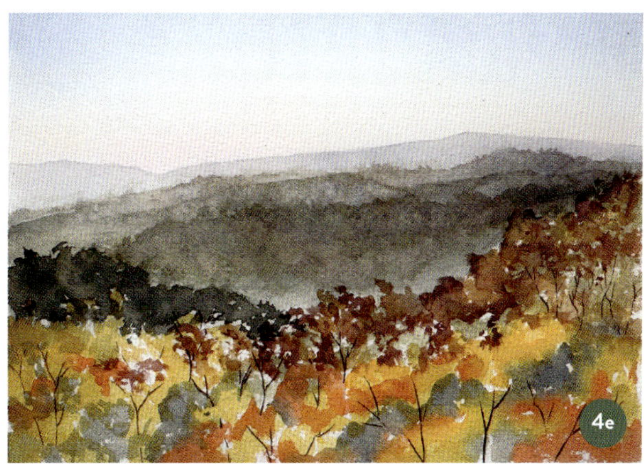

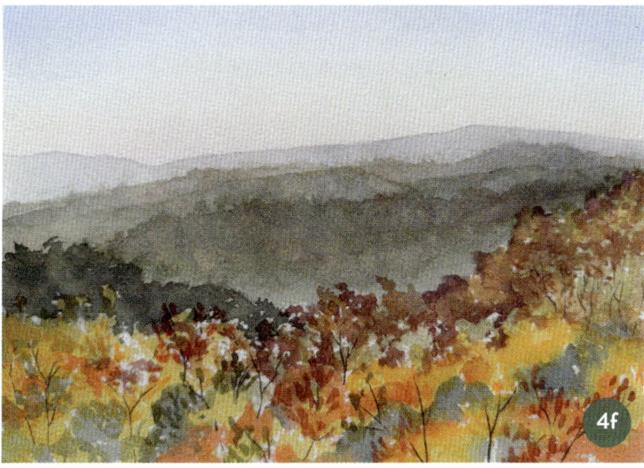

JOSHUA TREE

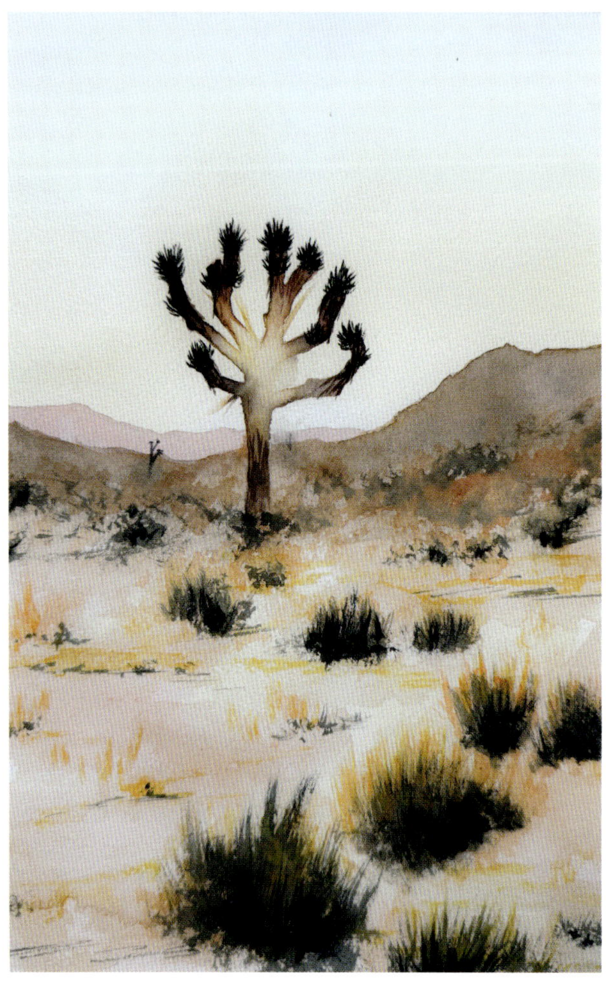

Joshua Tree National Park is home to some of the weirdest—and coolest—desert trees out there. Pay attention to the rhythmic placement of the foliage and the layers of light shining through the Joshua tree to create a stunning sunset scene.

BRUSHES
Round sizes 2 and 12; Foliage brush

COLOR PALETTE
New Gamboge, Pyrrol Scarlet, French Ultramarine, Hansa Yellow Light, Payne's Gray

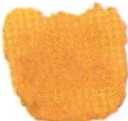 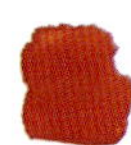 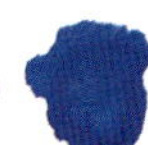  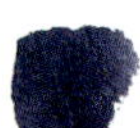

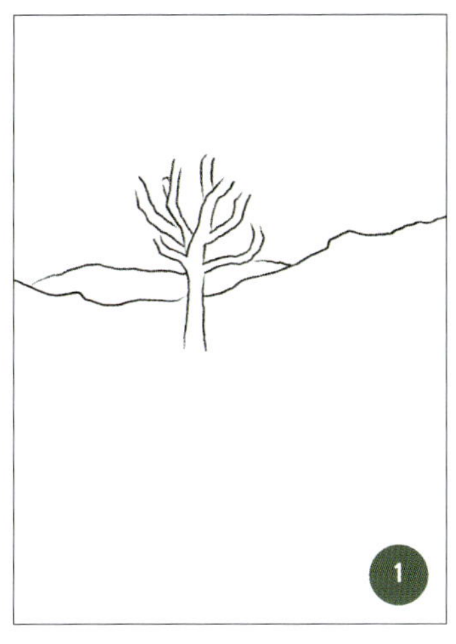

STEP 1: THE SKETCH

Sketch two relatively low mountain layers a bit higher than midway through the page. Then, sketch a Joshua tree with a relatively short trunk and short, thick branches jutting out in all directions. You don't have to sketch the iconic bristles on the end yet—we'll just paint those later.

STEP 2: THE UNDERPAINTING

Layer a wash of clean water across the whole page, then mix a watery New Gamboge. Use a size 12 round brush to spread the watery New Gamboge in loose zigzags across the wet page, creating a luminous wash. Make the sky mostly all yellow, with a pretty visible zigzag under the mountains, across the landscape. Leave behind plenty of white space! Rinse your brush, then mix a light-value orange-brown (New Gamboge + Pyrrol Scarlet + a hint of French Ultramarine). Use a size 12 round brush to tap the watery orange-brown paint into the mountain layers and to the side of the yellow zigzag, leaving bits of white between the colors. The goal here is a blend-y, pale underpainting so we can slowly add darker layers around the light. Let dry completely.

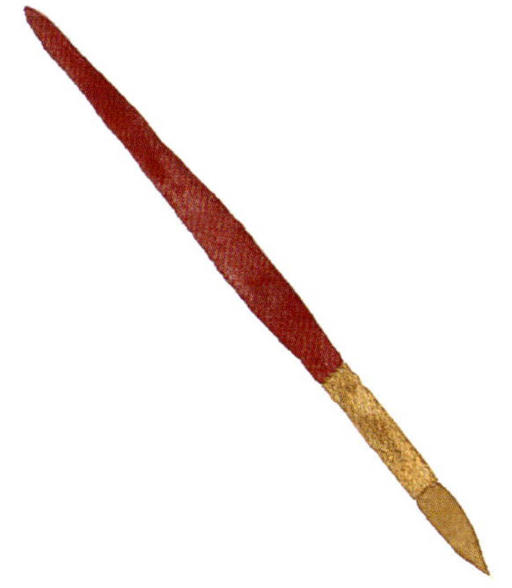

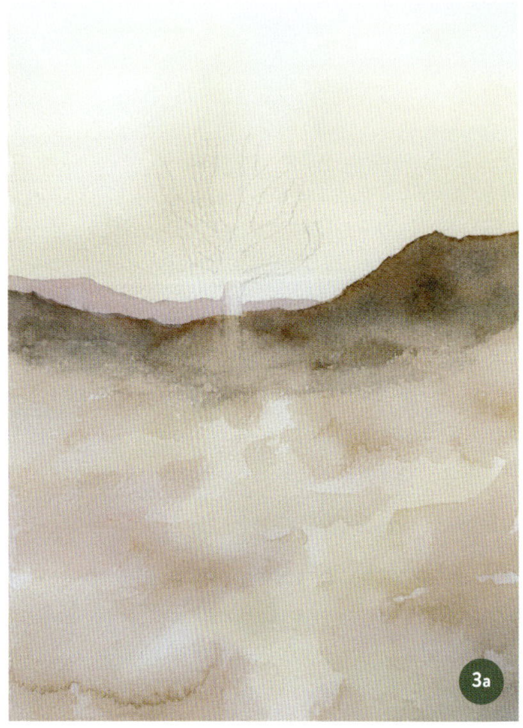

STEP 3: THE MOUNTAINS

Add a bit more paint to the orange-brown mix from Step 2 (still watery, just a bit more color), then paint the farthest mountain layer, using clean water to blend the edges down. Let dry completely, then add more yellow to the brown mix, and paint the midground mountain in watery, choppy strokes, leaving behind plenty of random textures and dry spaces. Paint all the way down the landscape as well, leaving most of the yellow zigzag dry. Make sure the paint is still quite watery—we're just adding subtle texture while preserving the light value of the underpainting. While this layer is still wet, mix a light-value warm green (New Gamboge + French Ultramarine), and use a size 2 round brush to tap into the mountain layer, leaving hints of brush along the base. Optional: If you want the mountain layer a bit darker to contrast against the background layer, mix a slightly darker-value brown, then tap into the mountain.

Finally, to prepare for the layers ahead, mix a light-value orange (Pyrrol Scarlet + New Gamboge), and use a foliage brush to paint a loose zigzag of desert foliage—larger in the front (bottom of the page), gradually growing smaller toward the mountains. The swaying movement here is important, and remembering to paint in a loose zigzag will help!

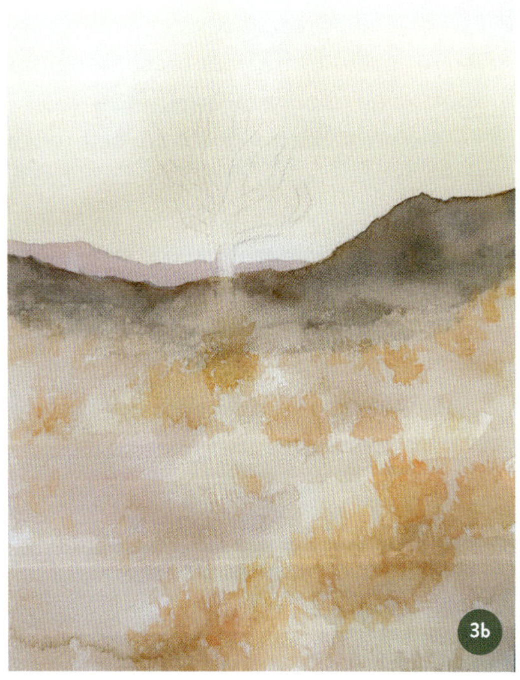

STEP 4: THE JOSHUA TREE

The Joshua tree will mostly be a silhouette, but we want to try to capture the look of sunlight piercing through the branches, almost making the tree partially invisible. The wet-on-wet technique (page 10) is perfect for this! Mix your paints, the watery warm brown from the previous step, and a neutral yellow mix (New Gamboge + Hansa Yellow Light). Then, use a size 2 round brush to layer a wash of clean water on the tree. Pick a spot on the right side of the trunk for the sun, and make sure to keep that spot free from paint as much as possible, either by lifting with a thirsty brush (page 11) or pushing away the paint as we drop it in. Start light, with watery New Gamboge paint, and drop it around that white spot on the wet trunk.

Then, drop in the warm brown, carefully pushing away any paint that might muddy up the yellow. The key is to use a small brush with only a little water in the paint and on the brush—too much water here will make the paint unwieldy. It's going to be a bit messy! It's okay if you need to mop up the wet paint with a towel and start over or fuss with it a few times. Optional: While the trunk is still wet, you can paint thin, wispy strokes in watery New Gamboge coming out from the sun spot to look like visible sun rays.

(continued)

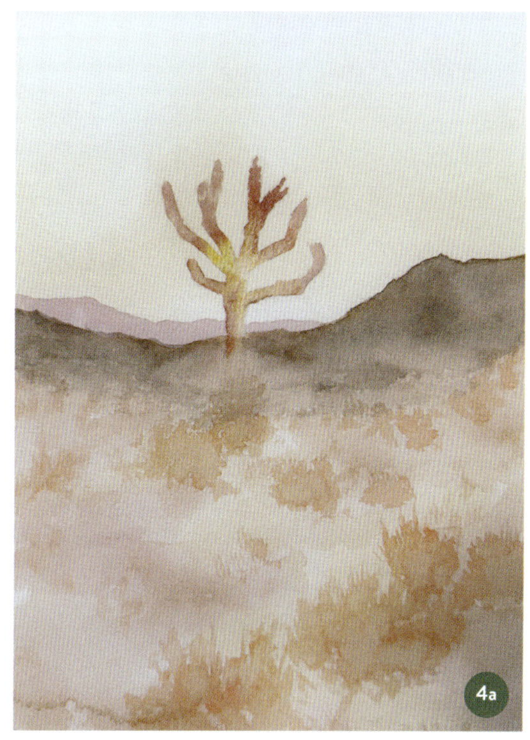

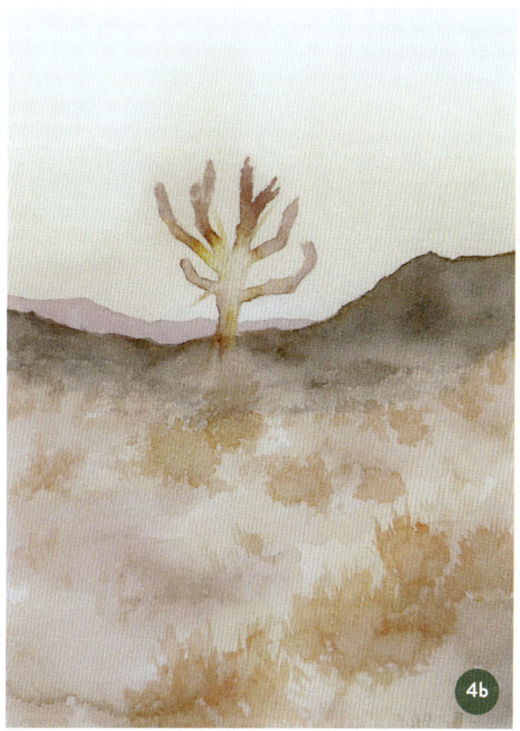

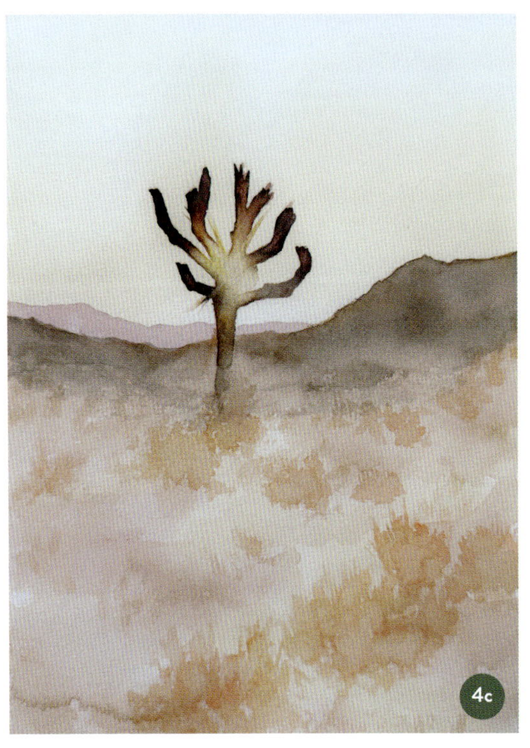

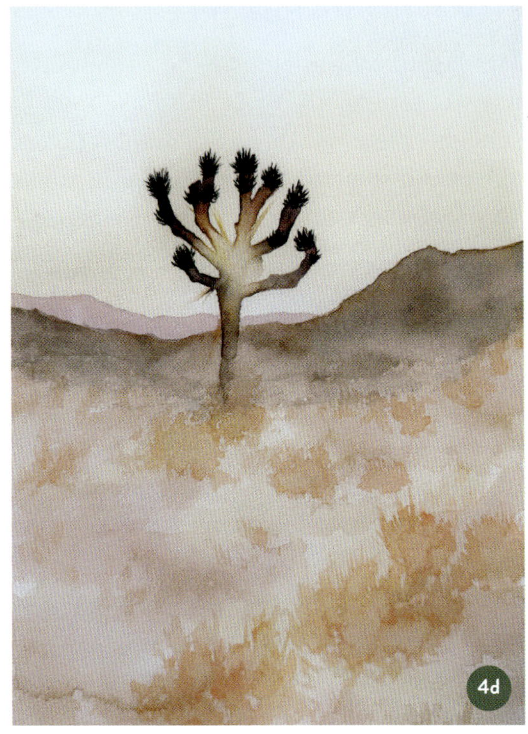

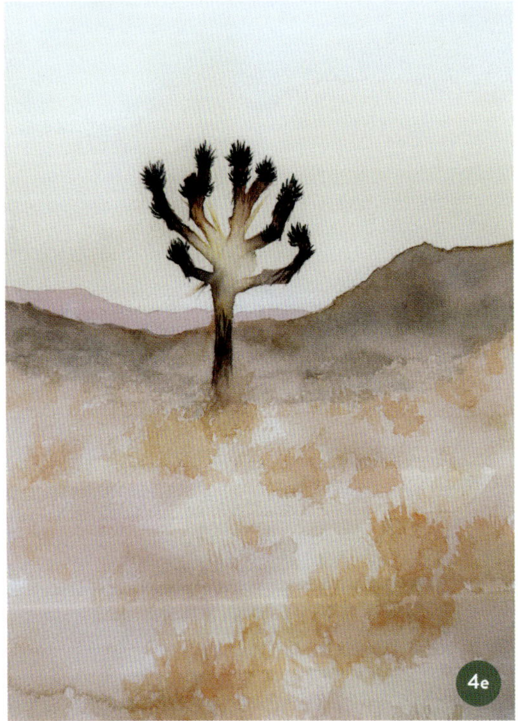

Next, mix a darker-value brown (more paint and more French Ultramarine), then use a size 2 round brush to tap into the far edges of each branch, letting the dark paint blend into the rest of the tree. You may need to rewet the tree at this point before painting to achieve a wet-on-wet gradient effect. Let dry.

Finally, mix a dark green (Payne's Gray + a bit of New Gamboge), and paint the spiky foliage on the tip of each branch with a size 2 round brush. Then, use the dark brown to paint small, spiky strokes on the edges of the branches and the bottom of the trunk to capture another Joshua tree feature. This is mainly a silhouette, so we don't need too many details—it's enough to emphasize one or two key characteristics.

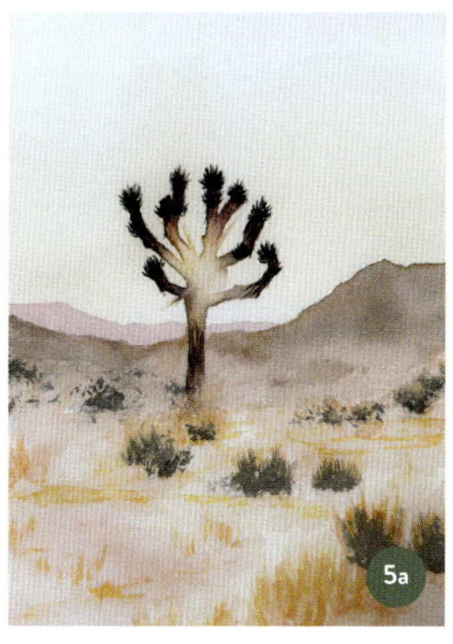

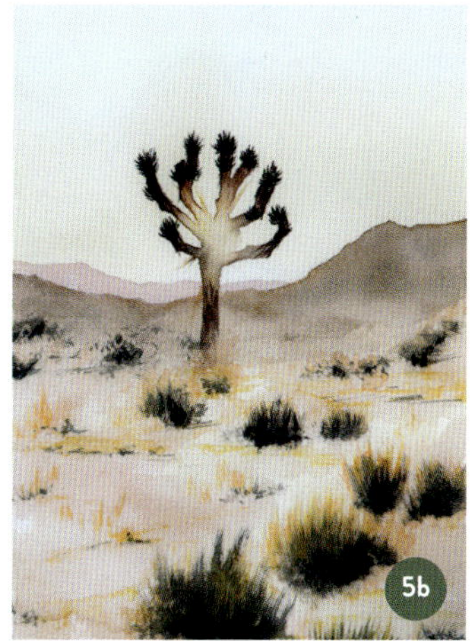

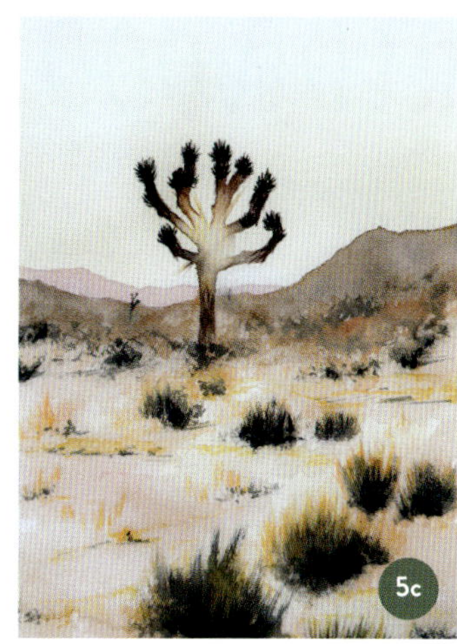

STEP 5: THE LANDSCAPE

Build out the rest of the landscape, paying careful attention to layer light to dark and maintain the illusion of depth with size (small in the back, large in the front). Use a foliage brush with the watery dark green mix from the previous step to add more color to the foliage clusters from the previous layers, leaving the top edges yellow (to imply the glow of golden hour skirting over the top). Use a mix of tapping and flicking upward to create blades of grass. Add more Payne's Gray to the green mix, and repeat, keeping the dark-value strokes even lower so we can see both the golden tops and the lighter green (layers!).

Finally, use a size 2 round brush with various shades of yellow, green, and orange to add dry brush (page 12) texture and blades of grass across the landscape and along the base of the mountain. Keep up the loose zigzag movement, and leave plenty of the underpainting showing to act as the pale desert ground. Lastly, mix a watery Payne's Gray, and starting at the base of the foliage clusters, flick downward to add cast shadows.

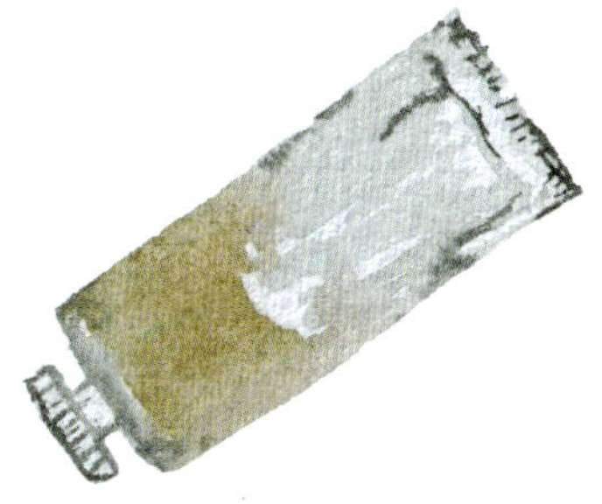

REDWOOD

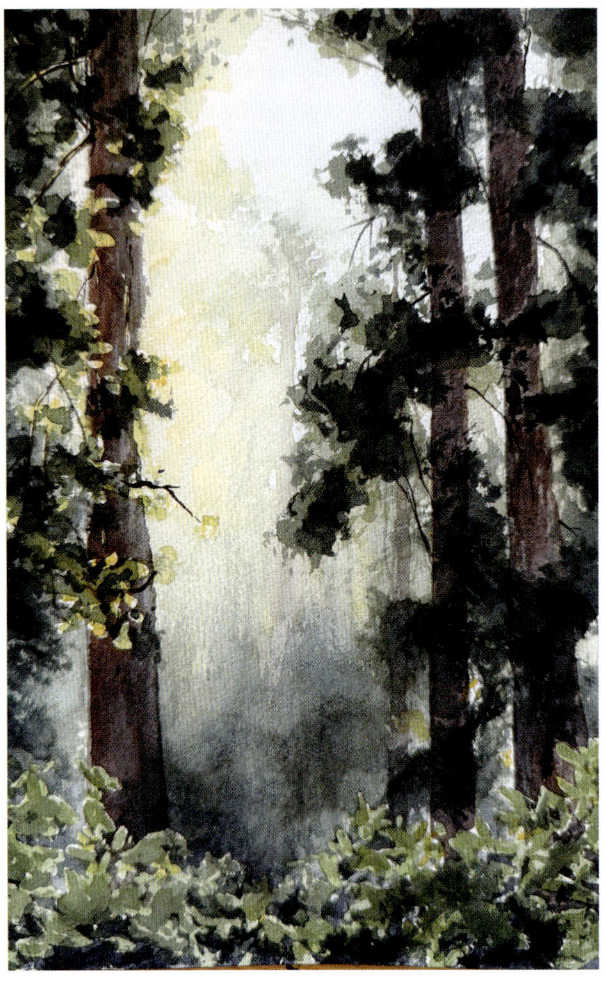

Deep in the Redwood National Park, surrounded by glimmering leaves and towering trees, how can you possibly feel anything other than a quiet sense of wonder? The trick here is a slow build of values—start with light, blurry layers in the background, then darker and more textured in the foreground. Remember: Especially when capturing light, we don't need perfection! Courage and curiosity will capture the magic much more effectively.

BRUSHES
Round sizes 2 and 12; Foliage brush; Masking fluid brush

COLOR PALETTE
French Ultramarine, Phthalo Blue (Green Shade), New Gamboge, Payne's Gray, Pyrrol Scarlet

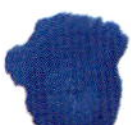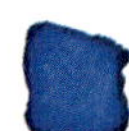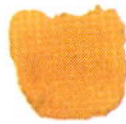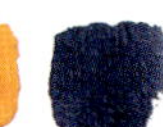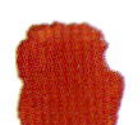

Note: This project uses masking fluid.

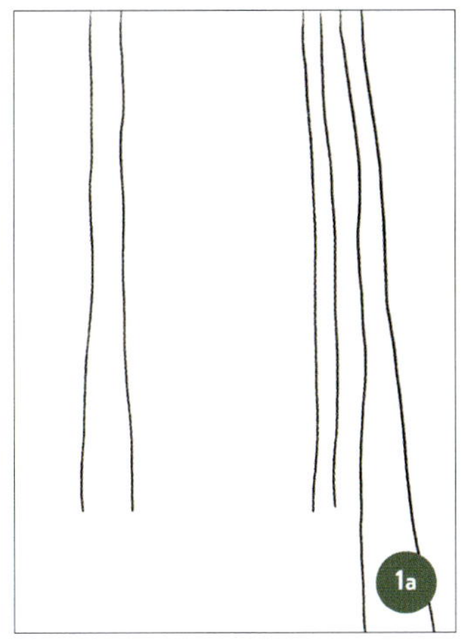

STEP 1: THE SKETCH

Start by sketching three tree trunks, one on the left side of the page and two slightly smaller ones on the right side of the page. The lines should be wobbly (more realistic!) and slightly tapered as they go up the page. Then, use your masking fluid brush prepped with soap and masking fluid (page 15) to paint leaf-like foliage texture along the bottom quarter of the page. Paint in a few crossing lines of foliage texture across the largest tree trunk on the left side of the page. (Think a loose zigzag). Let dry for 30 minutes or until tacky.

STEP 2: THE UNDERPAINTING

Use a size 12 round brush with clean water to wet the entire page. Then, use a quite light-value (watery) mix of French Ultramarine and Phthalo Blue to spread around the top right of the wet page. Paint between the trees if you can, but they will eventually be much darker, so it's okay if some of the color bleeds. Let dry completely.

STEP 3: THE BACKGROUND TREES

Next, paint a shrouded, hazy layer of tree texture using a watery foliage brush. Since this is a background layer, we want very light values—which means very watery paint and not a lot of definition. Part of the background tree layer will accentuate the glowing in the foreground, so use more warm, yellow-green mixes (New Gamboge + a bit of French Ultramarine) in the middle space, and less yellow in the edge spaces. Tap the foliage brush around the foreground trunks as much as possible, but it's okay if there's a little overlap.

Paint one long, skinny line loosely in the center to imply the silhouette of a faraway tree trunk blending with the foliage layer. Leave a space in the top right corner of the page blue, for the sky peeking between the trees. Before it dries but after you've painted the first round, add slightly more watery New Gamboge to the middle.

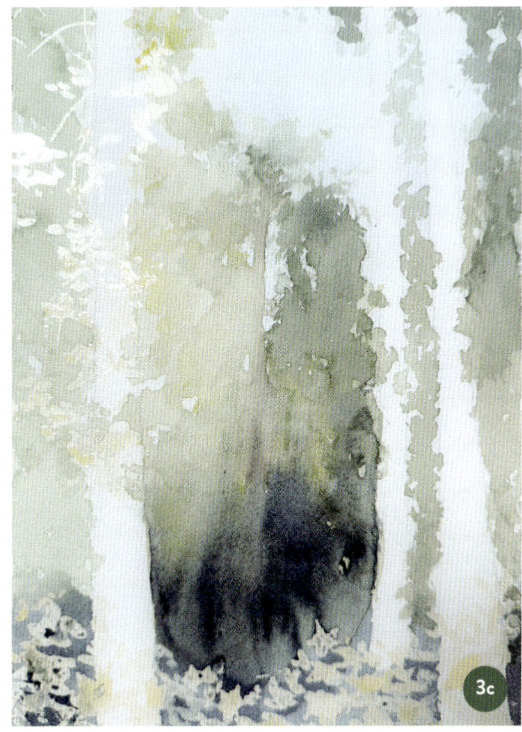

Then, use a foliage brush with clean water to wet the bottom of the page (where the masked leaves are), connecting the wet foliage layer with the bottom. Use the foliage brush with a darker, neutral green (Payne's Gray + the green mixture of New Gamboge and French Ultramarine) to gently flick your paintbrush up from the leafy ground into the damp, yellow foliage layer. Note that while darker than before, this green mixture should still be a watery and relatively light value. The paper around the masked leaves should be shadowy, but the shadows should bleed upward in blurry vertical stripes into the light, yellow middle area, mimicking glimmers of light and sun rays. Let dry completely.

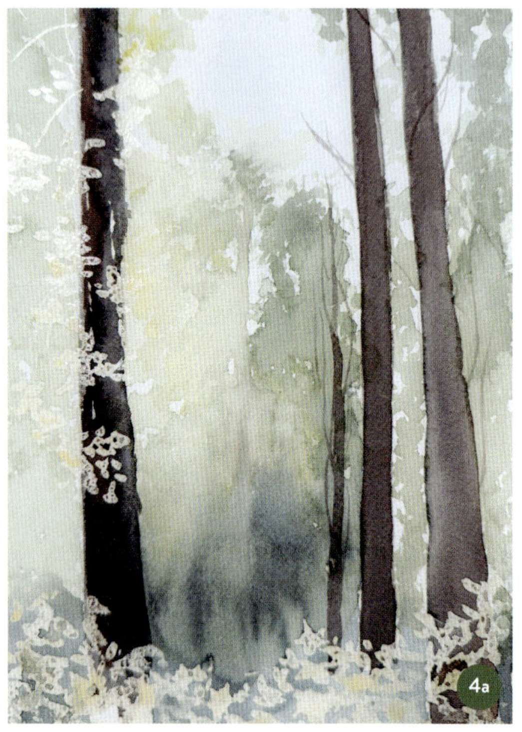

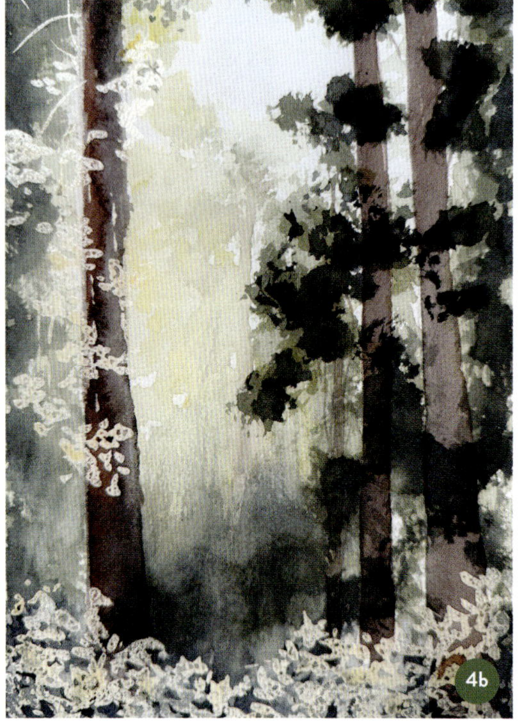

STEP 4: THE FOREGROUND TREES

Paint the foreground tree trunks using a brown mixture (French Ultramarine + Pyrrol Scarlet + a little bit of New Gamboge). Use a size 2 round brush to paint some branches coming out of the right side trunks and a small tree behind them. Start from the large trunk and lightly pull the detail brush upward to create thin, wispy branches. Let dry.

Use a foliage brush with darker-value greens (more paint to the mixture) to paint leaf clusters over the top of the right-side trees. Use a loose zigzag formation so the clusters move down the trunks into the leafy ground area. Then, starting from the center of the bottom of the page, use a foliage brush with just a bit of the watery dark green mix from the previous step to gently flick upward into the center, creating dry streaks into the light and creating shadows to imply starker sun rays. Use the foliage brush with the darker green mix to darken the left side of the left tree trunk, leaving some lighter edges around the masked leaf clusters and branches. We want the edge of the left side tree to be cast in shadow, but we want to leave behind lighter space around the masked leafy clusters so there's room to experiment with the glowing highlights later on. Let dry completely.

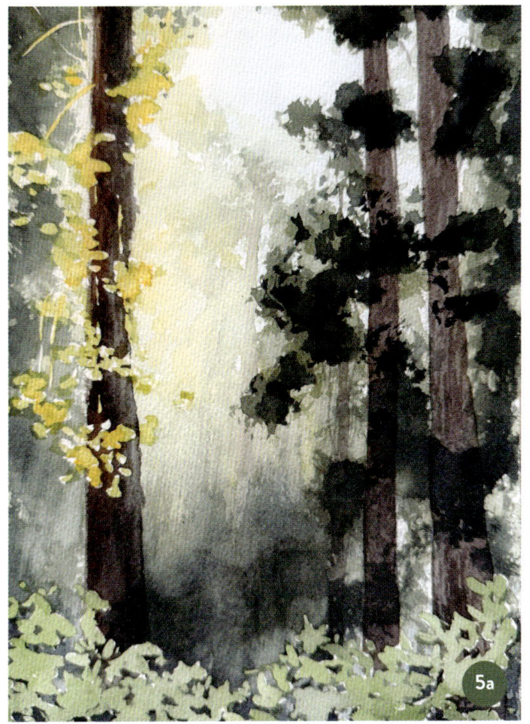

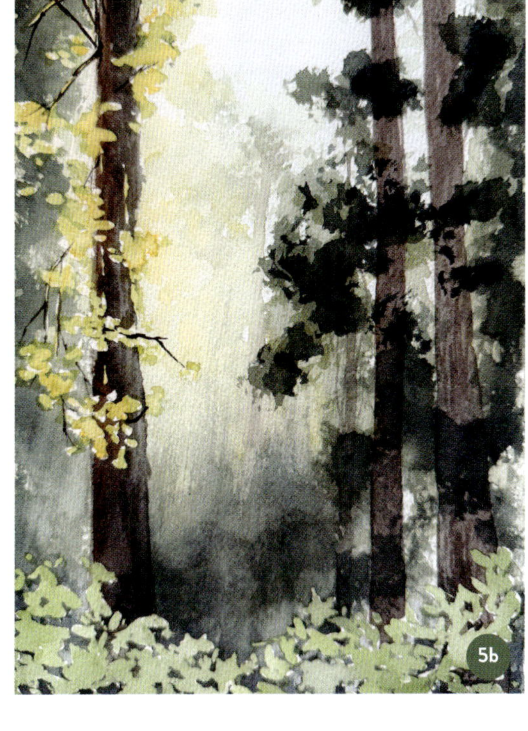

STEP 5: THE FOREGROUND LEAVES

Remove the masking fluid by gently rubbing it away with your finger or an eraser (page 15). Using watery paint on a small foliage brush, paint the leafy clusters on the left tree a yellow-green (New Gamboge + French Ultramarine), and then use a size 2 round brush to paint the leafy ground a more neutral watery green (same mix, but with more French Ultramarine). Both of these areas should be considerably lighter than the dark leaf clusters on the right side trees. Use a size 2 round brush with a dark brown mix (French Ultramarine + Pyrrol Scarlet + New Gamboge + a bit of Payne's Gray) to paint small, thin branches between some of the leaf clusters on the trees.

(continued)

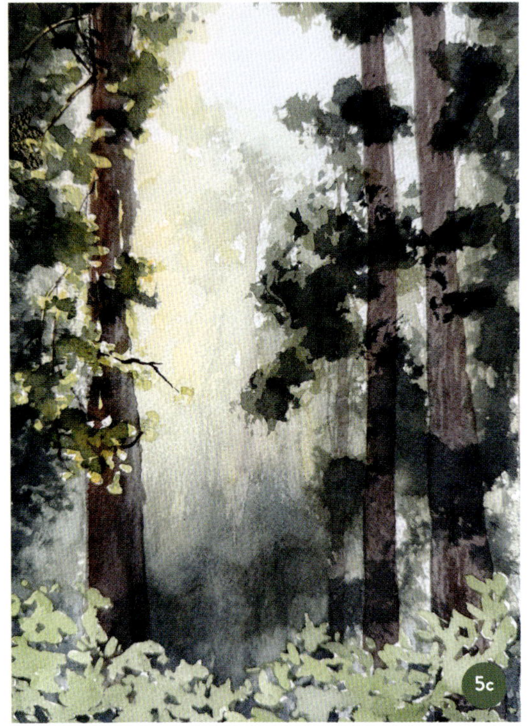

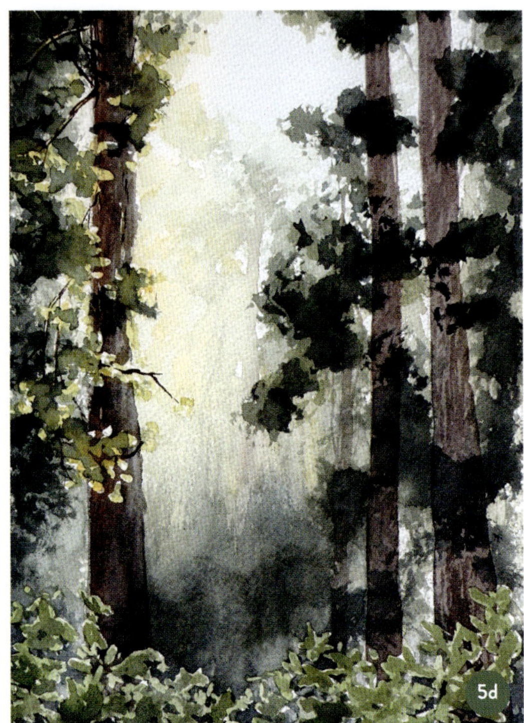

Then, use a foliage brush to lightly tap a slightly darker green over the top of the yellow green leaves on the left side tree, leaving behind peeks of the yellow on the edges of the foliage texture. Repeat for the ground leaves below. Finally, use an even darker green to add a few more darker foliage texture spots, more toward the edge of the page, on both sides. We're painting light to dark here, using less and less paint the darker we get to make the glimmers of yellow really pop.

STEP 6: FINAL DETAILS

If necessary, darken the trunks on the right side by painting a darker brown mix (add more Payne's Gray to the previous brown mix) around the leaf clusters, using choppy strokes to leave behind a bark-like texture. Use a foliage brush and a size 2 round brush with darker paint to add any final branches or small foliage shadows to add more movement and overall contrasting textures to make the layers snap together. The final result should be a light, watery layer in the background, slowly pulled forward by sharper and darker layers in the front.

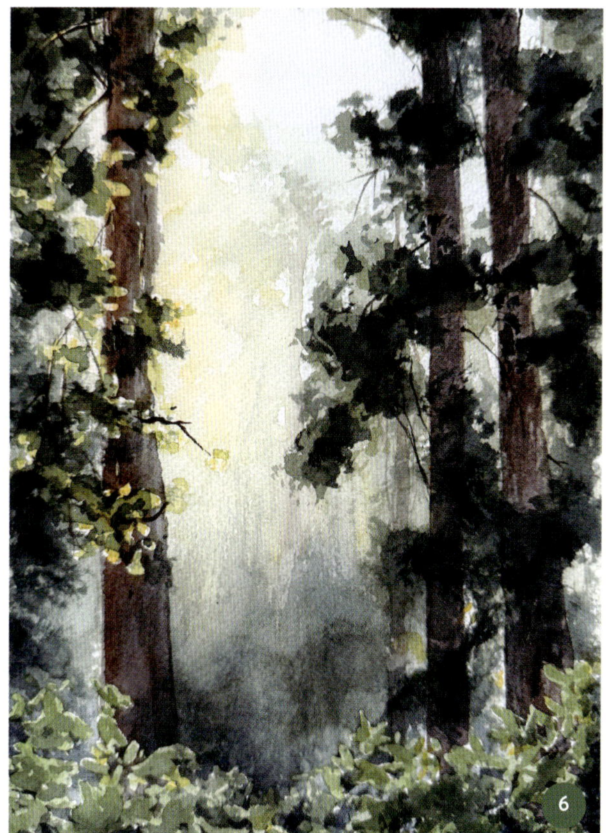

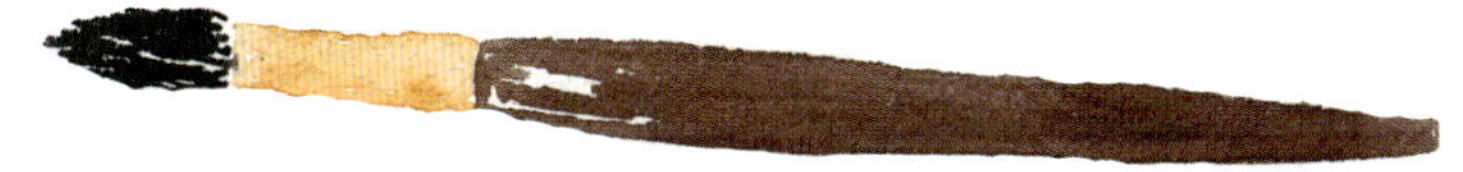

GREAT BASIN

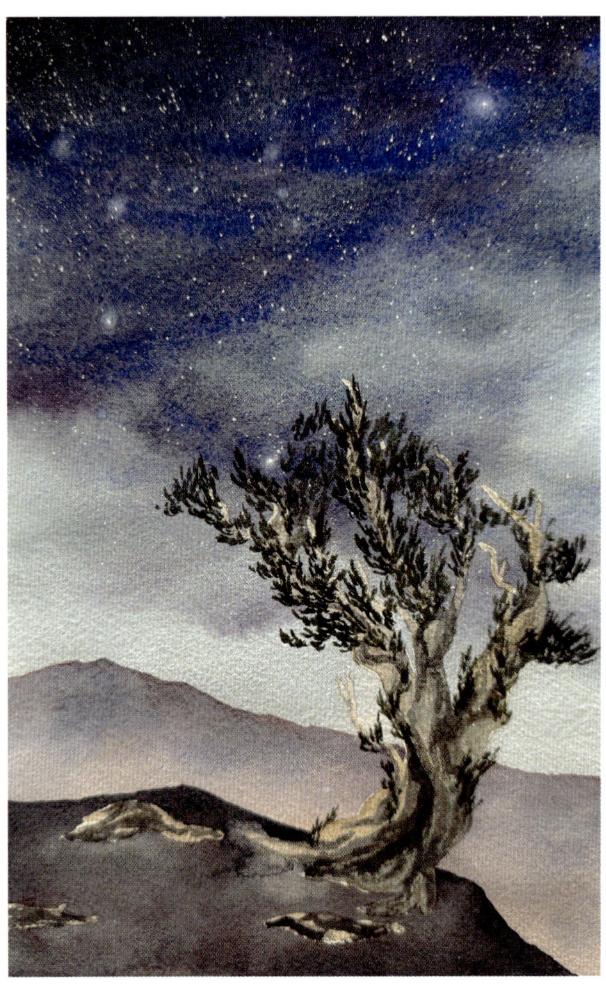

Bristlecone pines are said to be the oldest known living trees, and Great Basin National Park houses them in droves. With gnarled trunks twisting high on rocky mountaintops, these weathered species knows how to withstand the test of time—and with subtle layers of texture and value, you can capture a piece of that hardened wisdom in your studio.

BRUSHES
Round sizes 2, 6, and 12; Masking fluid brush

COLOR PALETTE
French Ultramarine, Phthalo Blue (Green Shade), Payne's Gray, Quinacridone Rose, white gouache, Pyrrol Scarlet, New Gamboge

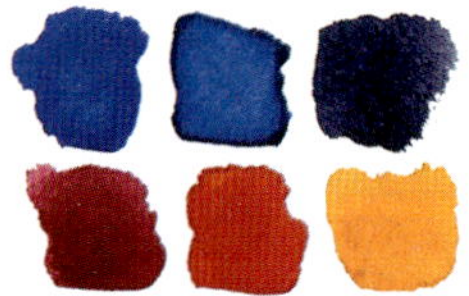

Note: This project uses masking fluid.

STEP 1: THE SKETCH

Sketch the flat mountain overlook with a loosely-angled C-curve (page 13) starting on the left edge of the page and curving down the bottom right edge. Then, sketch a mountain ridge about a third of the way up from the bottom, and a wobbly horizontal line with a couple sloping hills. Next, sketch the bristlecone pine. Start your lines on the ground, and gently pull your pencil up in twisty lines. We want the overall shape of the tree to be a loose C-curve—like it's bending to the wind—with a thick trunk and slowly tapering branches. Sketch a few thicker branches, then even more thin lines in forks coming out from the thicker branches.

Finally, use your masking fluid brush prepped with soap and masking fluid (page 15) to paint the tree. Paint a few loose S-curves (page 13) to the left of the tree on the flat mountain edge for roots that are pushing above ground. Let dry for 30 minutes or until tacky.

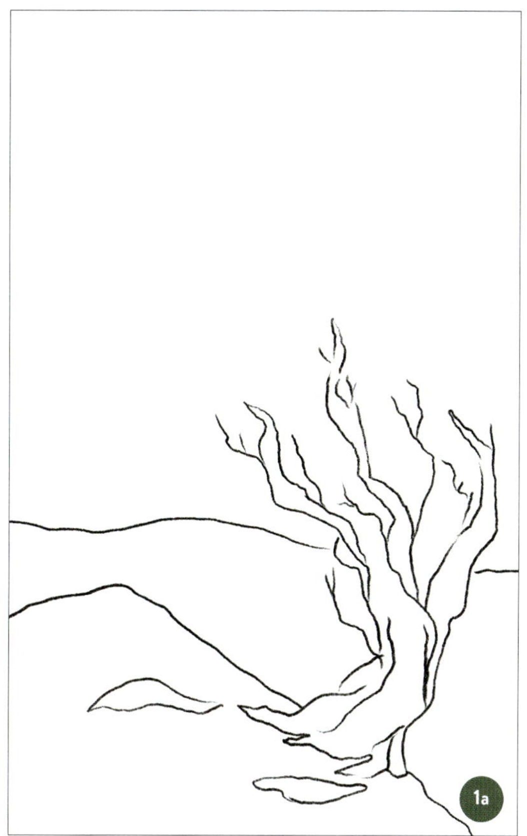

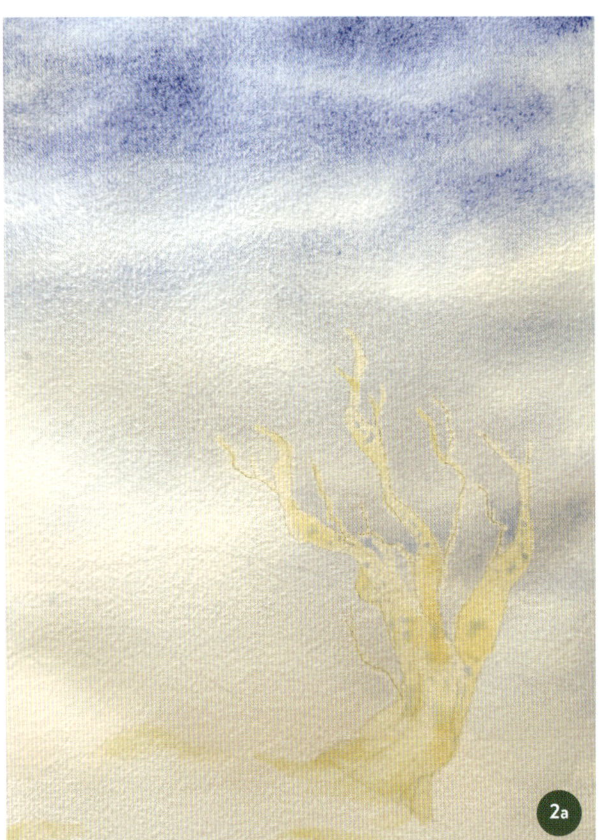

STEP 2: THE SKY

Paint a starry night sky with variations of blue and indigo. Layer a wash of clean water across the sky and into the distant mountain layer. With a size 12 round brush, paint medium-value French Ultramarine into the wet wash, starting at the top, alternating coming in from either side of the page so you leave behind thin, wispy slivers of white space—leaving more white space as you get to the bottom of the sky and into the mountain layer. Add a few strokes of Phthalo Blue. Let dry, then rewet with clean water, and repeat with a size 6 round brush this time. Add Payne's Gray to the top of the sky especially. The idea is to create a softly textured night sky with glimmers of various blues and wisps of white space.

Mix a deep violet (Payne's Gray + Quinacridone Rose), then tap the mix into the sky in a loose zigzag from the bottom of the sky up to the top. Add more French Ultramarine for a pop of blue. This should be a fun painting dance! Most important is to make sure the top of the sky is dark and gradually grows lighter toward the bottom.

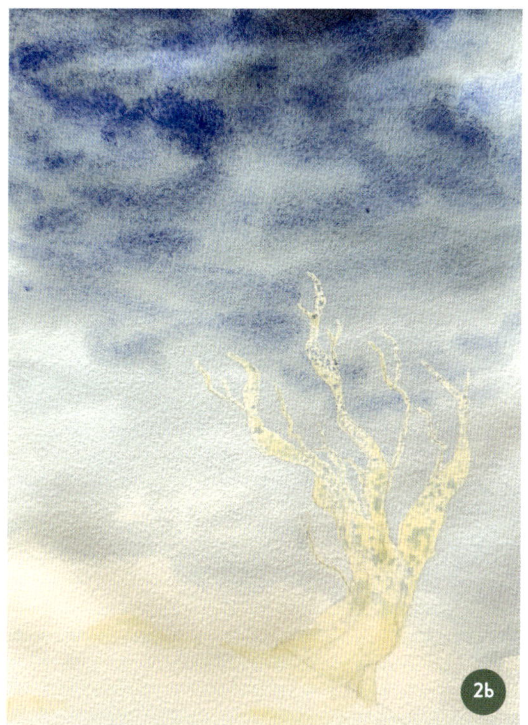

2b

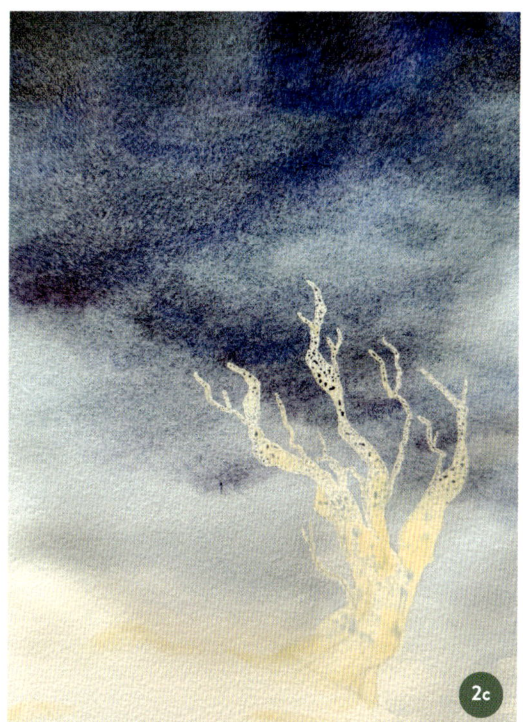

2c

While the sky is still mostly wet, use a size 2 round brush to add just a bit of water to your white gouache, then hold the brush over the sky with your non-dominant hand, and tap firmly with your dominant hand to splatter stars over the sky. Splattering the first layer over a still-wet sky will make some stars blurry, which adds to the depth. In a few spots, tap some thick white gouache into the sky, creating slightly larger blurry white spots. Let dry completely, then splatter more stars, and tap a single white dot into the blurry star spots. Let dry.

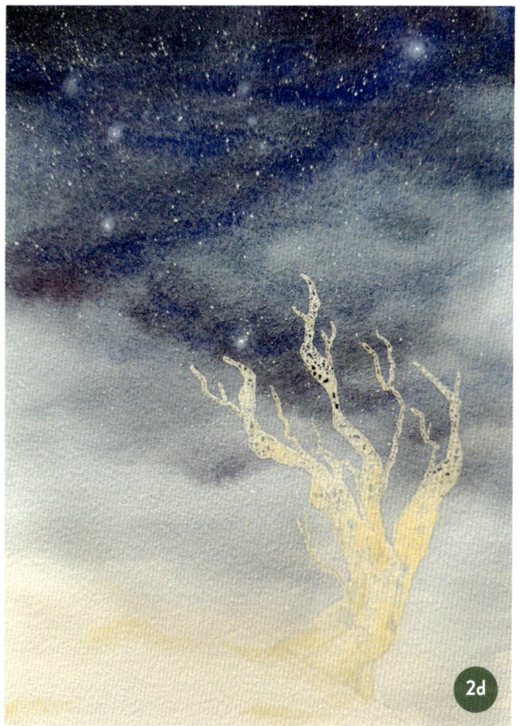

2d

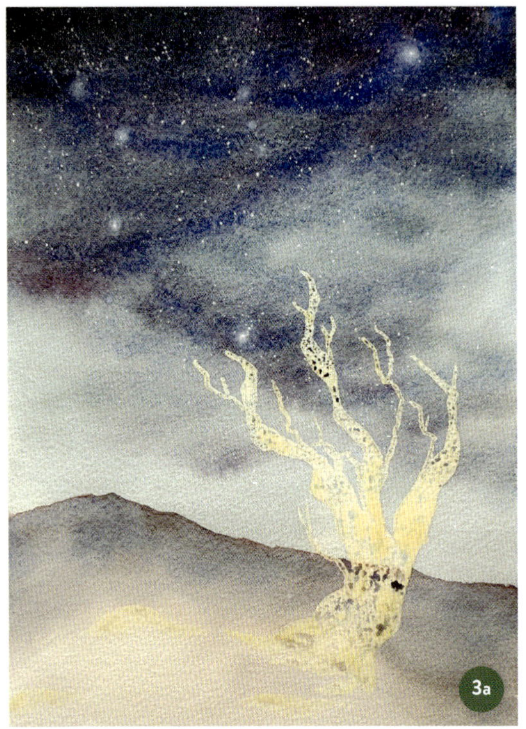

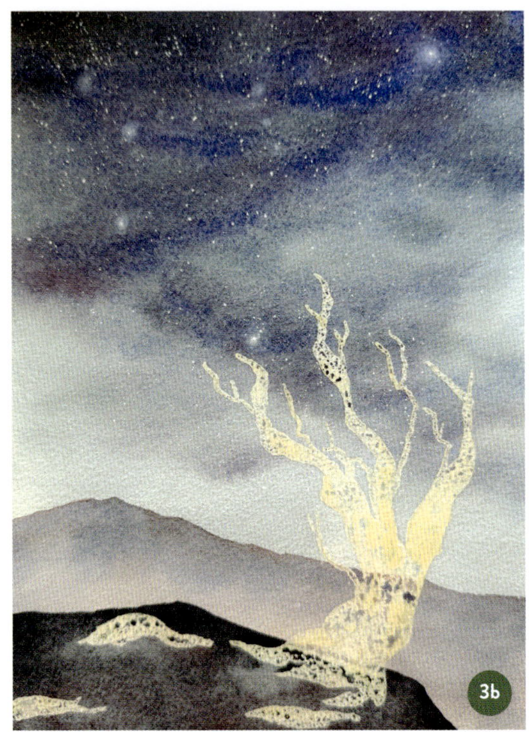

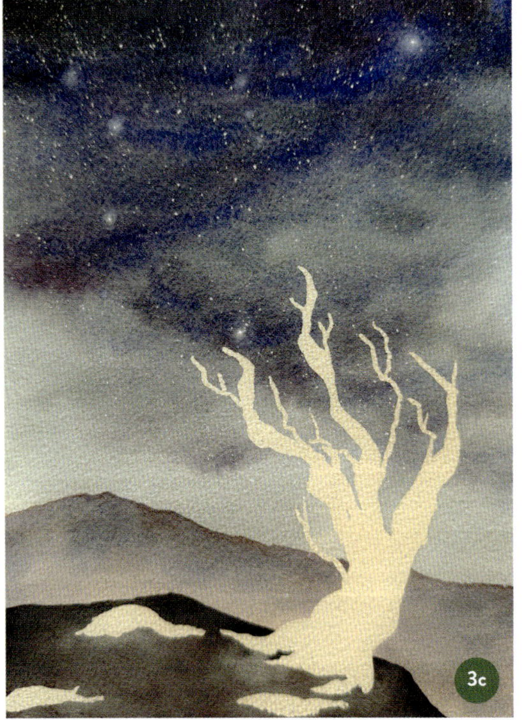

STEP 3: THE MOUNTAINS

Mix a watery, muted violet (French Ultramarine + Pyrrol Scarlet), then paint the first mountain layer, alternating between paint and water to make it luminous and light, especially toward the bottom of the layer. Let dry, then darken the mix by adding more paint and Payne's Gray. Paint the foreground mountain ledge. Tap a few strokes of Pyrrol Scarlet into the wet wash for added color variation.

Let dry completely, then remove the masking fluid by gently rubbing it away with your finger or an eraser (page 15).

STEP 4: THE BRISTLECONE PINE

Mix a watery, warm brown (New Gamboge + Pyrrol Scarlet + a hint of French Ultramarine). Use a size 2 round brush to paint the tree with clean water first, then tap the warm brown mix into the wet wash, allowing the paint to blend naturally. Paint the roots the same way. Take a bit of the dark violet mix from the previous step, add more water to it, and tap into the tree, just along the right side for a shadow. Let dry.

(continued)

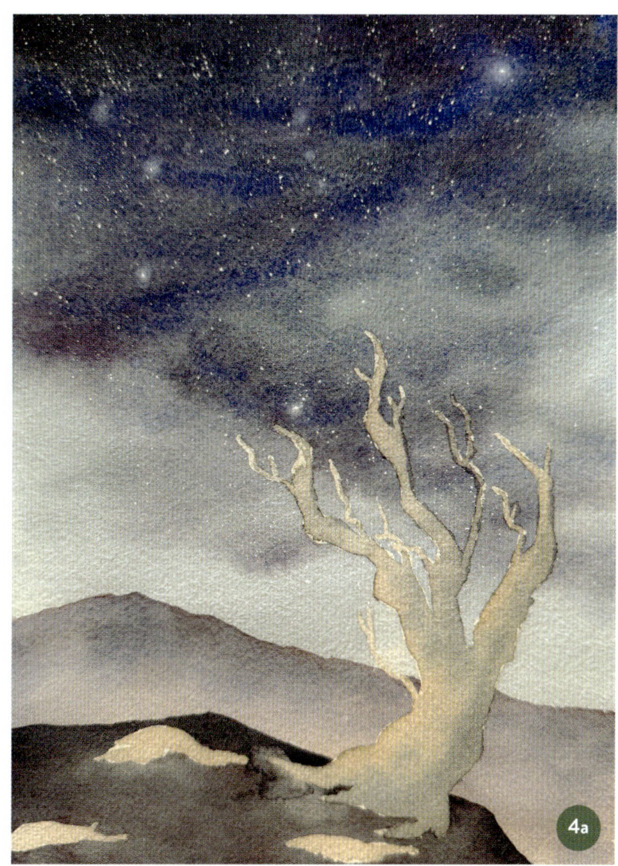

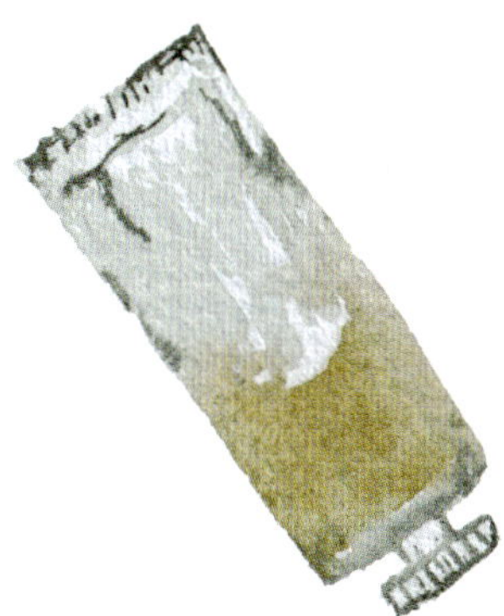

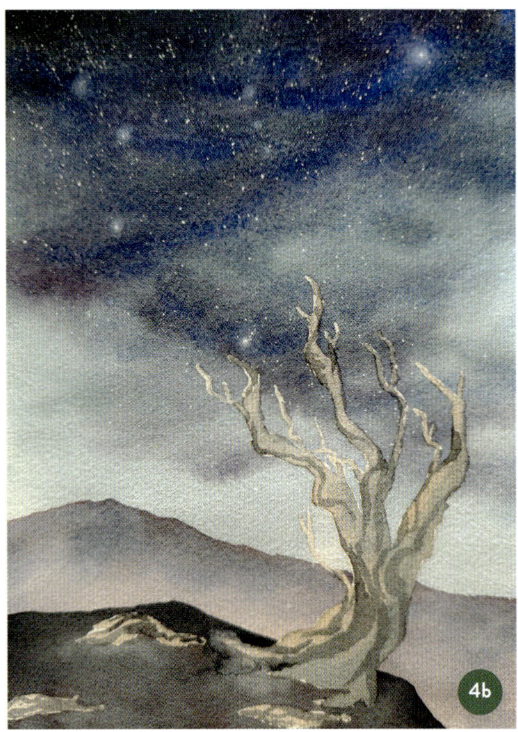

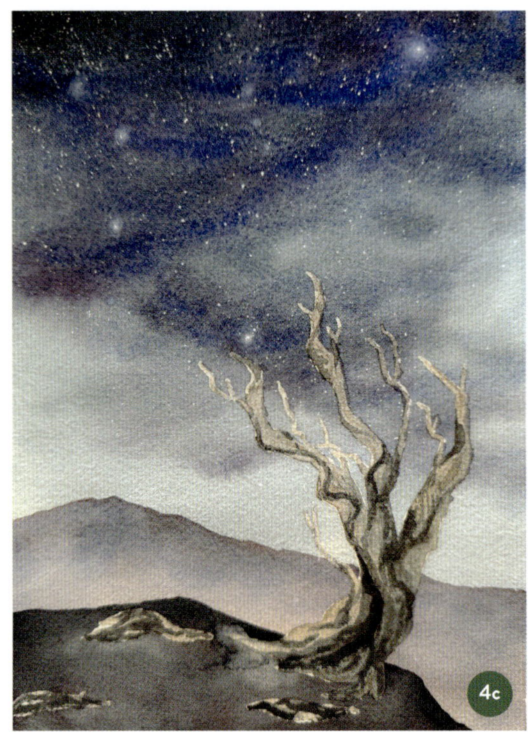

Next, paint defined gnarls into the dry bark with watery paint, starting at the base of the tree and pulling your brush up in loose C- and S-curves (page 13), leaving behind slivers of dry space. There is no right or wrong here! Have fun letting your brush play around—as long as there are wonky, curvy marks with spots of light space underneath, it's enough to imply the texture. Start with larger, lighter strokes and larger dry spaces first, then add thinner, darker strokes. Make sure there's at least one dark shadowy curve along the base of the trunk for depth.

Finally, mix a dark green (Payne's Gray + New Gamboge), and use a size 2 round brush to paint short, sharp marks in clusters around the branches and loosely along the trunk to complete the bristlecone pine effect. Remember to paint in clusters rather than thinking of them as individual needles to maintain a gnarled, more natural movement.

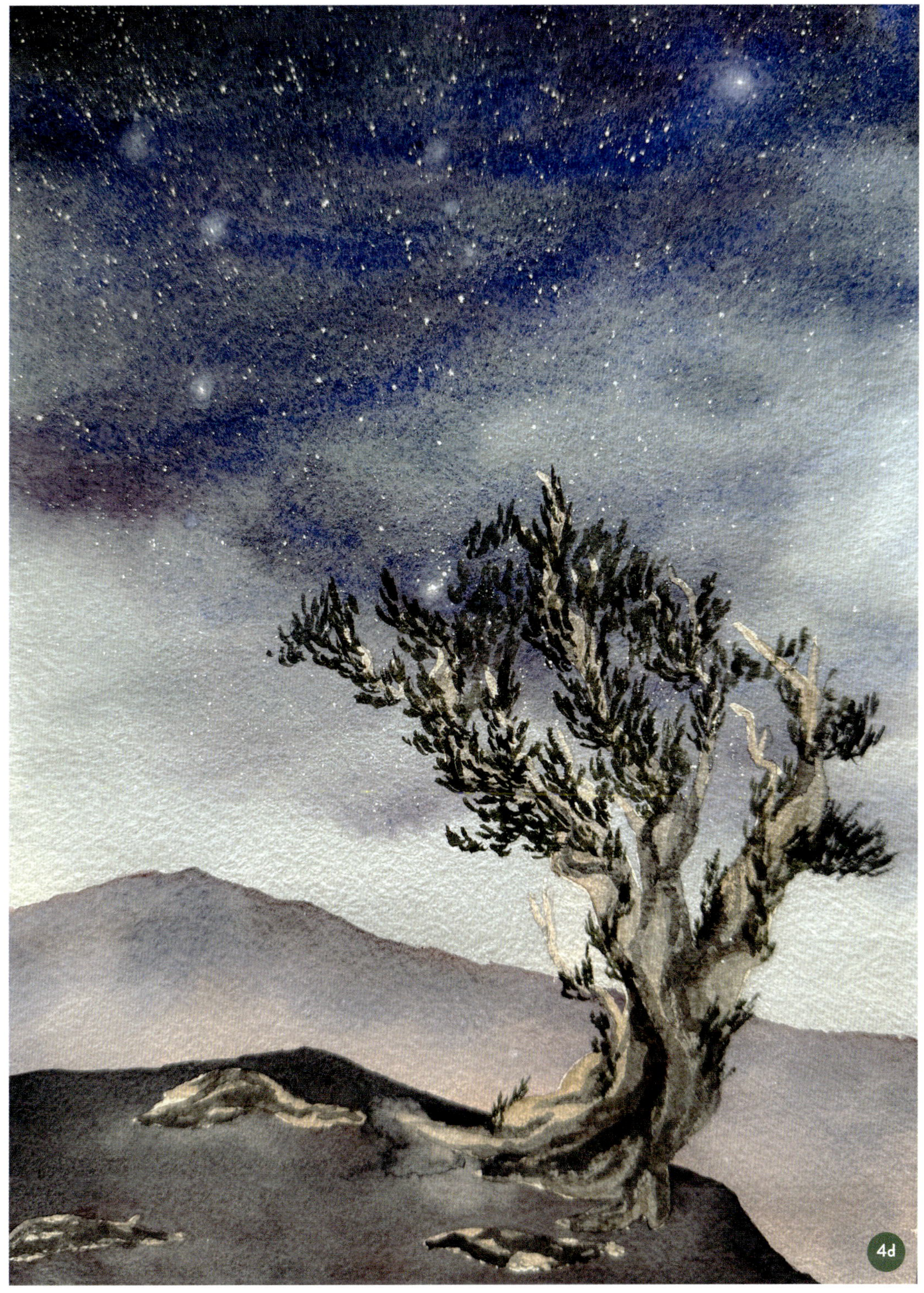

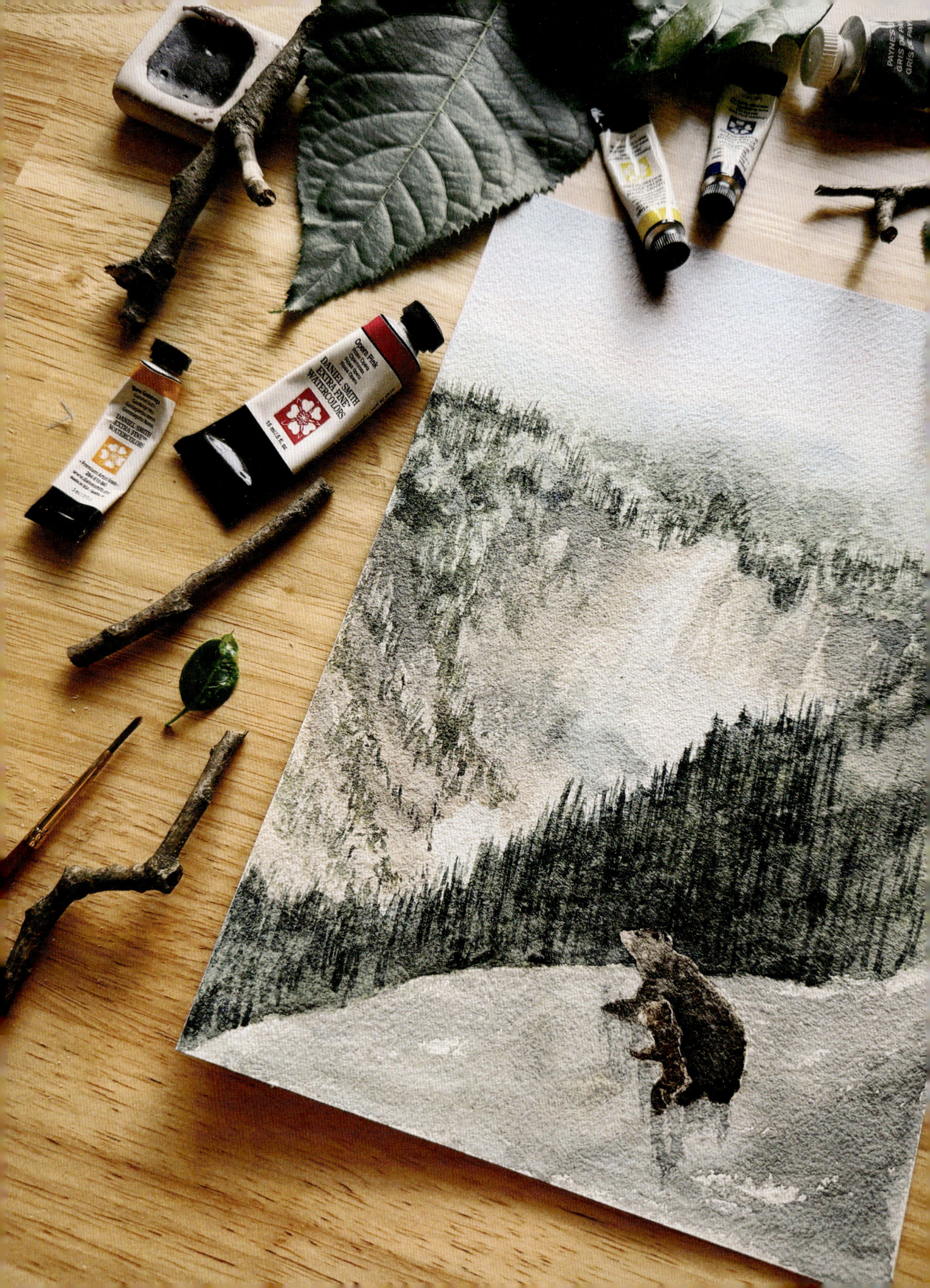

walking with the wildlife

"Wilderness without wildlife is just scenery."

—Lois Crisler

America's national parks are known for their idyllic landscapes, and part of the landscape are the animals that call these scenic views home. Let's paint some wildlife in their natural habitats while adventuring through a few parks in this chapter.

If using watercolor to paint wildlife (especially in a landscape book) feels overwhelming—I understand! That's why most of the animals featured in these projects are relatively simple and seamlessly integrated into a larger landscape scene. As ever, there's no need for perfection here; "good enough" is plenty to give you a magical creative experience.

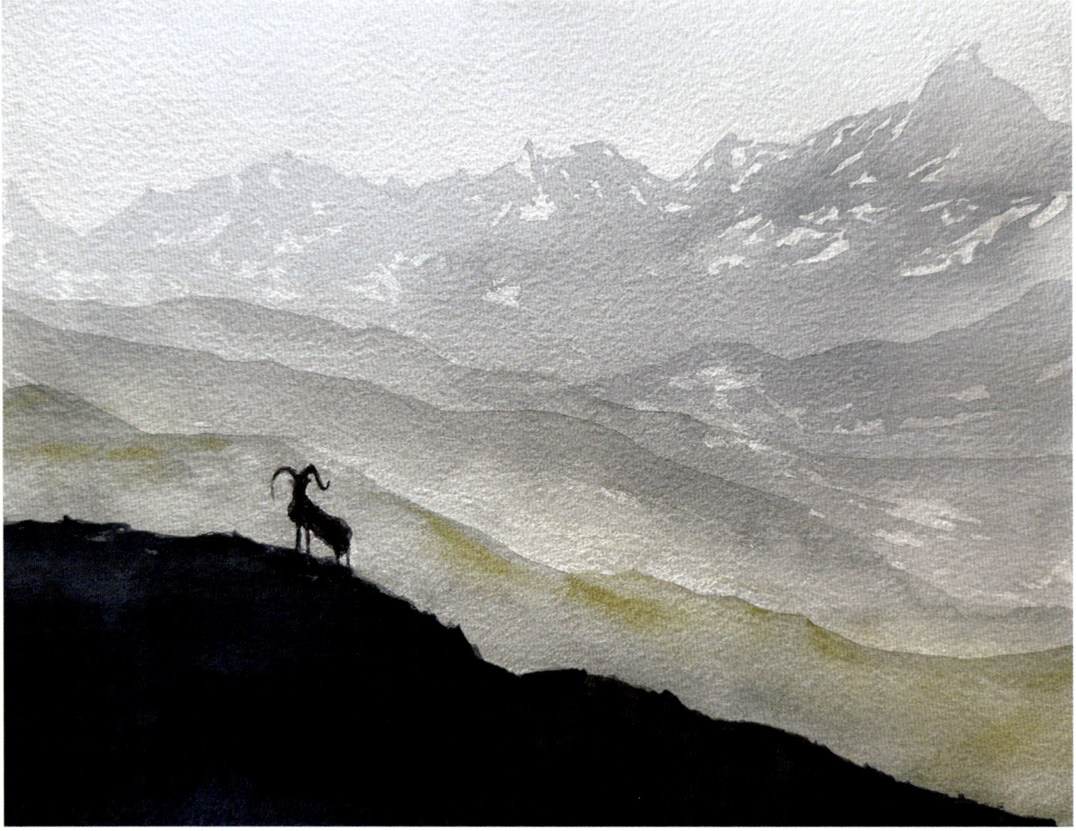

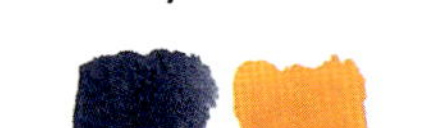

BRUSHES
Round sizes 2 and 12; Foliage brush; Masking fluid brush

COLOR PALETTE
Payne's Gray, New Gamboge

Note: This project uses masking fluid.

Home to the highest peak in North America (Mount McKinley), there's no better place to catch sight of a fearless Dall ram than in Denali National Park and Preserve. Let's paint a scene with pale mountain layers against a stark silhouette, bringing depth and perspective typical of such high elevations.

Sketch the mountain layers and a small ram. Start with a craggy mountain layer near the top of the page with a large peak to the right, moving up and down in jagged strokes all the way across. Then, sketch a few overlapping sloping curves down the page, with a final layer beginning about a third of the way up from the bottom to the left and sloping down to the bottom right. Sketch a ram looking out toward the mountain range—a rectangular-like body with curving lines for four legs, and a small head with visible ears. Sketch the horns, using C- or S-curves (page 13) to spiral out from the head and ending in points. Remember that we are not aiming for precision! It's okay to sketch a "good enough" ram. Finally, use your masking fluid brush prepped with soap and masking fluid (page 15) to paint the ram, preserving it for the final layer. Let dry for 30 minutes or until tacky.

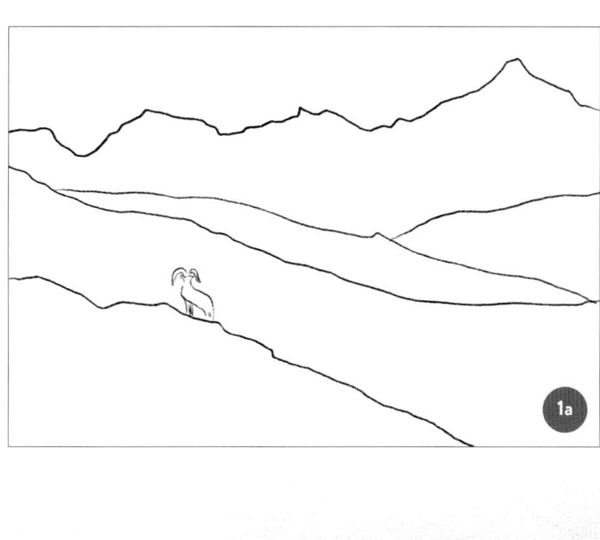

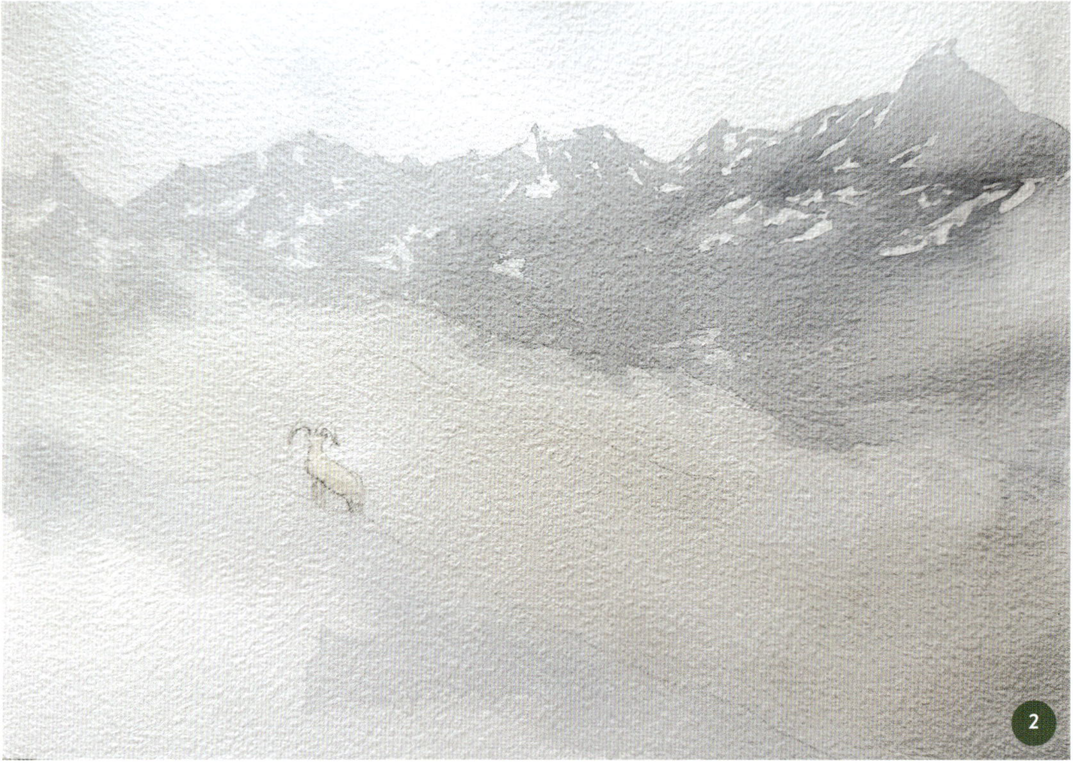

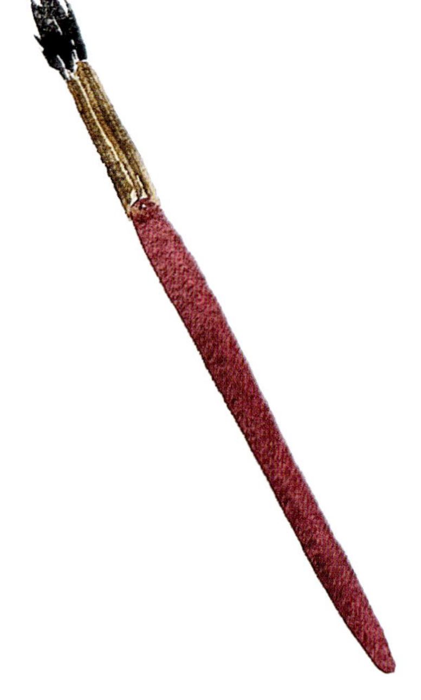

STEP 2: THE UNDERPAINTING

Layer a wash of clean water across the page with a size 12 round brush, then mix various shades of gray and green using Payne's Gray and New Gamboge. Paint the sky and the top mountain layer areas with more light-value grays and the lower mountain layers with more greens and yellows. The foreground mountain layer will be a dark-value silhouette, so it doesn't really matter what paint ends up there for now. Let dry completely.

Add a bit more Payne's Gray to the watery mix (still fairly watery, though), and paint the craggy background mountain layer using a foliage brush (which will make it easier to leave behind strips of white space for added texture). Let dry, then continue painting the lower mountain layers, gradually growing both darker in value and greener in color (though every layer should still be quite light). Make sure to leave behind long and somewhat random dry, light stripes in each layer.

Note: The previous layer must be completely dry before painting the next. For the closest mountain layer (that's not the silhouette), add more yellow into the green wash, creating glimmers of color variation.

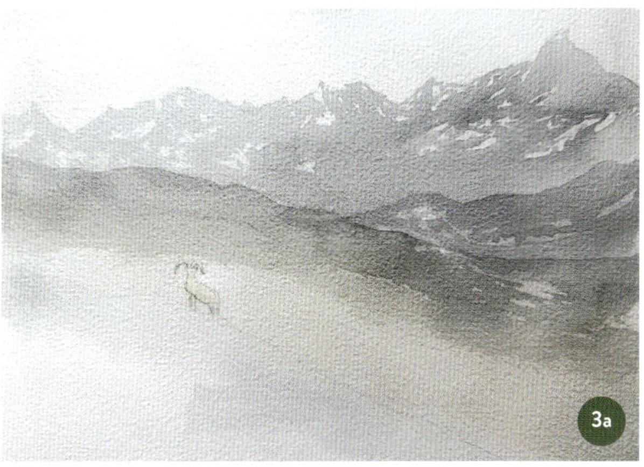

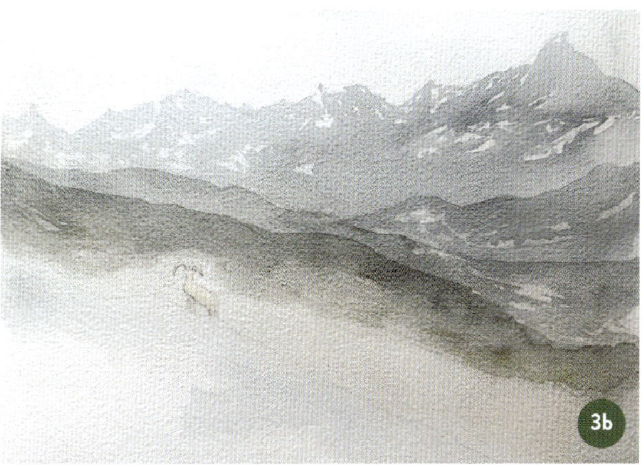

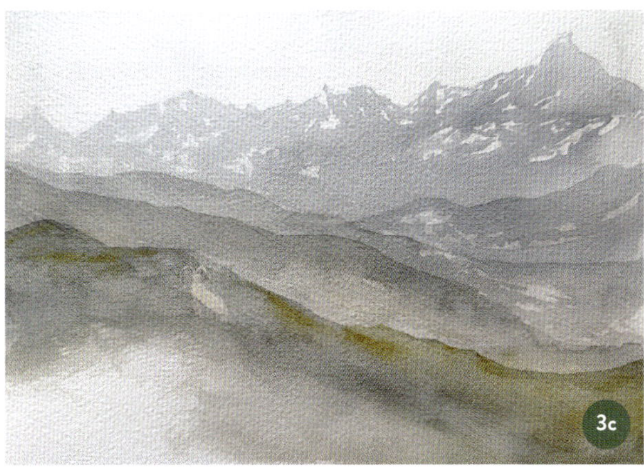

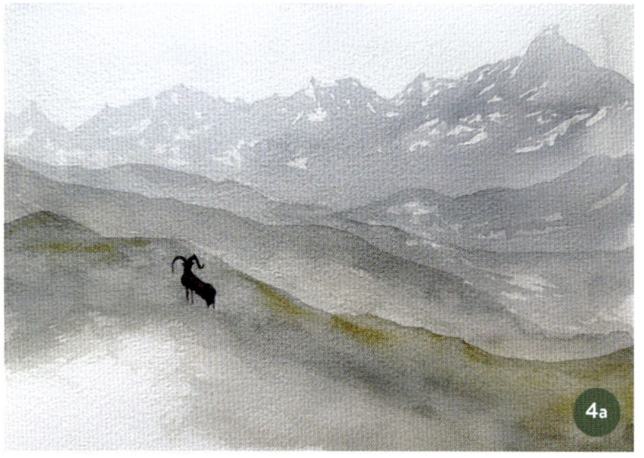

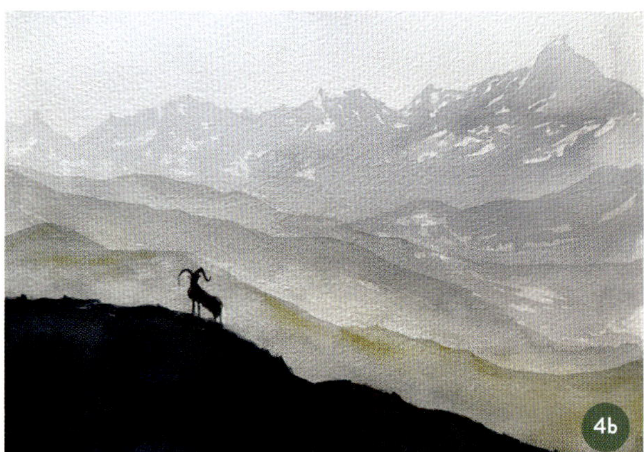

STEP 4: THE RAM

Let the mountain layers dry completely, then remove the masking fluid from the ram by gently rubbing it away with your finger or an eraser (page 15). Use dark-value Payne's Gray to paint the ram with a size 2 round brush, leaving slivers of white space along the edges for a highlight. Paint the foreground mountain layer dark-value Payne's Gray. This doesn't need to be a super smooth wash—a little texture will add to the depth.

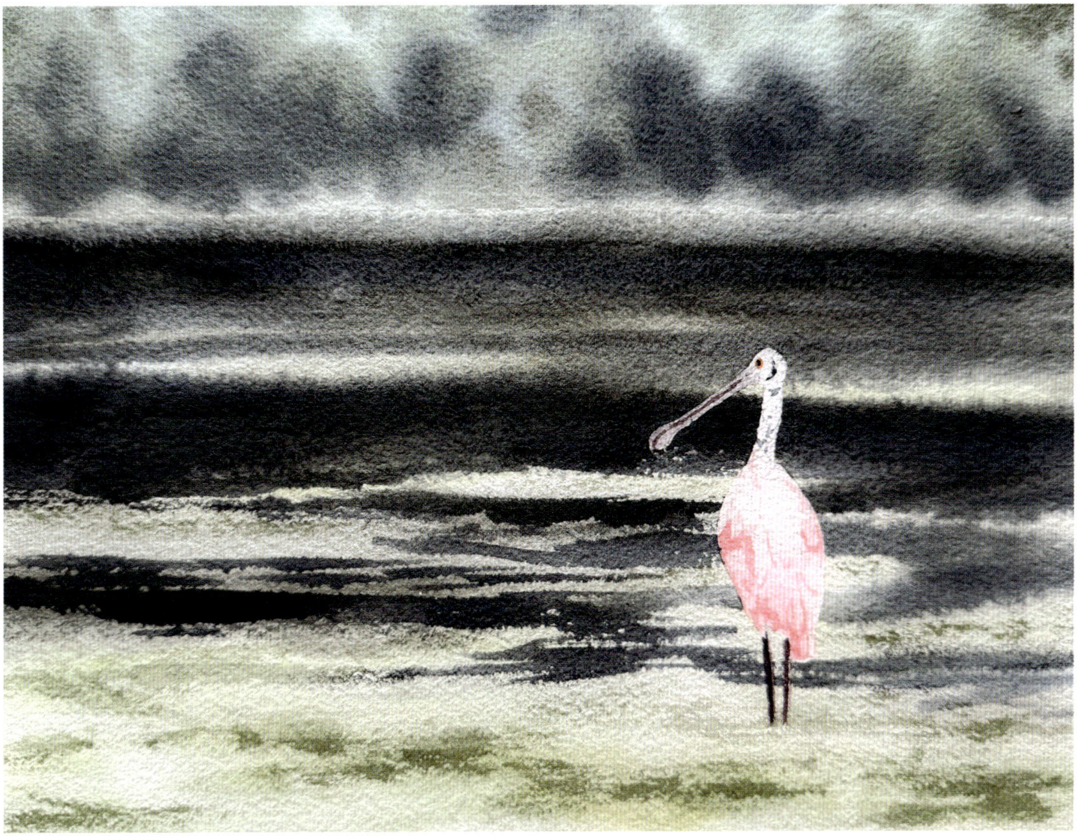

EVERGLADES

BRUSHES
Round sizes 2 and 12; Foliage brush; Masking fluid brush

COLOR PALETTE
French Ultramarine, Hansa Yellow Light, Payne's Gray, Opera Pink, white gouache, New Gamboge

  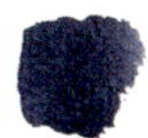  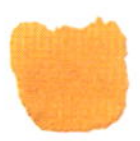

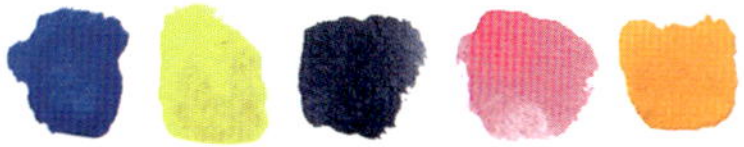

Note: This project uses masking fluid.

Set against the lush greenery of the Everglades, the roseate spoonbill makes for a colorful addition to the watery Florida landscape. The flash of pink set against the green mossy surface will make this scene pop! Don't worry—even though this creature will be one of the most detailed animals in the book, you have everything you need by starting light and blurry, then adding just a few dark and detailed marks to bring it all together.

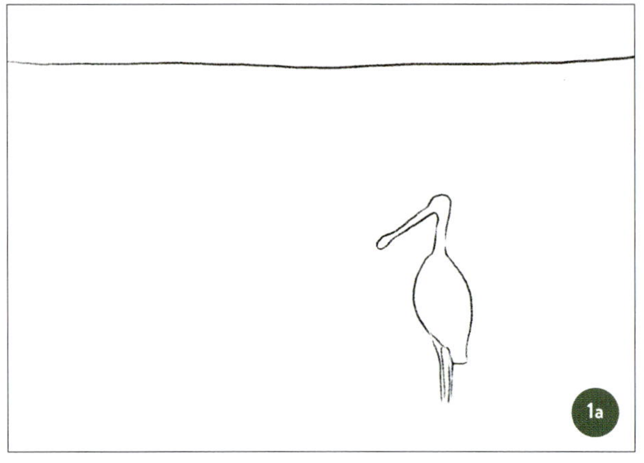

STEP 1: THE SKETCH

Sketch an outline of the spoonbill with an almond-shaped body, long neck, and a long, skinny bill that flares slightly at the end. Then, sketch a line about a fourth of the way down from the top of the page to separate the water from the trees behind it. Finally, use your masking fluid brush prepped with soap and masking fluid (page 15) to paint over the sketch of the spoonbill. This will preserve the white space so we can paint the water first, then the spoonbill after. Let dry for 30 minutes or until tacky.

STEP 2: THE LANDSCAPE

Layer a wash of clean water across the whole page. Then use a size 12 round brush to paint loose, zigzag strokes of yellow-green (French Ultramarine + Hansa Yellow Light) across the bottom of the page, leaving behind plenty of white space. Use a foliage brush to paint various darker greens (any combinations of Hansa Yellow Light, New Gamboge, and Payne's Gray you want to try) above the water, in the forest area at the top of the page. Let dry completely.

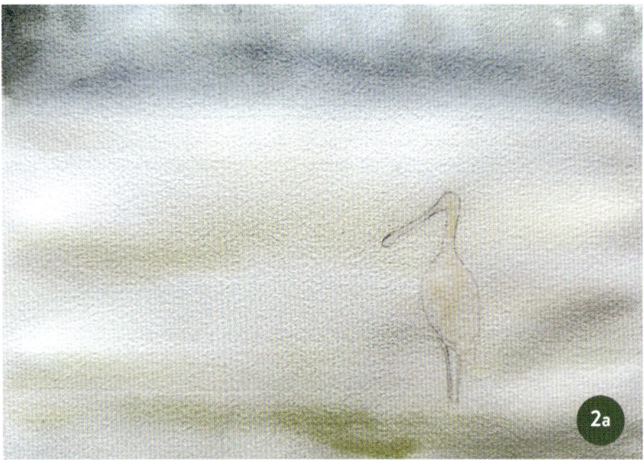

Rewet the water area, then create a dark green mixture (Payne's Gray + French Ultramarine + Hansa Yellow Light). Use a size 12 round brush to paint the area just below the trees dark green, leaving behind small slivers of the previous layer in some spots. If the color isn't quite dark enough, add more paint, and then use a smaller brush to paint. The layer might be drying toward the bottom at this point, and that works in our favor! The closer we get to the bottom, the more defined and smaller we want the dark ripples, and any dry brush (page 12) texture will look like sparkles in the water. Paint the dark green in loose, swooping strokes around the light green areas, trickling off into subtle ripples the closer you get to the bottom of the page, so it looks like loose zigzags of light and dark.

Next, rewet the forest area, and repeat the previous layer (use a foliage brush to add different shades of green) with slightly darker paint, leaving behind small bits of white space for depth. Paint just above the shoreline so there's a thin, natural strip of blurry white space between the water and the trees. Let dry completely.

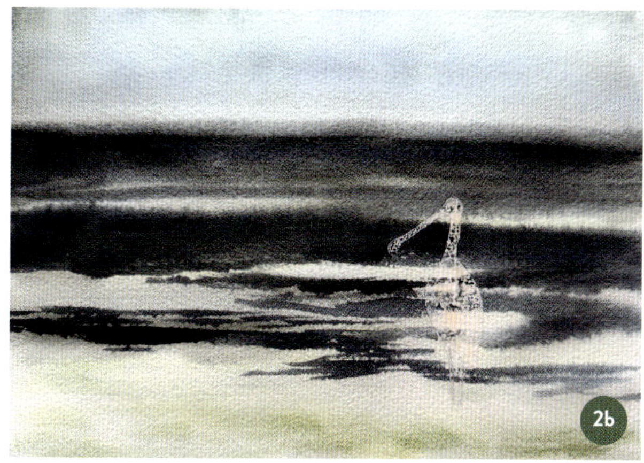

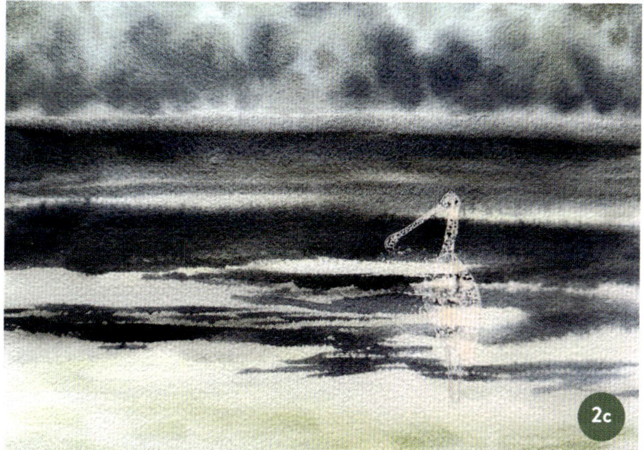

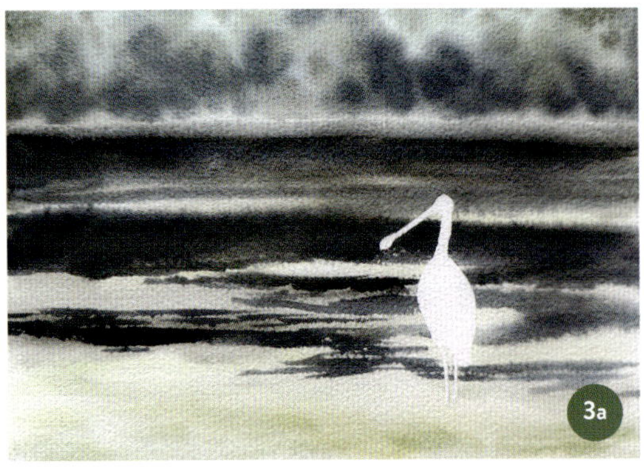

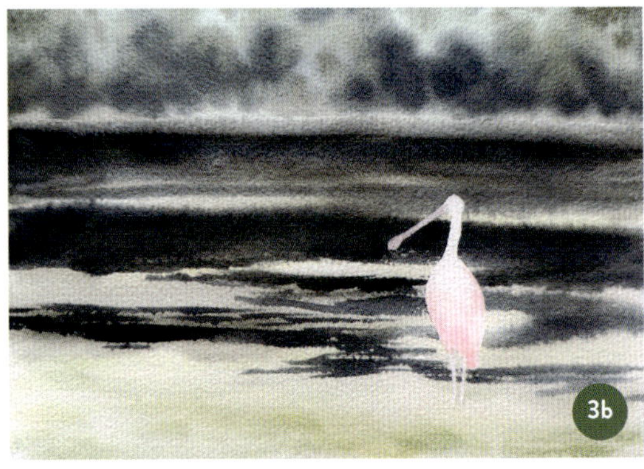

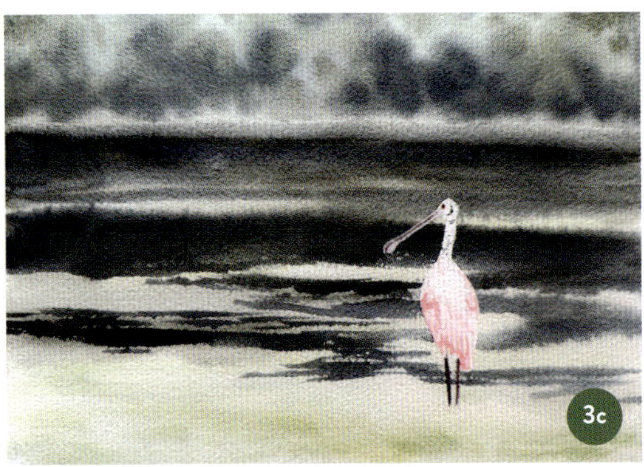

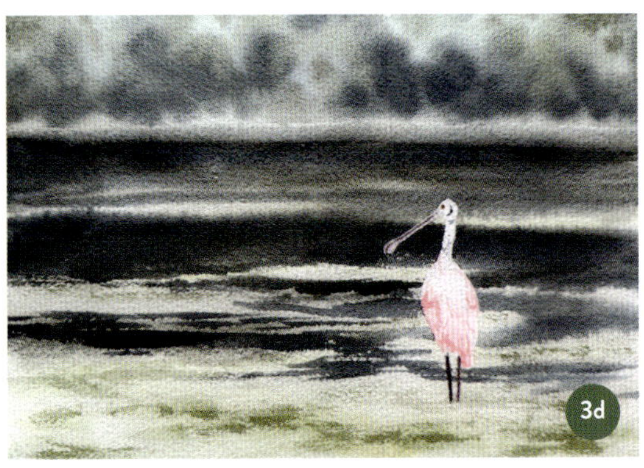

STEP 3: THE SPOONBILL

Remove the masking fluid from the spoonbill by gently rubbing it away with your finger or an eraser (page 15). Create a pink mix (Opera Pink + a bit of Hansa Yellow Light). Then, use a size 2 round brush to layer a wash of clean water on the bird. Tap the pink mixture along the bottom and sides of the body, using the wet-on-wet technique (page 10) to encourage natural blends and shadows. Paint the beak a very watery gray (mix a bunch of random colors together with a bit of Payne's Gray). Let dry completely, then use a size 2 round brush to paint jagged feathery shadows along the bottom and sides of the body. Remember: We're implying texture here, so creating realistic feathers is not necessary! Use a slightly darker gray to paint a thin line on the beak, separating the top and the bottom, curving a bit at the end. Paint a small orange circle (Hansa Yellow Light + Opera Pink) for the eye, then a few odd Payne's Gray marks along the neck for some detail. (They're supposed to look random and varied!) Complete the spoonbill with a small Payne's Gray dot in the center of the eye, an even smaller white gouache dot on top of that and to the side (for a highlight), and thin, dark legs coming down from the body going into the water.

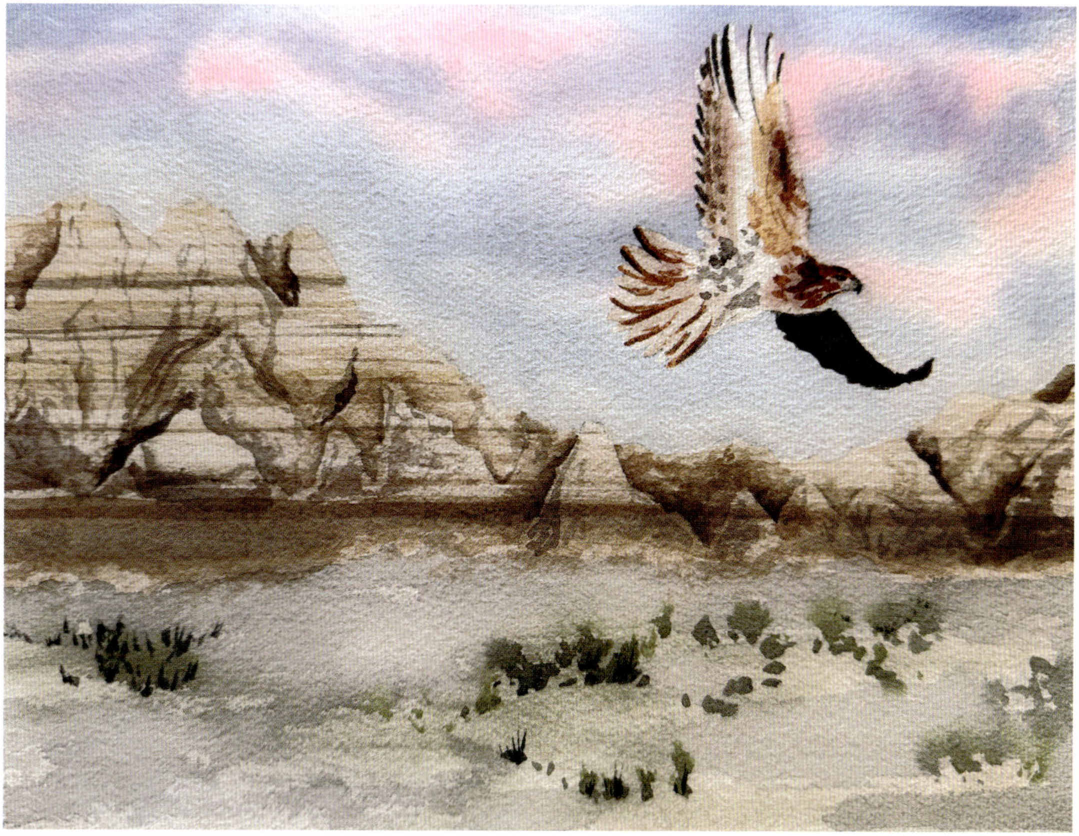

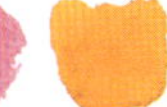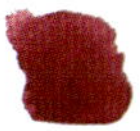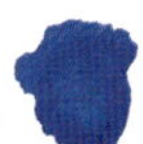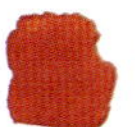

BADLANDS

BRUSHES
Round sizes 2, 6, and 12; Foliage brush;
Masking fluid brush

COLOR PALETTE
Opera Pink, New Gamboge, Quinacridone
Rose, French Ultramarine, Pyrrol Scarlet,
Payne's Gray

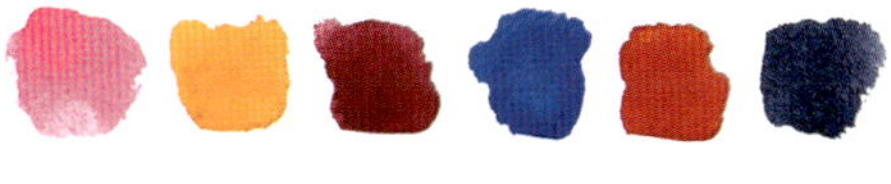

Note: This project uses masking
fluid.

With such starkly striped rock
formations that stand out against
the arid landscape, Badlands
National Park already makes an
impression. Add a red-tailed hawk
soaring over the scene, and you
have a moment in nature you
won't soon forget. We're playing
with a lot of different textures
here—remember that it's meant to
be fun! Paint what speaks to you,
and simplify what doesn't.

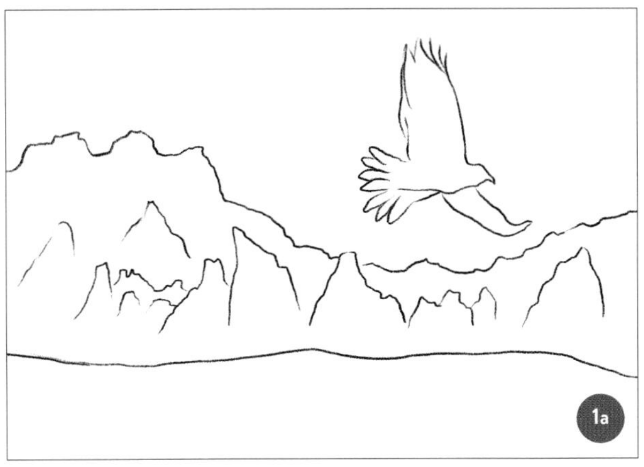

STEP 1: THE SKETCH

Sketch the mountain formations, leaving a space in the top right corner for a large red-tailed hawk. Start with a craggy horizontal line just below the top of the left side of the page, moving up and down in sharp lines, and then sloping down through the center and to the right of the page—carving out space in the sky for the hawk. Sketch more layers of rock formations using loose triangle-shaped marks of various sizes in front of the larger mountain layer, stopping about a third of the way up from the bottom of the page.

Finally, sketch an outline of the hawk—we want it large to add perspective, as if it's flying close to us with the mountain far away. Sketch a small rounded head with a curved beak, one large wing with curves for feathers oriented vertically, another smaller wing curved and to the right side. Then, sketch the tail feathers fanning out straight across from the head. Shaky strokes are okay at any point! Use a masking fluid brush prepped with soap and masking fluid (page 15) to paint over the hawk. Let dry for 30 minutes or until tacky.

STEP 2: THE SKY

Start with a wash of clean water across the sky with a size 12 round brush, carefully painting around the mountain ridge. Create various mixes of pinks and oranges with Opera Pink, New Gamboge, and Quinacridone Rose, and then tap into the wet sky in loose horizontal strokes. While still wet, tap watery French Ultramarine in the spaces around the pink clouds, leaving behind a soft mix of pink, white, and blue. Let dry completely, then erase the pencil marks along the top mountain ridge if possible before moving on.

STEP 3: THE MOUNTAINS

Mix various shades of brown (Pyrrol Scarlet + New Gamboge + French Ultramarine) and green (any combination of yellow and blue). Use a size 12 round brush to paint the mountain and the land below the mountain in a watery brown layer. Then use a size 6 round brush to add a few long strokes of green just above the bottom of the page and a violet-brown (add more French Ultramarine) along the lower layer of the rock formations.

(continued)

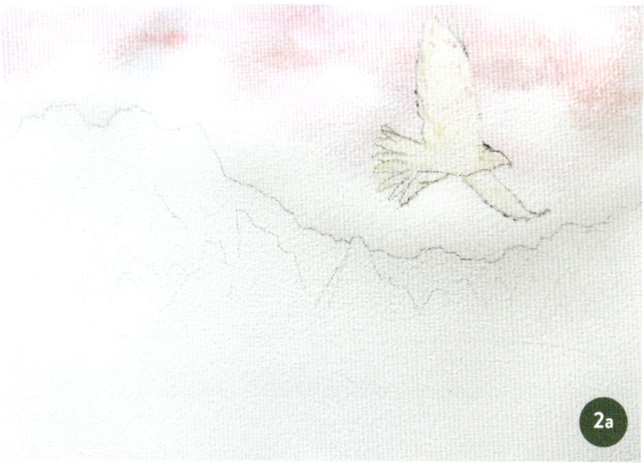

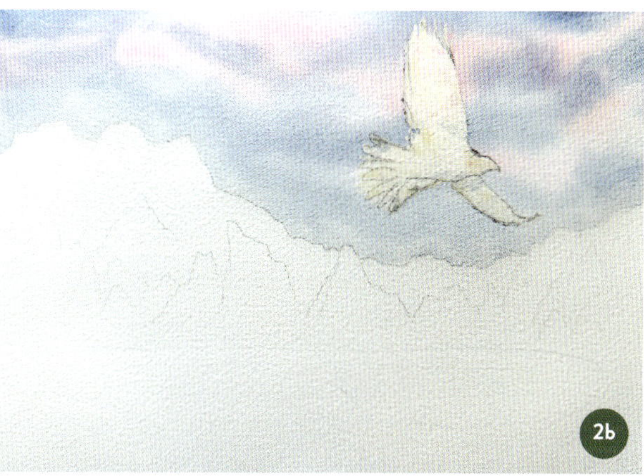

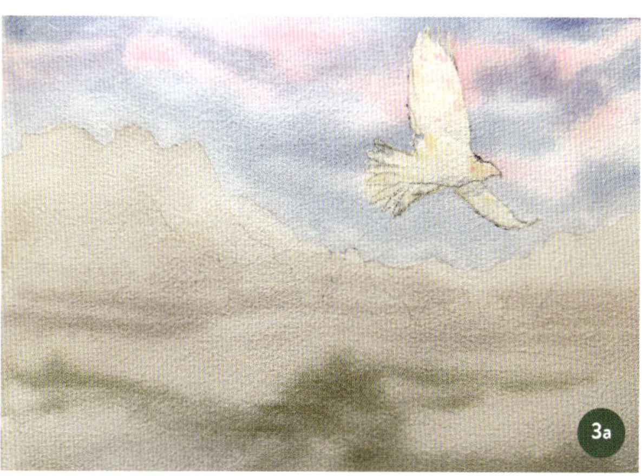

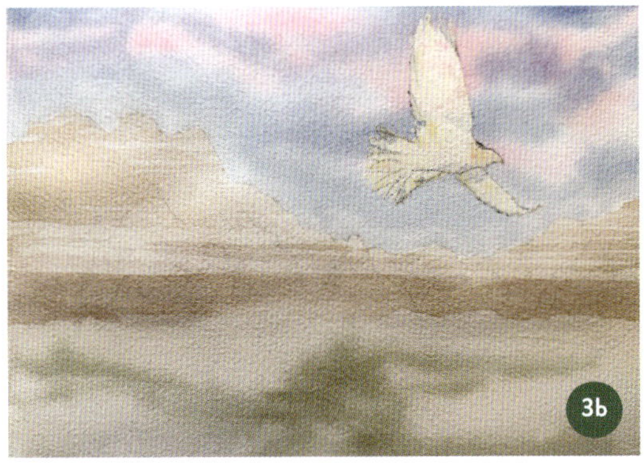

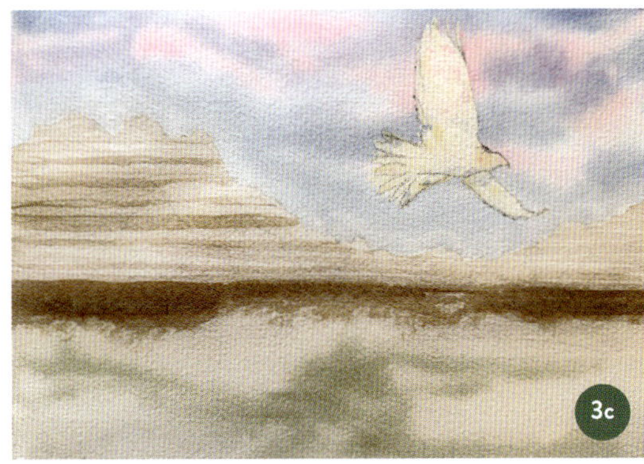

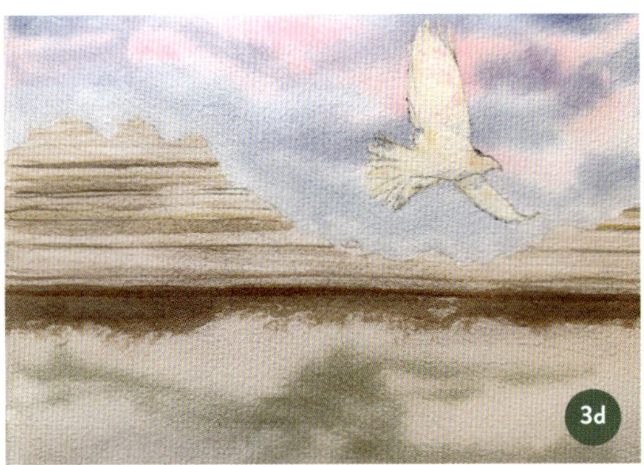

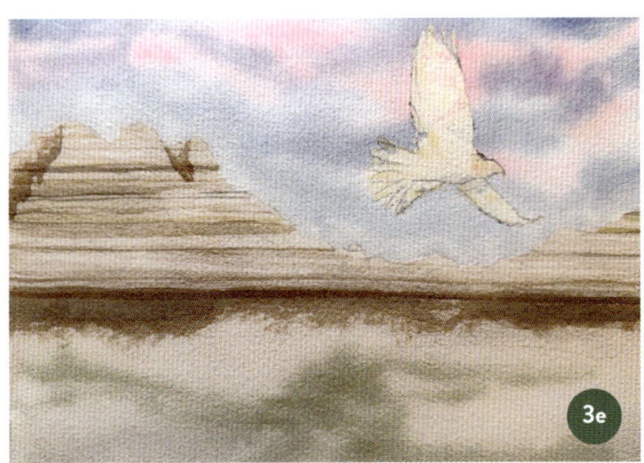

Let dry, then use a size 6 round brush to paint watery brown mixes in horizontal lines across the mountains, leaving behind stripes of the light layer beneath. Make the stripes toward the top thinner—with one chunky stripe along the bottom of the area—using a kind of jagged edge to help blend into the ground. Repeat with both slightly darker-value paint and light-value yellow-brown paint (more New Gamboge in the mix), and use a foliage brush to blend the bottom into the landscape. Let dry completely.

Next, use the watery brown mix with a size 2 round brush to begin carving out the rock formations with the negative space technique (page 15). Paint a jagged line down the side of the mountain, and lightly blend it out to one side, or paint a "v" shape between two peaks and blend it up in the middle. As you get to the bottom triangle-shape formations, use the negative space technique to paint around the outline of the rock formations, painting their shadows in order to give shape to the structures. Start with watery lines, then blend slightly upward or out in the dry layer. This will start to feel messy pretty quickly!

Continue carving out various shapes (even veering from your original sketch as you feel inclined), using the same method. It's okay if the shadows appear to go to nowhere—we're just trying to imply texture, not capture accuracy.

(continued)

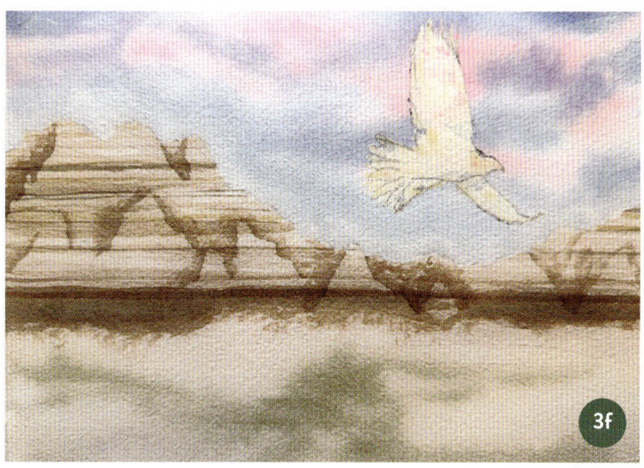

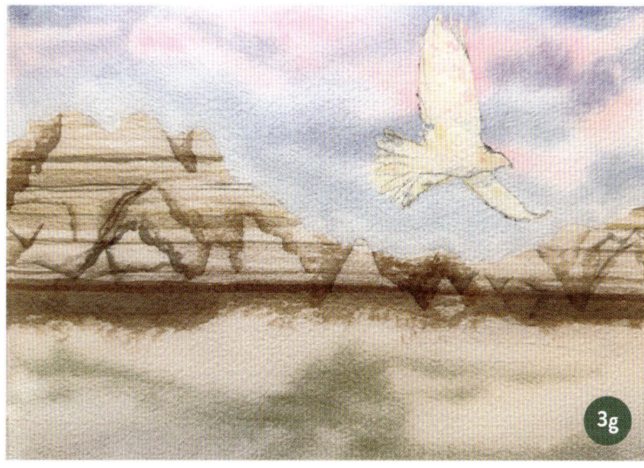

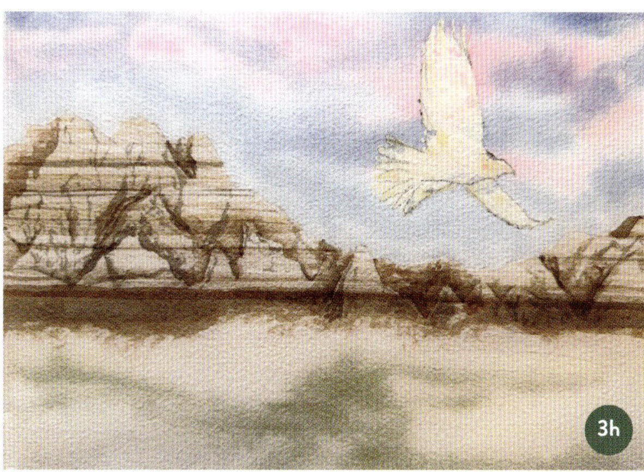

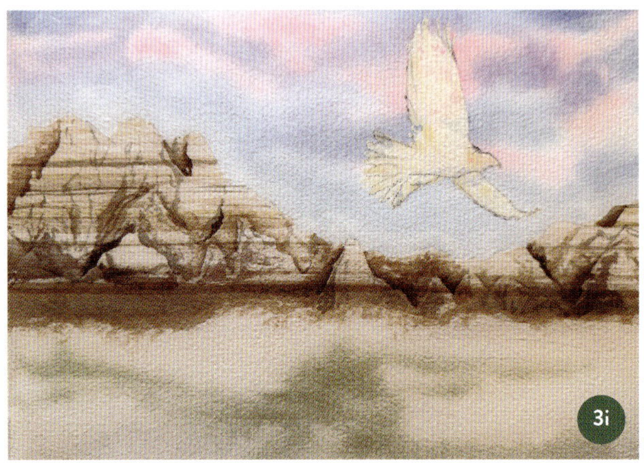

Use a size 2 round brush to add thin lines and shadows across the mountain ridge, adding more depth and texture to the various rocky areas. Finally, mix a darker-value brown, and darken some of the shadows behind or between select rock formations (you choose which ones!), highlighting the depth even more.

STEP 4: THE LANDSCAPE

Mix a watery, muted green (New Gamboge + French Ultramarine + a bit of Payne's Gray), then use a size 6 round brush to gently brush across the landscape, adding textured strokes. Mix a darker-value green (New Gamboge + French Ultramarine), and use a size 2 round brush to paint a few scattered upward marks to imply desert foliage. We don't need these to have much detail—the hawk will have more detail, and we don't want to have too many layers competing for the spotlight!

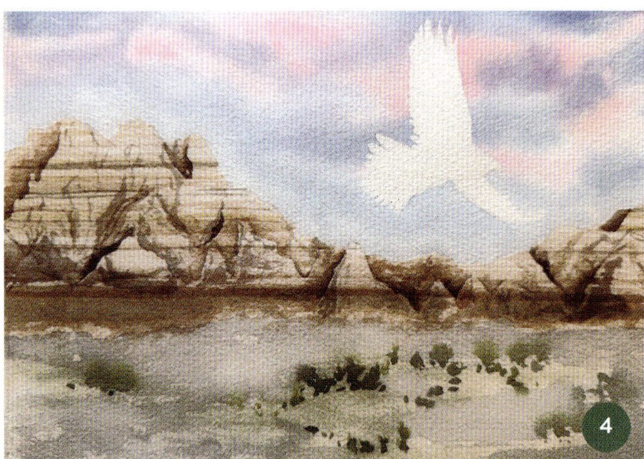

To prepare for the next step, remove the masking fluid from the hawk by gently rubbing it away with your finger or an eraser (page 15).

STEP 5: THE RED-TAILED HAWK + FINAL DETAILS

Mix a red-brown (Pyrrol Scarlet with just a bit of New Gamboge and French Ultramarine). Use a size 2 round brush to wet the entire hawk area with clean water, then gently tap the red-brown paint into the body, near the head and along the tail feathers and upper wing especially. Leave the beak white as well as a few white stripes on the feathers. Let dry, then start adding texture. You don't have to know what you're doing here! Paint a few loose C-curves (page 13) along the feathers and some dots along the outer edges of the wings. Paint the beak light gray (add a bit of Payne's Gray to brown, and mix a lot more water). With the red-brown mix, create a feather-like texture around the head with a few strokes. Add some yellow and brown marks. Animals are supposed to have variation—just make sure to leave behind some white space! Paint the lower wing a dark-value red-brown, as if it's cast in shadow.

Finally, add more Payne's Gray to the green mix from the previous step, and use a round size 2 brush to paint a few darker shadows along the bottom of the foliage on the landscape, creating more depth and contrast.

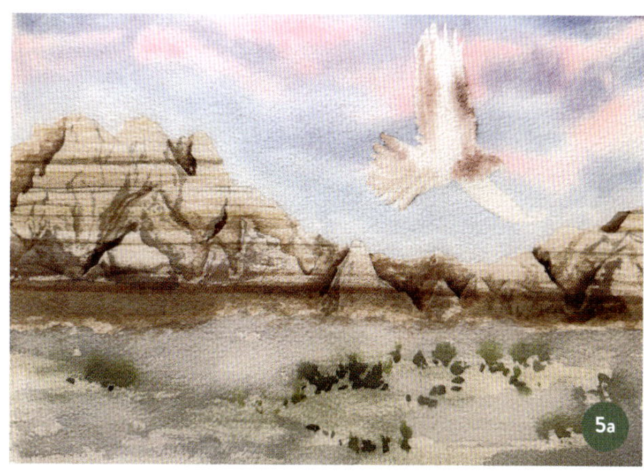

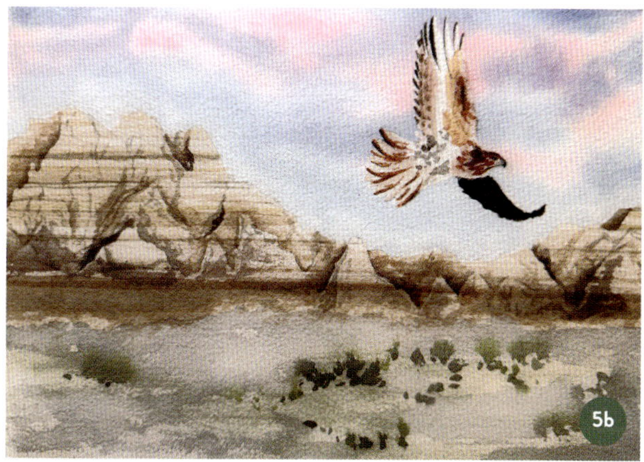

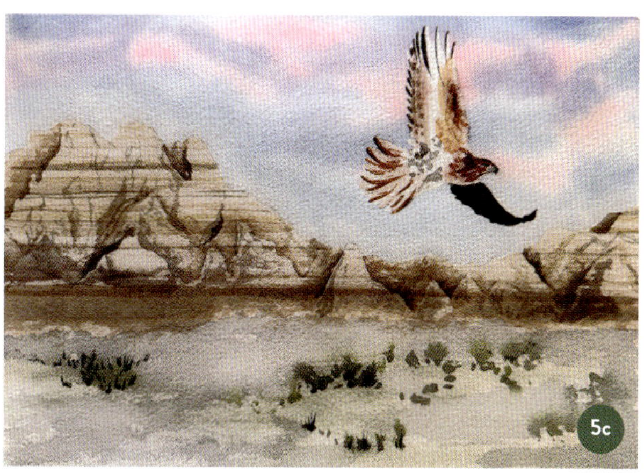

YELLOWSTONE

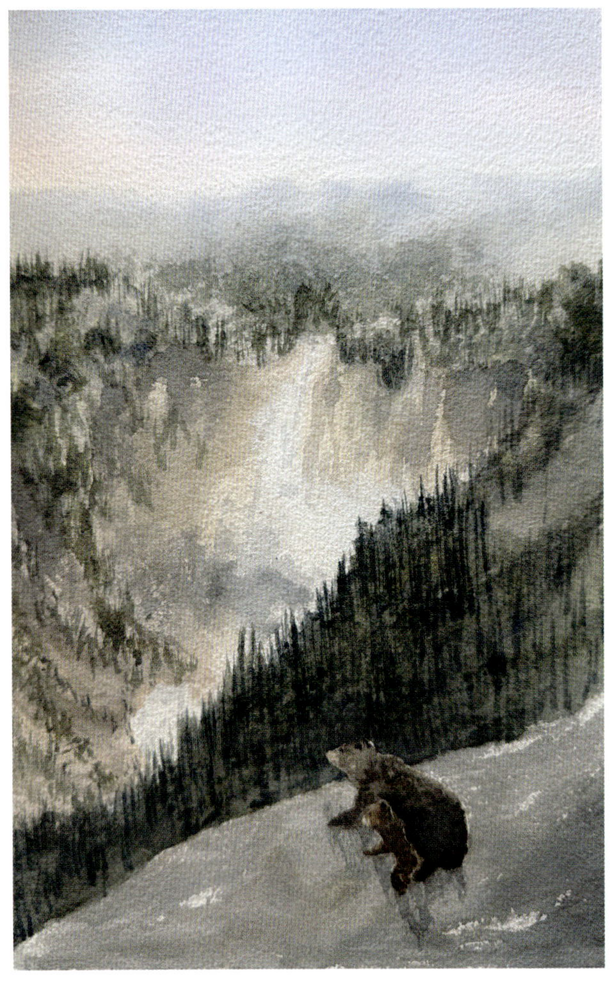

The Grand Canyon of the Yellowstone is a little piece of wonder tucked into an already awe-inspiring place. What would it look like for even Yellowstone's iconic bears to take a moment to reflect on how beautiful the scenery is? Let's paint it and find out—just remember that less is definitely more when it comes to small wildlife in big scenes! We don't need "perfect" bears— just brown smudges with ears will do!

BRUSHES

Round sizes 2, 6, and 12; Foliage brush; Masking fluid brush

COLOR PALETTE

Quinacridone Rose, French Ultramarine, Payne's Gray, New Gamboge, Pyrrol Scarlet

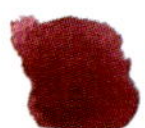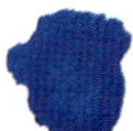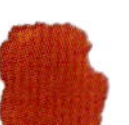

Note: This project uses masking fluid.

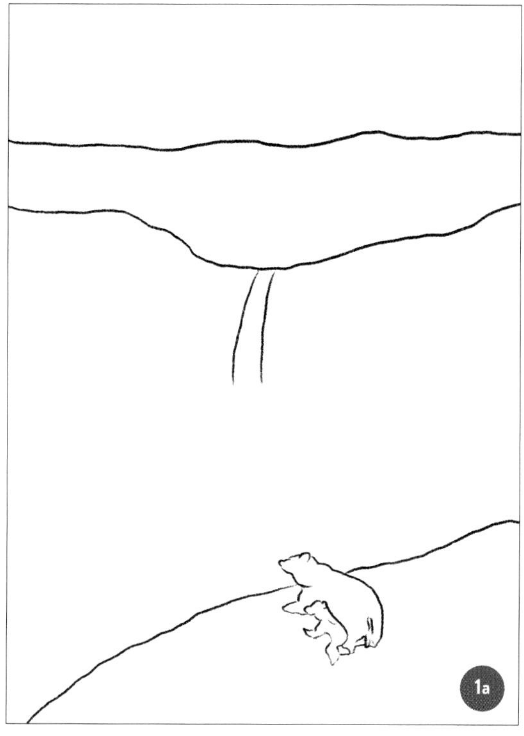

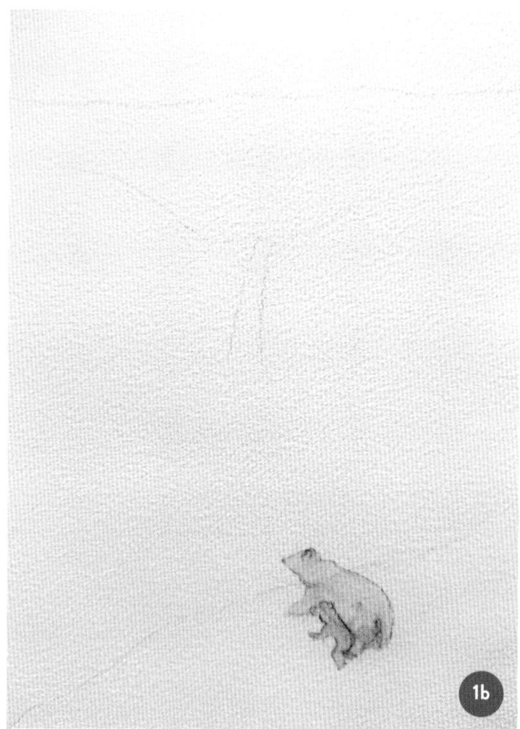

STEP 1: THE SKETCH

Separate the sketch into three distinct sections: the sky, the valley, and the foreground mountain ledge with the two bears. Start with a wobbly horizontal line a bit below the top of the page, then sketch a side C-curve (page 13) dipping down a bit under that (to distinguish the background mountains from the midground area). Sketch two gently sloping, vertical lines down from the center of the curve for a small, distant waterfall, landing at about the center of the page. Finally, sketch a sloping line from the right side of the page down to the bottom left corner for the foreground mountain ledge, and add outlines for two bears (a mama and baby). Remember: You don't have to be an expert in animal anatomy! "Looks *kind of* like a bear" is plenty good enough here. Sketch a small head with a slightly elongated nose and round ears, tapering out into a wider, rounded backside, and legs that bend slightly. The baby bear can be nestled into the side of the mama bear, and its proportions will be a little more symmetrical (the backside is about the same as the front).

Finally, use a masking fluid brush prepped with soap and masking fluid (page 15) to paint the bears, ensuring they remain white. Let dry for 30 minutes or until tacky.

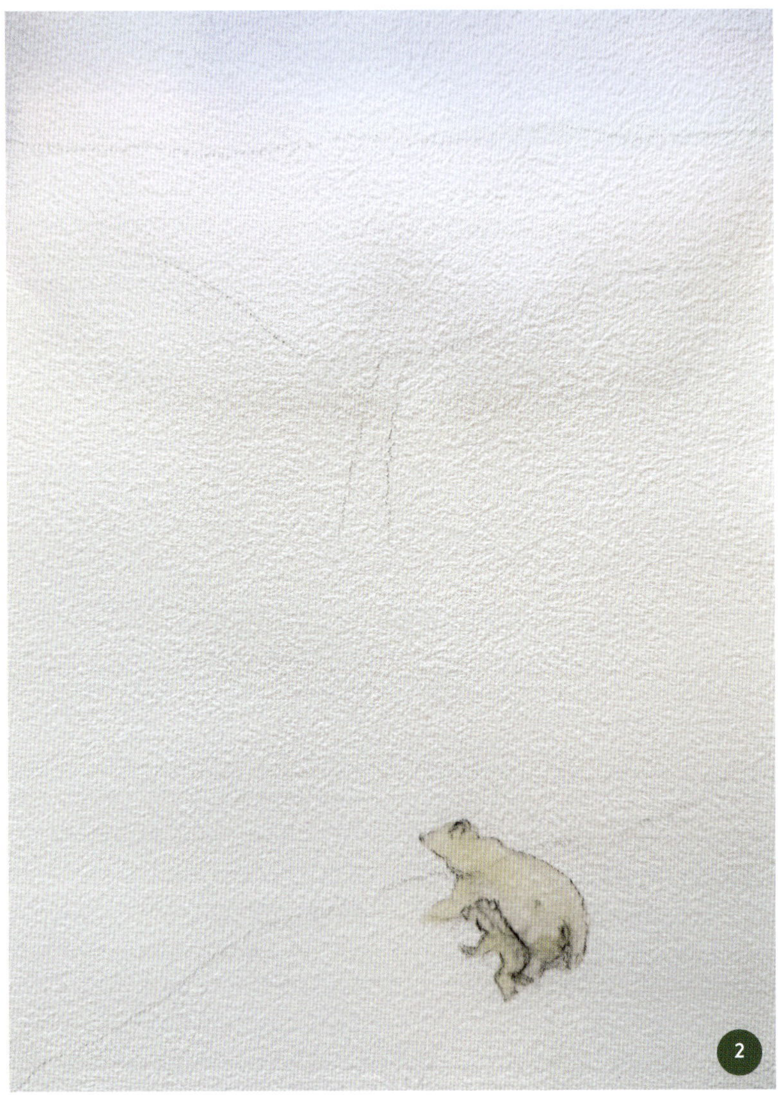

STEP 2: THE SKY

Layer a wash of clean water across the sky and feathered (page 12) into the background mountain layer. Mix light-value (watery) Quinacridone Rose and French Ultramarine, then use a size 12 round brush to tap into the wet wash in loose, horizontal strokes, creating a pale blue-violet sky with subtle flickers of rose.

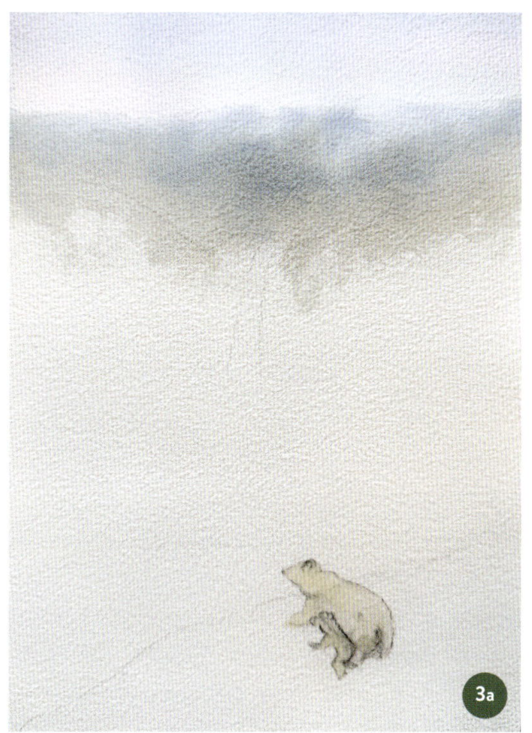

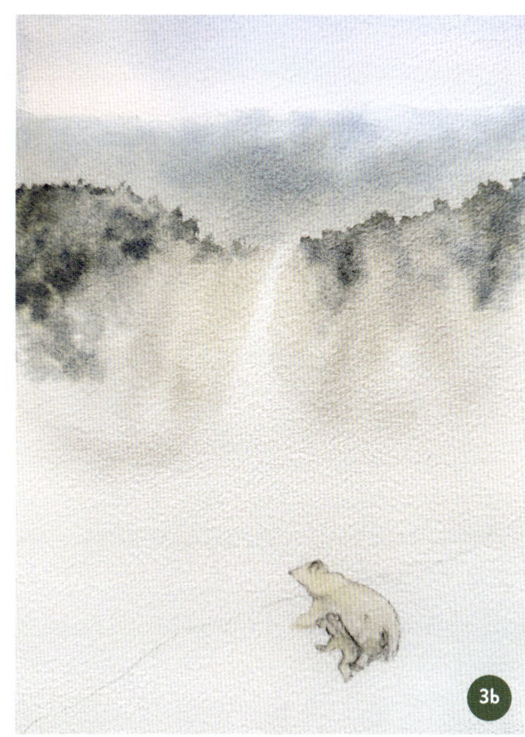

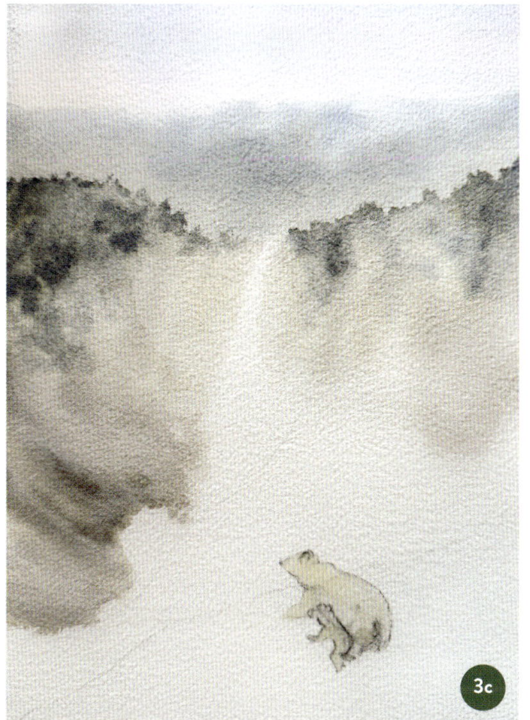

STEP 3: THE BACKGROUND MOUNTAIN

Let the sky dry completely, then add a bit of Payne's Gray to a watery blue-violet mix (French Ultramarine + Quinacridone Rose), then a watery warm green (French Ultramarine + a bit of New Gamboge). Layer a wash of clean water across the background mountain—be careful not to venture into the midground mountain quite yet. Use a foliage brush to tap the watery blue-violet into the top of the mountain. Rinse, then tap the warm green into the bottom of the mountain, using the foliage texture as the edge (to help blend into the next layer eventually). Make sure to leave the waterfall clear of any paint if possible. Let dry completely.

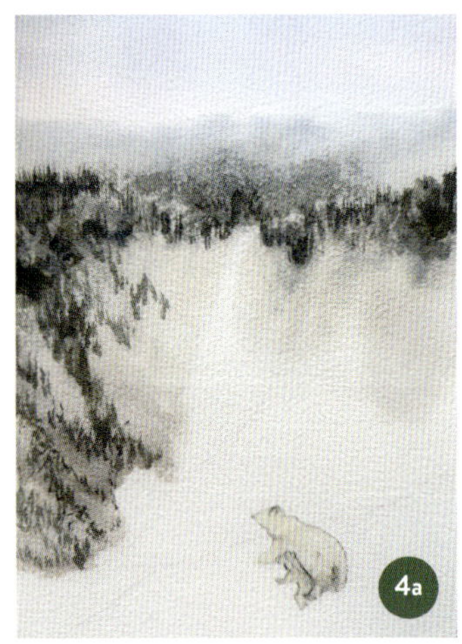 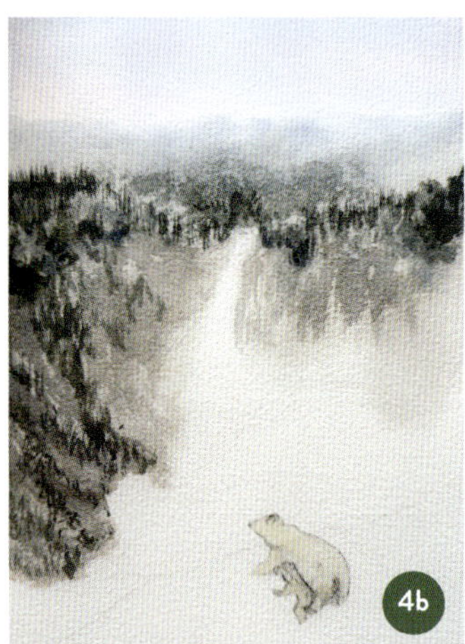 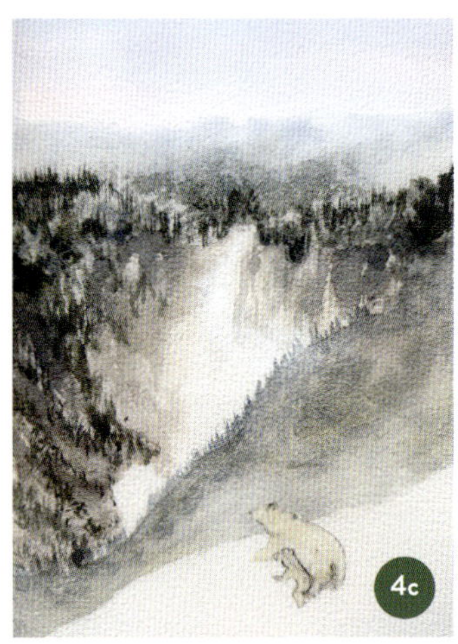

STEP 4: THE MIDGROUND MOUNTAIN AND VALLEY

Mix a watery warm brown (Pyrrol Scarlet + New Gamboge + a hint of French Ultramarine). Layer a wash of clean water over the midground mountain, making sure to leave the waterfall dry. Use a size 6 round brush to tap the warm brown into the wet wash, letting it blend naturally in a luminous layer. Mix a slightly darker-value green (a bit of Payne's Gray into the warm green mix from the previous step and more New Gamboge if it becomes too gray), then use a foliage brush to tap into the still-wet wash along the top ridge and along the far sides, creating a kind of sideways gradient (green on the edges into brown toward the center). Extend the warm brown down to the left side of the valley, leaving rough white edges for splashes of white water. Mix a slightly darker warm brown (a little more paint than water), then use a size 2 round brush to paint from the rough edge upward in swooping C-curve (page 13) motions, emphasizing a downhill movement to imply depth to the valley.

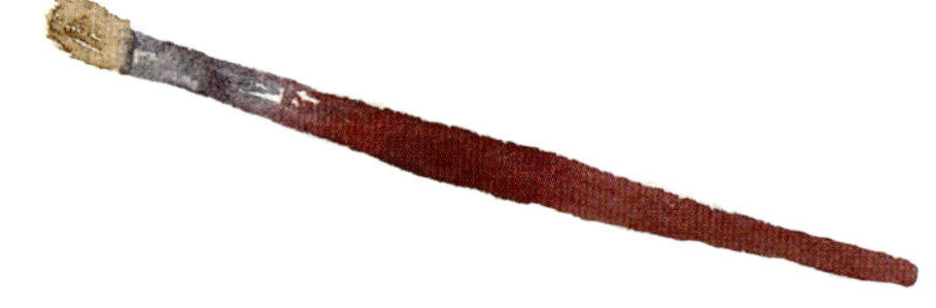

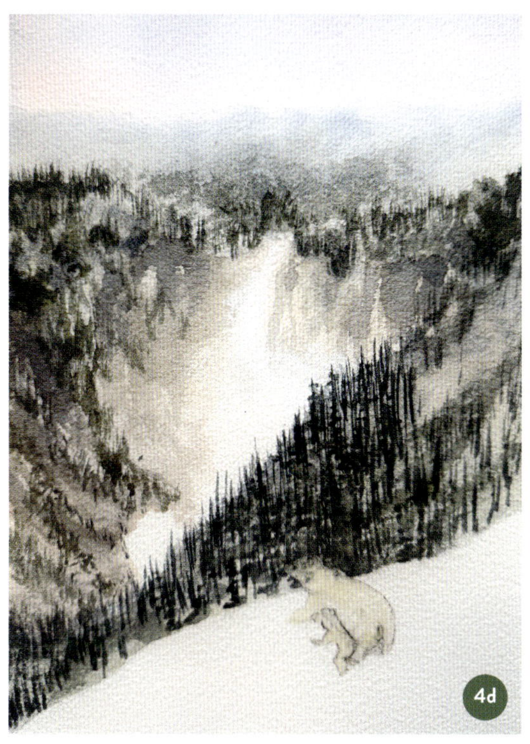

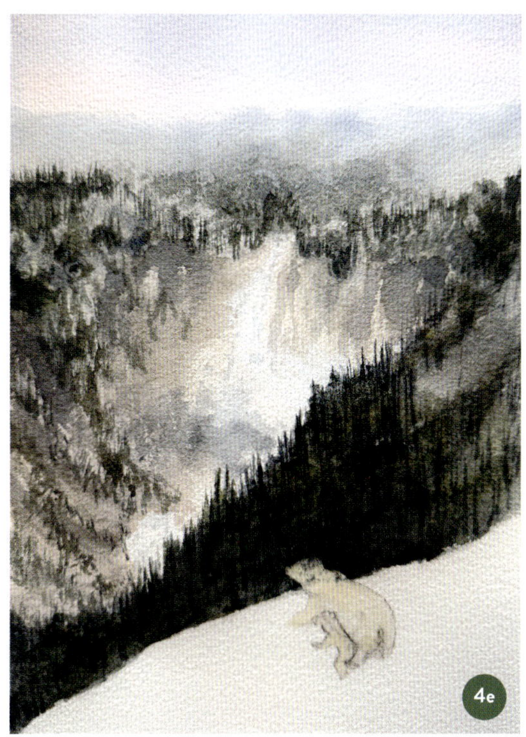

Let dry, then use the warm green mix with a foliage brush and a size 2 round brush to create clusters of small evergreen trees—small, vertical flicks to create tiny tree-like marks. We want the trees to look like they're cascading down the valley in clusters, so use the sloping curves from the previous layer to paint loose lines of trees (growing smaller as you go deeper into the valley). Let dry, then use a size 2 round brush to paint watery brown in rough, dry brush (page 12) textures across the mountain and valley areas, leaving behind random strokes of the lighter layer beneath. Let dry.

Next, use a size 12 round brush with somewhat watery green to paint a layer of trees between the foreground and the valley. Start in the top right edge of the midground mountain and slope downward, landing just above the left corner of the page. The contrast in value and color here will also help the white space from the previous layer turn into sprays of water and fog from the waterfall. While the green layer is still wet, use a foliage brush to paint small, vertical tree marks along the ridge. Mix a darker-value green, and use a foliage brush and/or a size 2 round brush to paint a mix of foliage texture and small vertical strokes for tree trunks across the layer, leaving behind one or two spots clear along the right edge for a little breathing room. Let dry, then paint a layer of watery green (add more New Gamboge and French Ultramarine to the mix) on top of the trees, helping blend everything together to look like a full forest with hints of texture. Let dry completely.

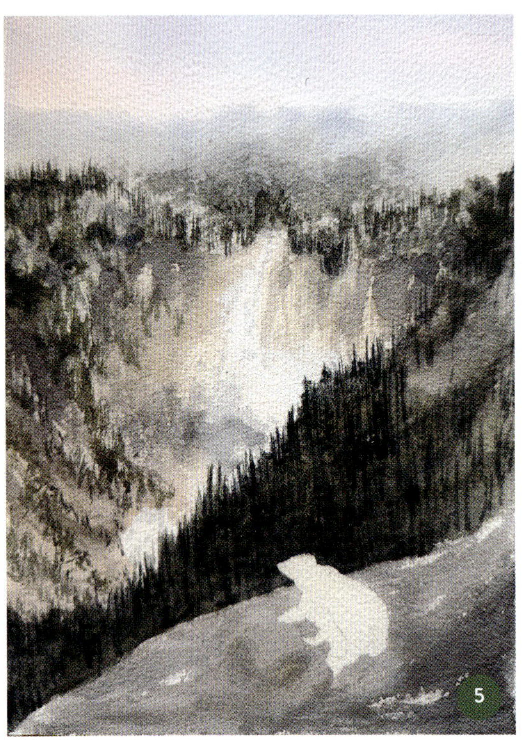

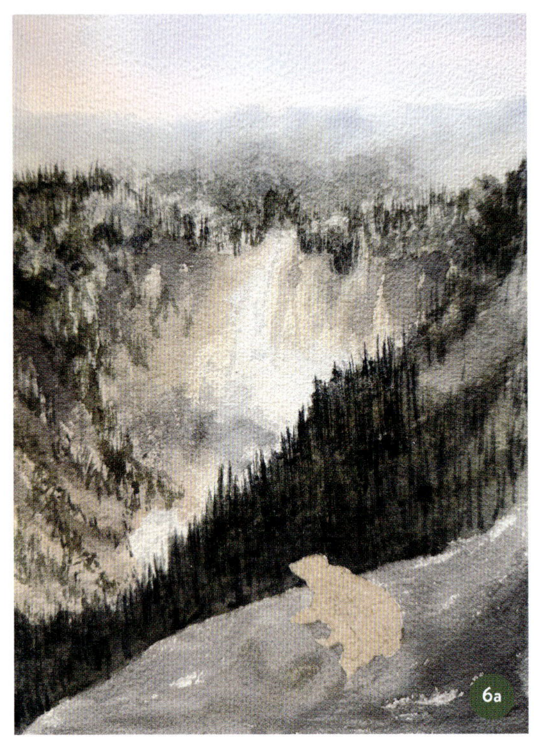

STEP 5: THE FOREGROUND MOUNTAIN

Mix a neutral gray (Payne's Gray + a bit of Pyrrol Scarlet + New Gamboge, and lots of water), then use a size 12 round brush to paint a textured wash using the dry brush technique (page 12) across the dry foreground mountain area. We don't want too much watery paint on the brush, otherwise it'll be difficult to leave behind the small slivers of textured white space. Tap watery brown into the wash in a few places for color variation.

Let the previous layer dry completely, then remove the masking fluid by gently rubbing it away with your finger or an eraser (page 15).

STEP 6: THE BEARS

Before we paint the bears, remember that we're not shooting for accuracy here! "Looks kind of like a bear" is good enough. One trick is to mix two slightly different browns for each bear, so they're easier to tell apart.

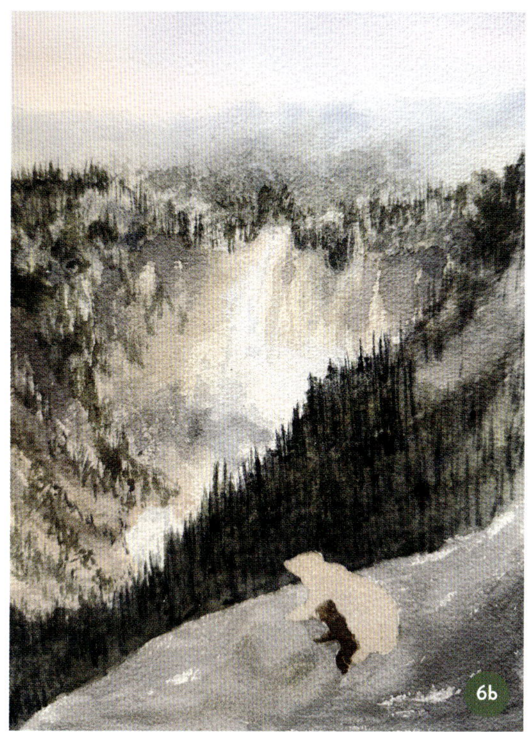 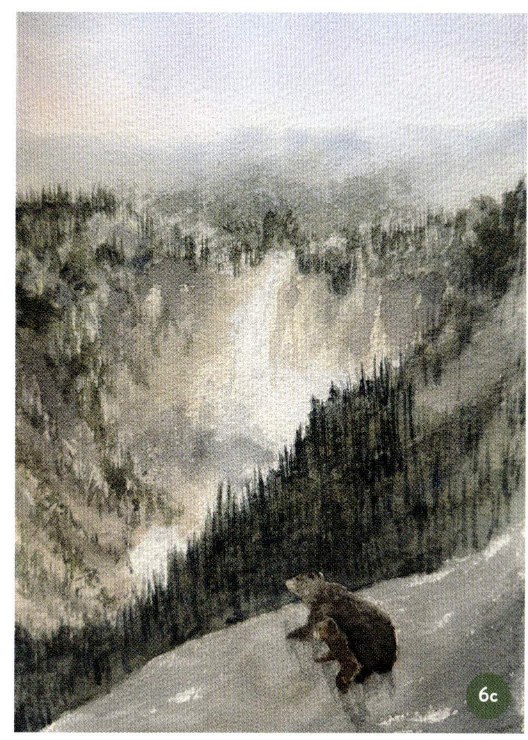

Start with a wash of light-value brown (French Ultramarine + Pyrrol Scarlet + New Gamboge) across both bears with a size 2 round brush. Let dry, then paint the small bear with a darker-value brown—leave the nose unpainted, so it looks lighter. Then use a slightly different brown (add a bit more Pyrrol Scarlet to the brown mix) and paint the mama bear, carefully leaving an edge of lighter space around the small bear's body, and another dry edge between the top of the mama bear and the mountain layer. Leave the nose clear, again, so it's lighter than the rest of the body. Mix a slightly darker-value brown, and lightly tap into the backside of the mama bear and around the edges of the baby bear so there's some shadowy contrast. Let dry, then use Payne's Gray to add tiny dots for eyes and a slightly larger dot for the inside of the ears. Finally, mix a watery Payne's Gray and flick just beneath the bears (on the ground) for a subtle cast shadow.

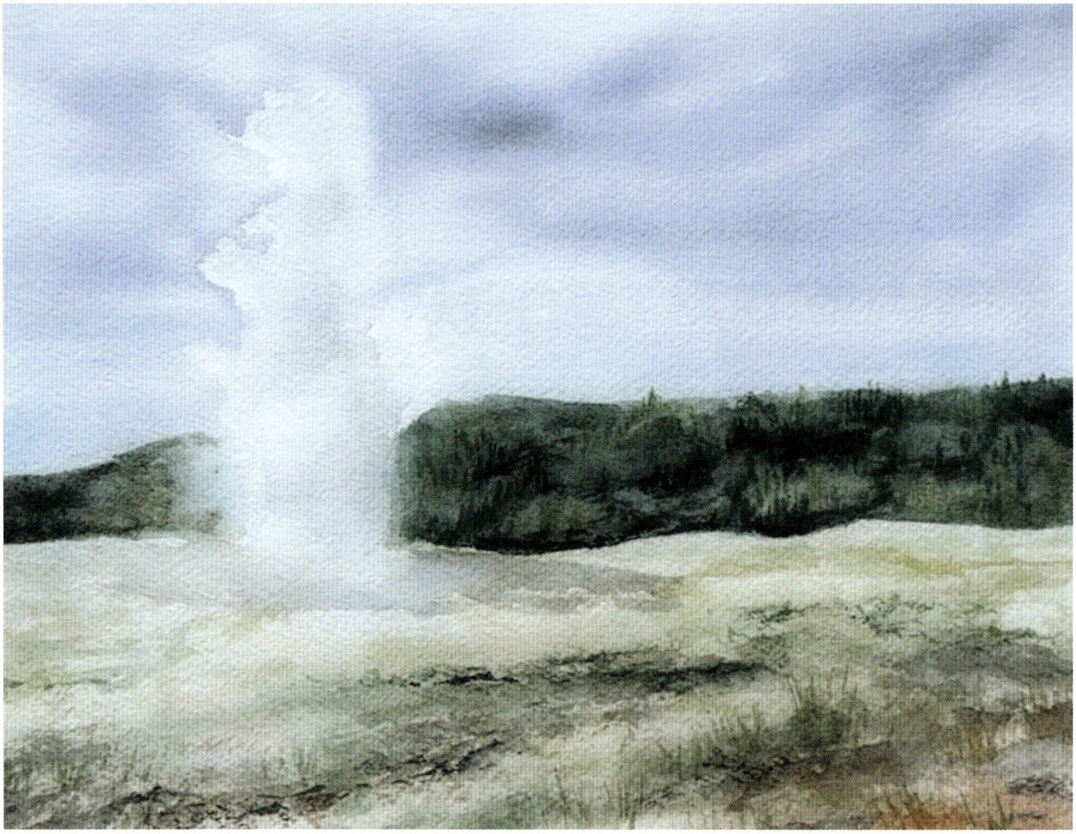

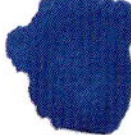

OLD FAITHFUL

BRUSHES
Round sizes 2, 6, and 12; Foliage brush

COLOR PALETTE
French Ultramarine, Phthalo Blue (Green Shade), Payne's Gray, Hansa Yellow Light, Pyrrol Scarlet, New Gamboge

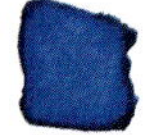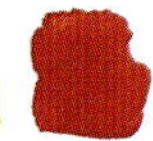

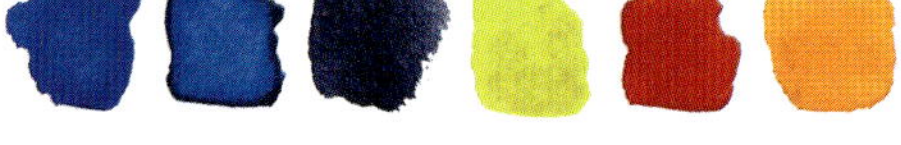

Sometimes, the most breathtaking forces of nature are also the most comforting. Old Faithful is a geyser in Yellowstone National Park named not only for shooting streams of hot water from the earth but for doing it consistently for as long as humans can remember. Let's use serene colors and subtle contrasts to depict Old Faithful on a stormy day.

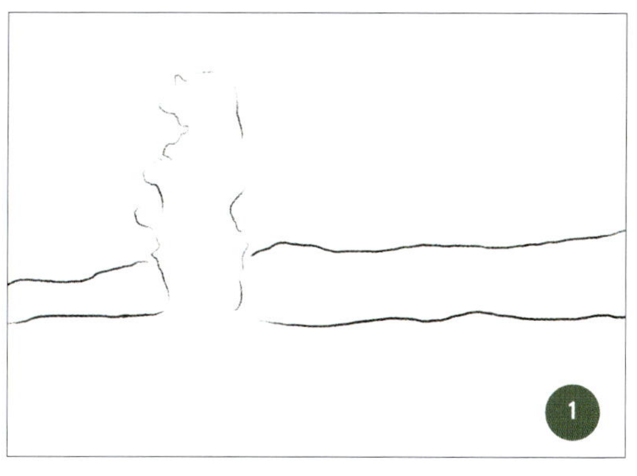

STEP 1: THE SKETCH

Start with a loose sketch separating the sky, the trees, the landscape, and the geyser cutting into the layers. Draw a kind of wavy horizontal line across the bottom third of the page (for the landscape), then draw another choppy line just above that, slightly sloping upward, for the distant trees. Just below the tree line, lightly sketch the general outline for the geyser, cutting into the other layers. Erase the pencil marks that land inside the geyser.

STEP 2: THE UNDERPAINTING

With a size 12 round brush, wet the entire paper with clean water. Then, using the wet-on-wet technique (page 10), paint loose, watery strokes of sky blue (French Ultramarine + Phthalo Blue) along the bottom of the sky and Payne's Gray across the top third of the paper. Paint in wide slopes to create a luminous texture (page 10), allowing some white of the paper to shine through. While the paper is still wet, switch to a round size 6 brush, and use slightly less watery Payne's Gray (still wet, but more pigmented) to paint loose shadows, forming the bottoms of stormy clouds. Remember: Even if you're not sure what you're painting, the idea is to build contrast, starting light and growing a bit darker. Use thicker paint to ensure the shadows don't disappear into the wet wash.

(continued)

Continue with an underpainting for the rest of the scene. Rewet the page below the sky with clean water if necessary, then paint a small, loose section of a cool green (French Ultramarine + Hansa Yellow Light) across the center third of the scene. We're still using the wet-on-wet technique, so it will be messy! It's okay if some green bleeds into the sky a bit. Use a watery brown mix (Pyrrol Scarlet + New Gamboge + French Ultramarine) and Hansa Yellow Light to paint a luminous foreground texture—streaks of blurry paint with some white peeking through. Use a thirsty brush (page 11) to corral the wet paint if necessary by taking the clean, damp brush and lifting away any stray edges.

Make sure the entire page is still wet (re-wet and reapply paint if necessary), then use a clean towel to lift the pigment (page 16) just off the left side of the scene to form the geyser. With the towel in hand, firmly press into the wet wash several times to create a vertical shape with cloudy texture along the left side. Use a thirsty brush to clean up the edges if necessary. Finally, if the foreground area is still wet, add a few strokes of a more pigmented green and brown to add some loose contrast to the underlayer. Let the layer dry entirely.

You can also use a round size 2 brush to tap watery Payne's Gray along the outside edges of the geyser to further enhance the white of the steam against the sky.

STEP 3: THE LANDSCAPE

Next, use the dry brush technique (page 12) with a size 6 round brush to loosely scrape light-value (watery) paint across the dry layer to form a foliage-like texture to the foreground. Consider the bottom right corner of the page the closest portion of the scene, and adjust accordingly, gradually growing smaller and lighter the closer to the background and geyser. Use light-value (watery) strokes of green, brown, and Hansa Yellow Light to make the front strokes darker and larger, and the strokes in the back smaller and lighter. Mix Payne's Gray with the green mix, and use a bit of that to create a handful of shadows along the land. Then, use a size 2 round brush to paint small, vertical flicks of paint, especially along the bottom of the page, to mimic grass. No need to paint grass everywhere—just a few clusters will work.

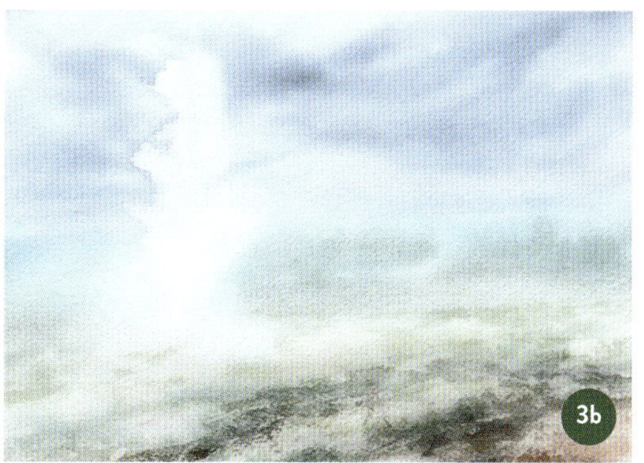

3b

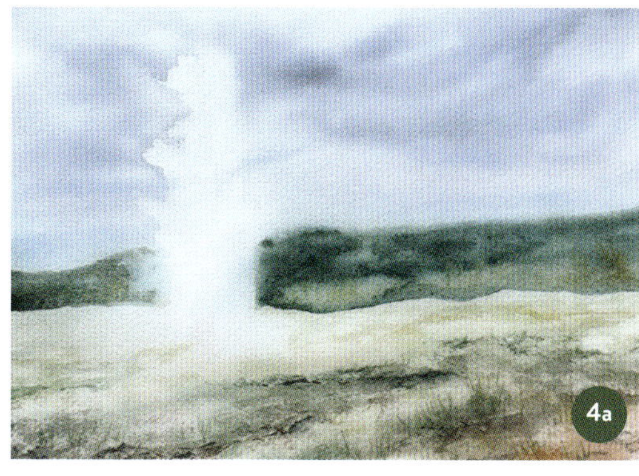

4a

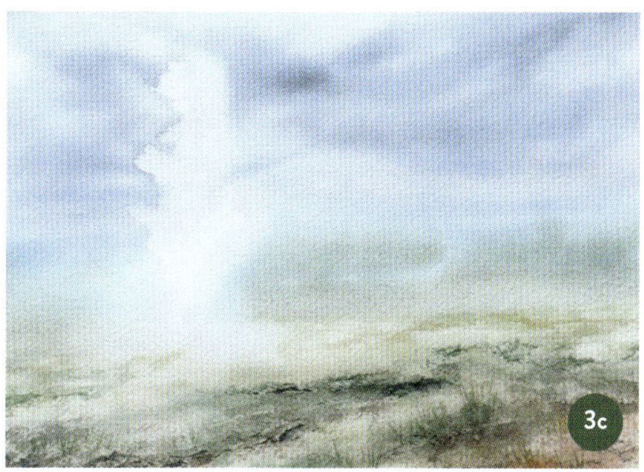

3c

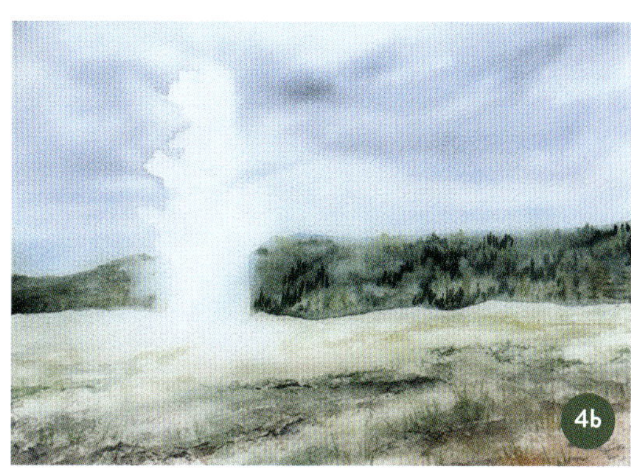

4b

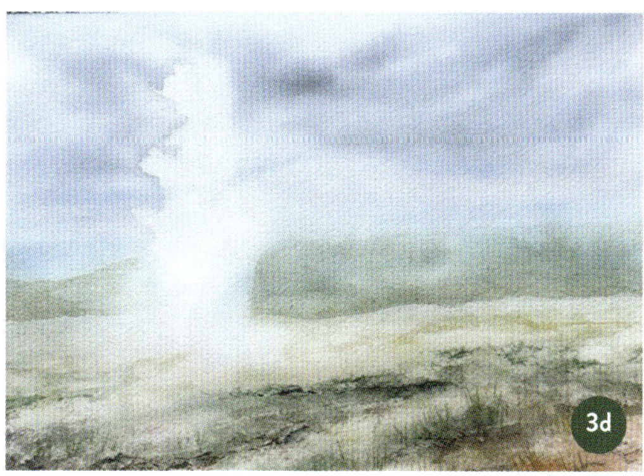

3d

STEP 4: THE BACKGROUND

To help highlight the geyser, we want this dark background layer to act as more of a contrast subject, not a detailed one. Rather than painting dozens of individual trees, we'll focus on values with some contrasting marks to imply the grand forest behind. Start with a light-value (watery) layer of the brown mix + New Gamboge, contained along the forest area outlined by the underlayer. Make sure to paint around the geyser, leaving that vertical area clear of paint. Use a towel to lift any stray paint as necessary.

(continued)

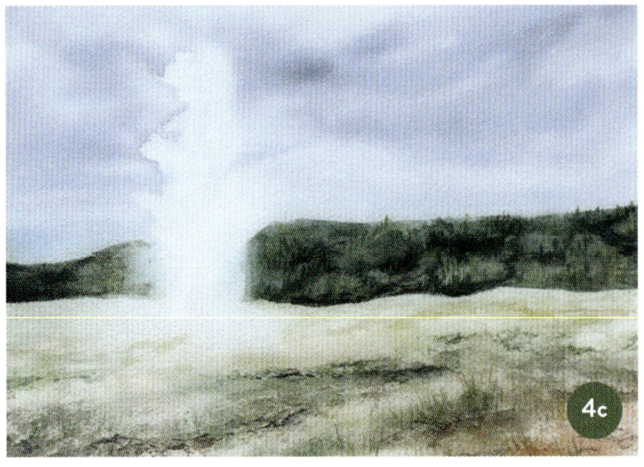

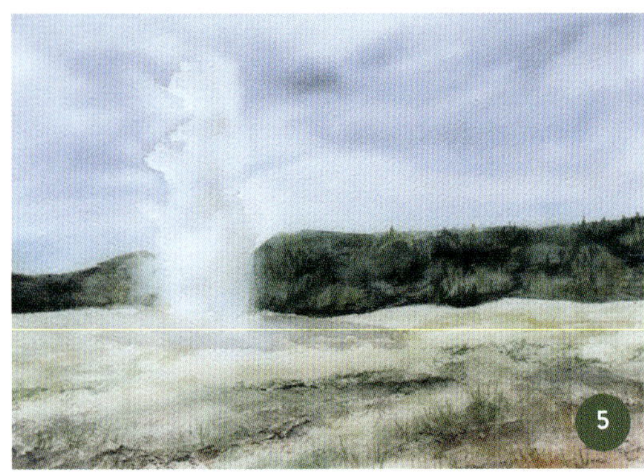

While the forest strip is still wet, drop in strokes of French Ultramarine and Hansa Yellow Light, especially along the longer right side. We want to create pockets of yellow-green and lighter washes surrounded by darker greens. Remember: The thicker your paint is, the more you'll be able to control it in a wet wash (page 22)—and we're not aiming for perfection here, just a loose contrast between light and dark.

The layer may start to dry in parts at this point. While it's partly dry, partly wet, use a round 2 brush to begin painting small vertical strokes in a green mix for distant trees, loosely spread throughout the layer. Let dry completely, then rewet the entire forest with clean water to subtly disturb the paint in the dried layer and create a hazier effect. Let dry.

STEP 5: THE GEYSER

Finally, add some warm shadows to the geyser. (This is optional—if you'd rather leave it alone, that's totally fine too!) Mix a bit of brown into Payne's Gray to make a warm gray, then add lots of water to the mixture.

Using a round size 6 brush or a round size 2 brush, carefully rewet the geyser, leaving the edges of the cloudy left side dry. Then, add just a few strokes of the warm gray mixture along the right side and the middle of the geyser. Use a thirsty brush to lift any stray paint and to lift away a few highlights. This will be messy! It's less of a precise technique and more of a dance—the warm gray is to contrast against the cool gray of the sky, but the shadows themselves are only to give more dimension to the water. Less is more.

Let dry, then use a watery Payne's Gray to paint a thin, horizontal shadow just under the bottom and right side of Old Faithful. Add just a few dry brushstrokes of Payne's Gray along the bottom of the scene to add any final bits of contrast to the foreground as necessary. Again—less is more!

SEQUOIA

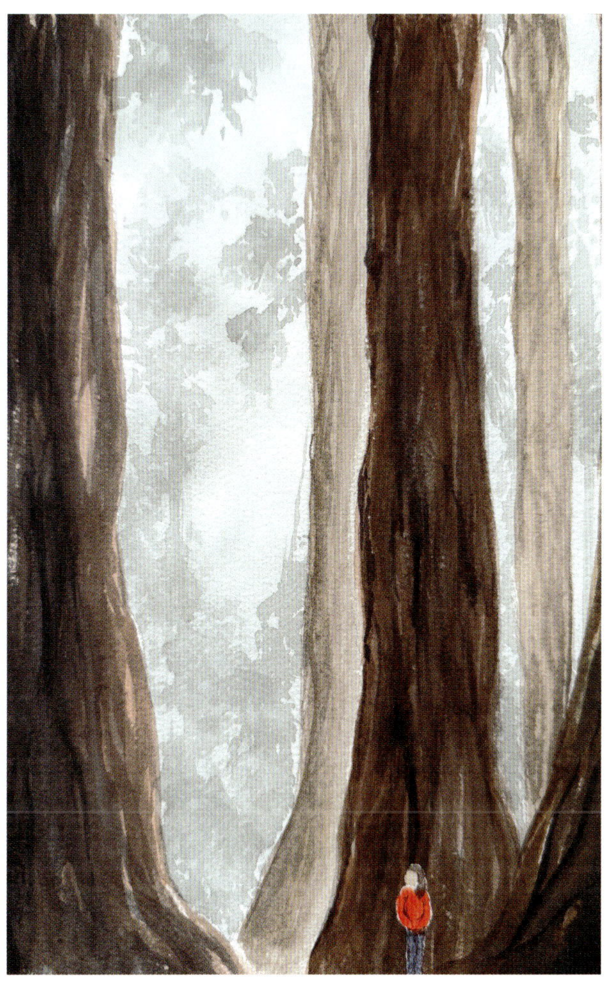

A specific type of redwood, Sequoia trees are so large you cannot possibly comprehend them without a tiny human figure for scale. Sequoia National Park contains forests full of these silent giants—and even if all your wandering is happening at your desk, I'm certain with creative color play and intentional scaling, we can recreate the majesty of these towering trees.

BRUSHES
Round sizes 2, 6, and 12; Foliage brush; Masking fluid brush

COLOR PALETTE
Payne's Gray, New Gamboge, Pyrrol Scarlet, French Ultramarine

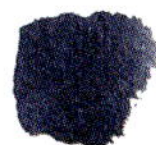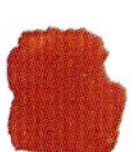

Note: This project uses masking fluid.

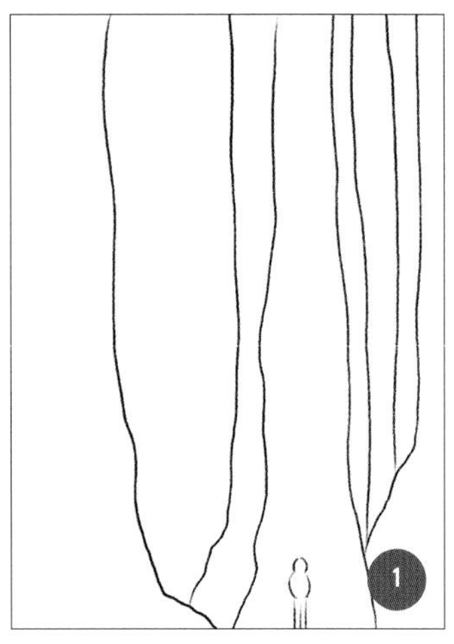 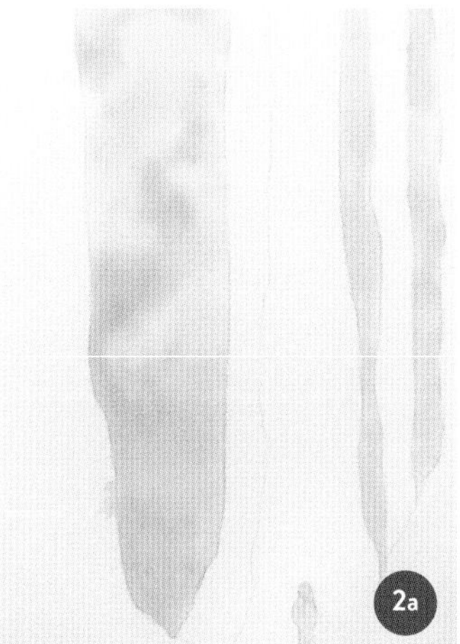 

STEP 1: THE SKETCH

Sketch long, vertical, and slightly wobbly lines for the big Sequoia trees, widening slightly as they reach the ground. Use either edge of the paper to denote trees only halfway in the scene, but make sure there's at least one fully visible tree in the foreground (slightly off-center and to the right in mine). Sketch a line or two for trees a layer behind as well. Then, sketch a human figure in front of a foreground tree—this is mainly to provide a scale of reference, so make the figure pretty small. Remember, we're not trying to master the human form—general shapes are okay. So, sketch a small, rounded head with two C-curves (page 13) on either side for the arms and two lines for legs in line with the head. Use a masking fluid brush prepped with soap and masking fluid (page 15) to paint the figure in order to preserve the white space for after the trees are all painted. Let dry for 30 minutes or until tacky.

STEP 2: THE BACKGROUND TREES

Paint the background with light-value, blurry tree shadows. Start with a layer of clean water in the windows behind the trees you've sketched using a size 12 round brush, then use a foliage brush to drop in light-value (very watery) Payne's Gray and dark green (Payne's Gray + a hint of New Gamboge). Use a foliage brush in the wet wash for blurry dark green spots to imply shadowy tree shapes. Let dry, then use a foliage brush on the dry layer to paint (still quite light-value) dark green tree shapes. Paint a few shaky vertical strokes for the trunks, then clusters of foliage for the trees. Make sure to leave the large foreground and midground tree areas clear.

Repeat once more as needed for even more depth, making sure the lighter layers beneath are still somewhat visible. Let dry.

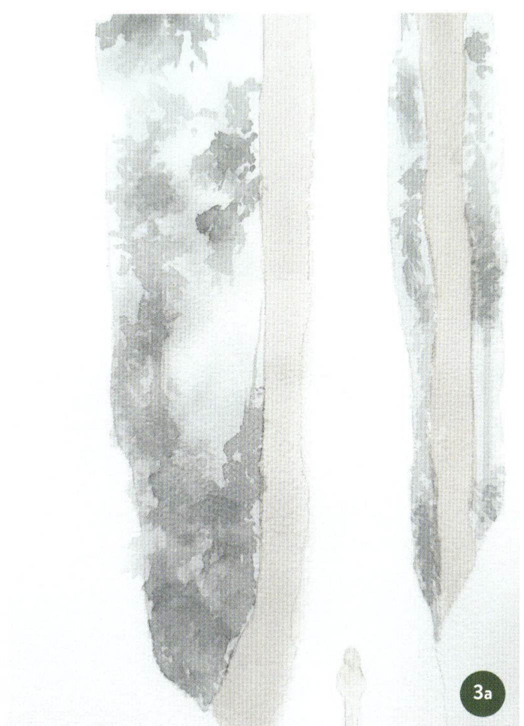

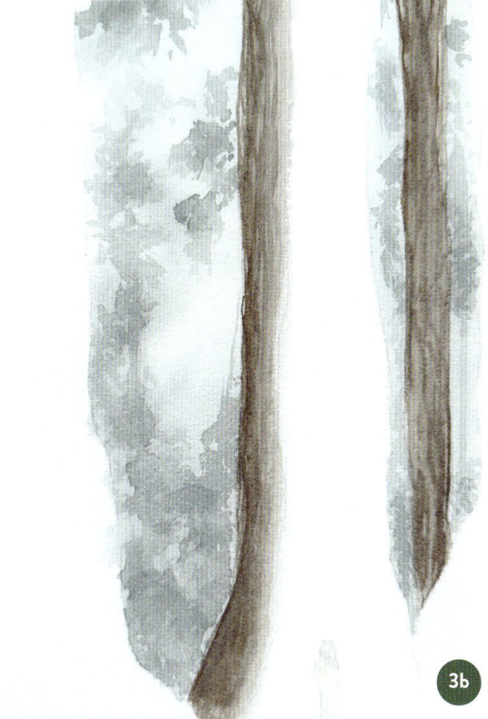

STEP 3: THE MIDGROUND TREES

Mix a watery, cool brown (New Gamboge + Pyrrol Scarlet + French Ultramarine, but with more blue), then paint the first layer of the midground Sequoias. Mix darker-value browns, then use a round size 2 or a foliage brush to paint long, vertical strokes up and down the trees. You can paint while the first layer is still wet so it looks a bit blurry. Add more brown to the far edge of the trunks, creating a subtle gradient. Not too much paint here! It's still the midground, so less is more to build contrast and depth. Let dry.

STEP 4: THE FOREGROUND TREES

Mix a watery, warm brown (more Pyrrol Scarlet than the others), and paint the first layer on the foreground Sequoias. Mix darker-value browns, then paint in long, vertical strokes with a round size 6 brush or a foliage brush, leaving behind strips of the layer beneath. It's okay if you get some dry brush (page 12) texture here! You can make the browns slightly different shades for added variation—it's just important that they're warmer than the midground trees. Add Payne's Gray to your mixes to make them an even darker value, and repeat, making the edges of the paper the darkest. Add more Payne's Gray to get a darker value still, then use a size 2 round brush to paint thinner shadows, creating more depth in the bark. You can vary the shapes here as well, maybe adding a few curves or whorls. Let dry.

(continued)

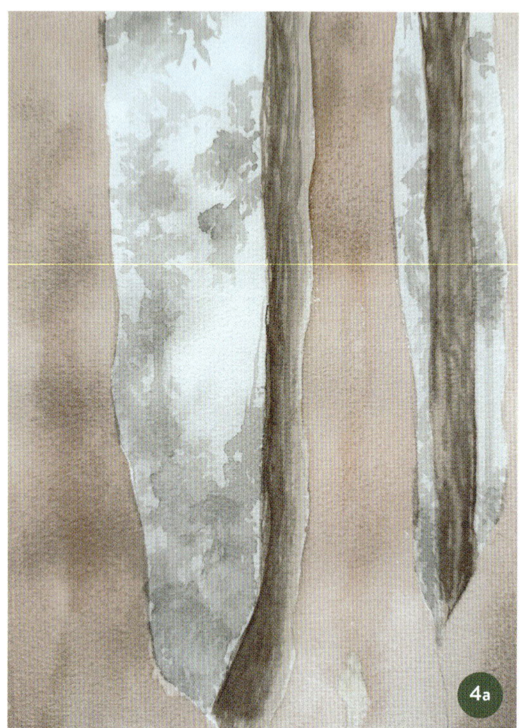
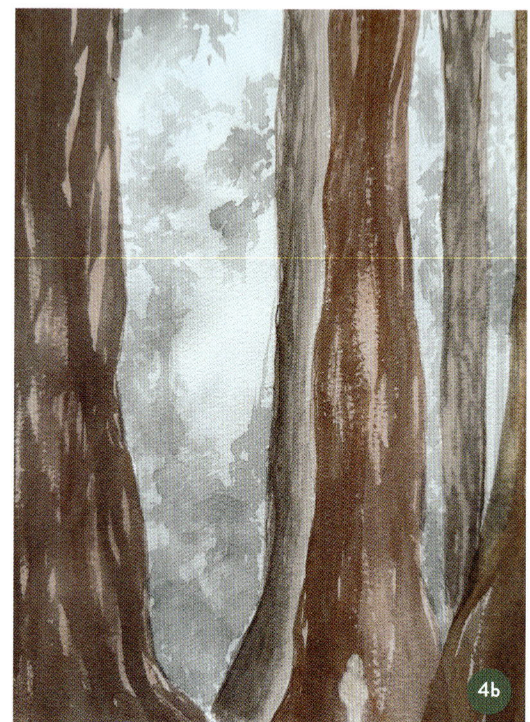
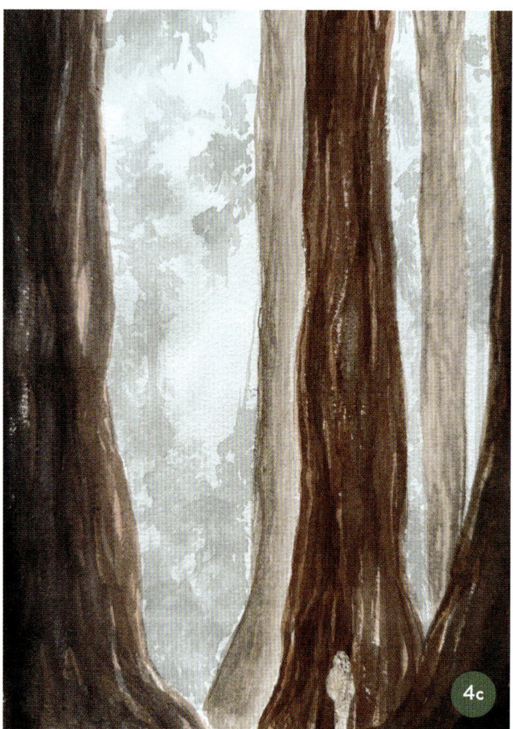
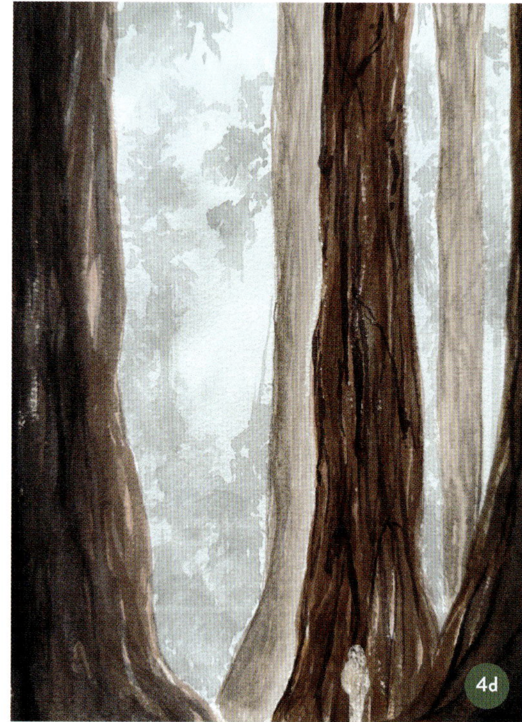

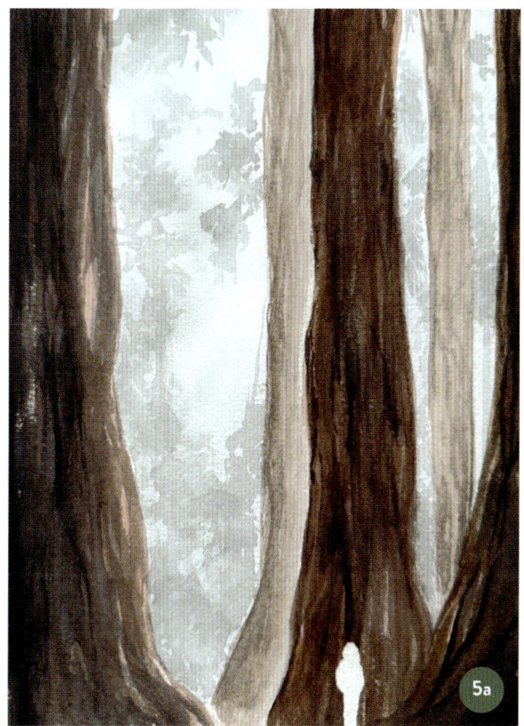

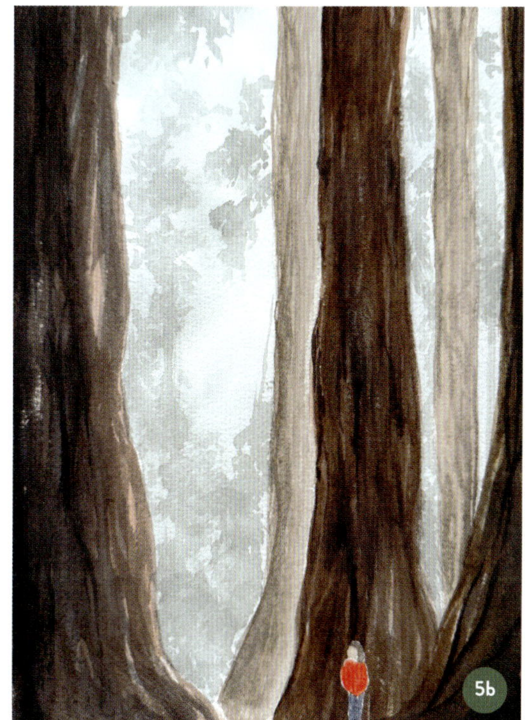

Then, if you like, use a size 12 round brush to paint some clean water over the top of the trees to slightly soften the layers, making them look more weathered. Let dry.

STEP 5: THE FIGURE

Remove the masking fluid by rubbing it away gently with your finger or an eraser (page 15). Then, use a size 2 round brush to paint the pants, shirt, and hair whichever colors feel right for you. Remember that we're not looking for accuracy—the figure is mainly here for scale purposes. Use slightly darker values (again, of whatever colors you chose) to add shadows along the sleeves and the pant legs for added dimension to the clothes.

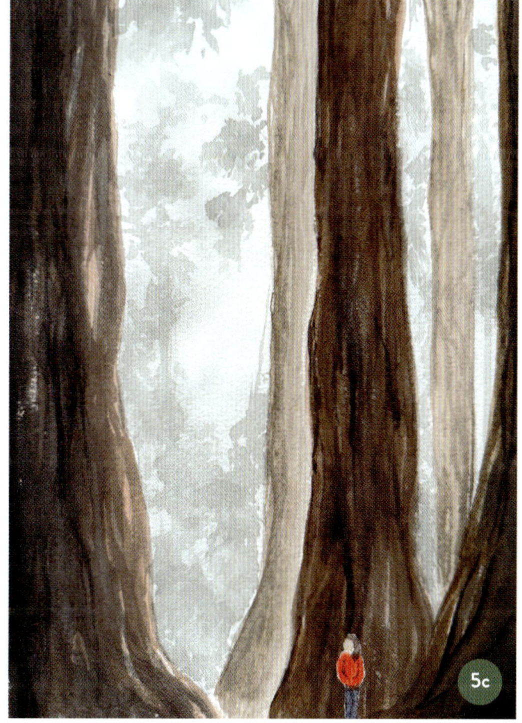

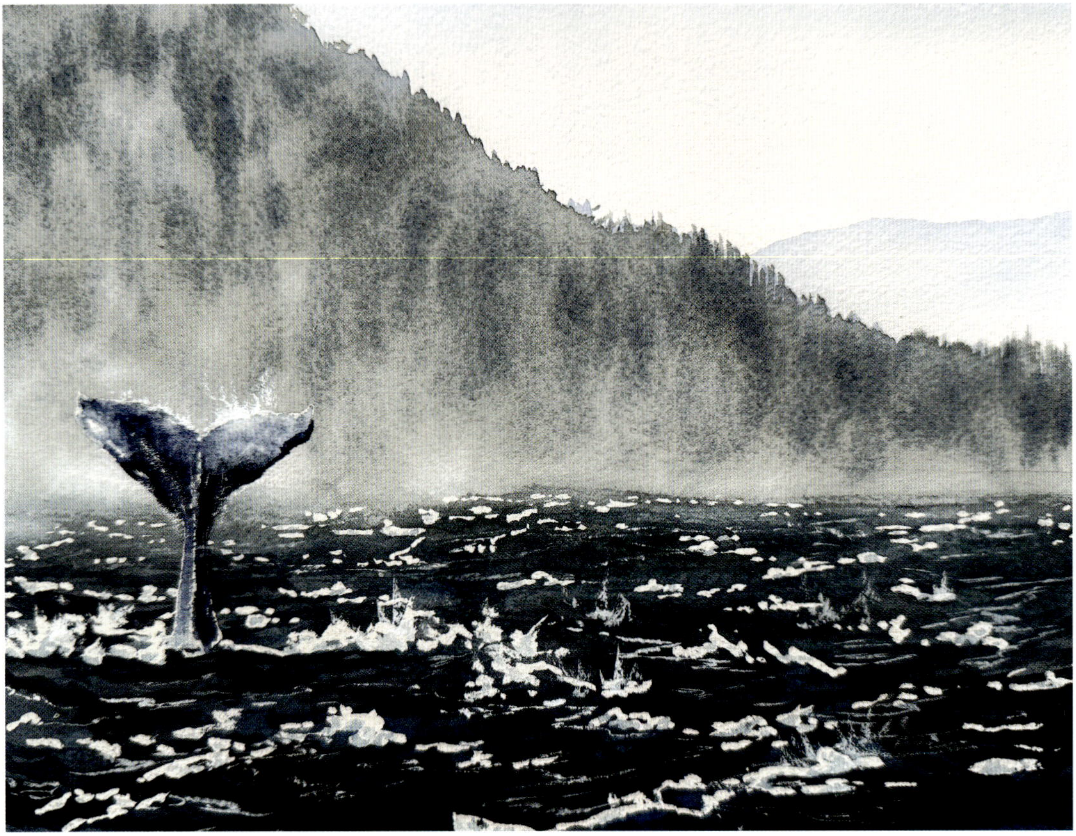

KATMAI

BRUSHES
Round sizes 2 and 12; Foliage brush; Masking
fluid brush

COLOR PALETTE
French Ultramarine, Quinacridone Rose,
New Gamboge, Payne's Gray, Phthalo Blue
(Green Shade), white gouache

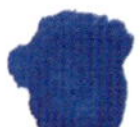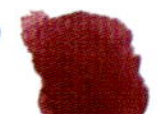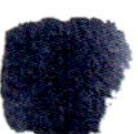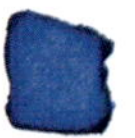

While Katmai National Park and Preserve is mainly known for its volcanoes, the area is also home to diverse wildlife—including pods of humpback whales waving hello to strangers on the rocky shore. Let's capture the pristine Alaskan wilderness and its friendly inhabitants with this choppy oceanic scene.

Note: This project uses masking fluid.

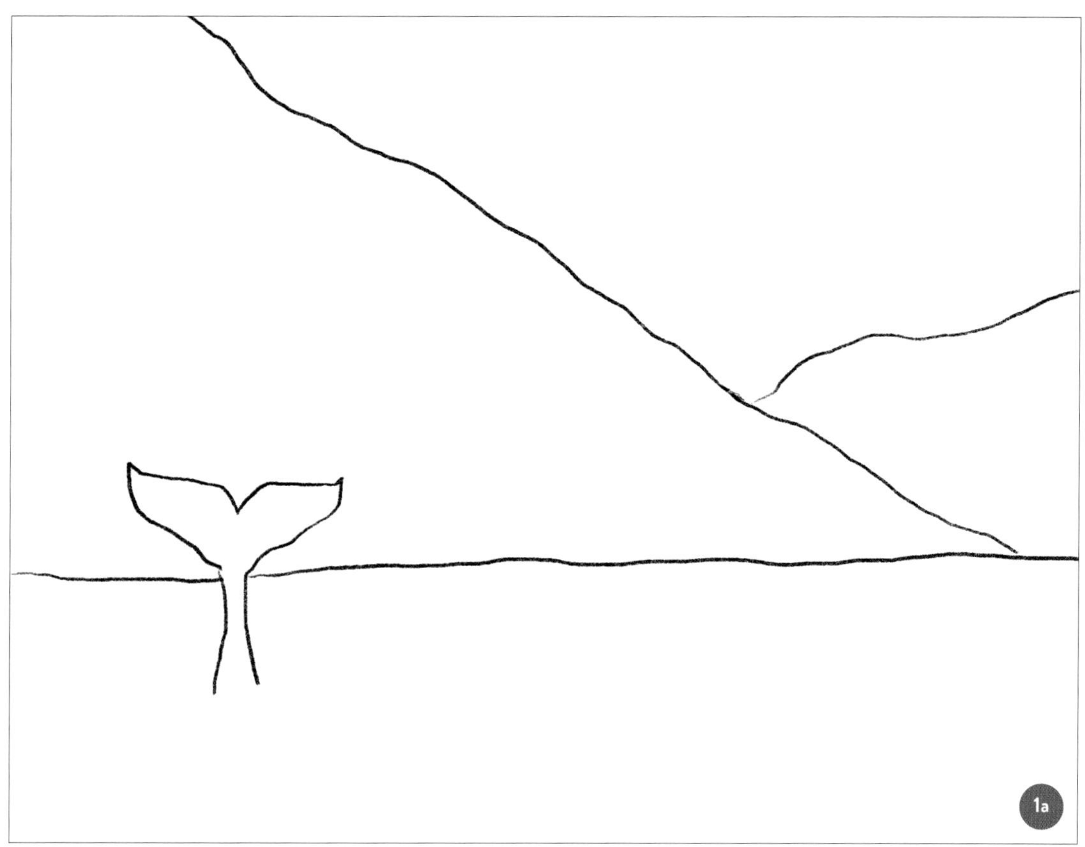

STEP 1: THE SKETCH

Sketch the mountain layers and the whale's tail coming out from the ocean. Start with a horizontal line about a third of the way up from the bottom of the page. Then, sketch a kind of jagged, swooping line starting at the top left and moving down to about the center right of the page. Behind that layer, sketch a small curve starting at the base of the large mountain and sloping upward to the right side for the background mountain layer.

For the whale's tale, sketch two gently curving vertical lines tapering toward the top and two elongated S-curves (page 13) coming up and out of each side. Then add two more S-curves in a flipped orientation connecting the tail inward.

(continued)

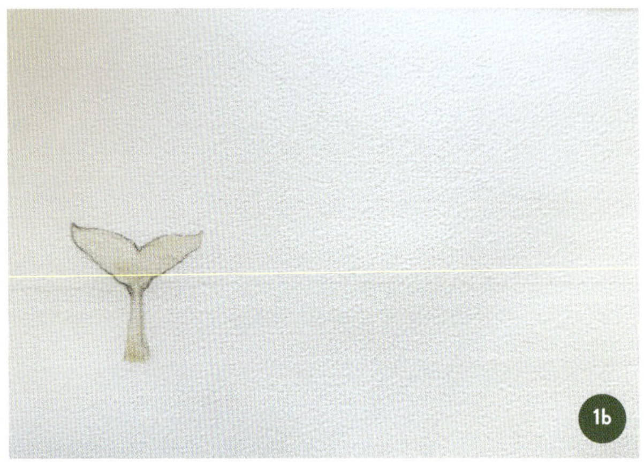

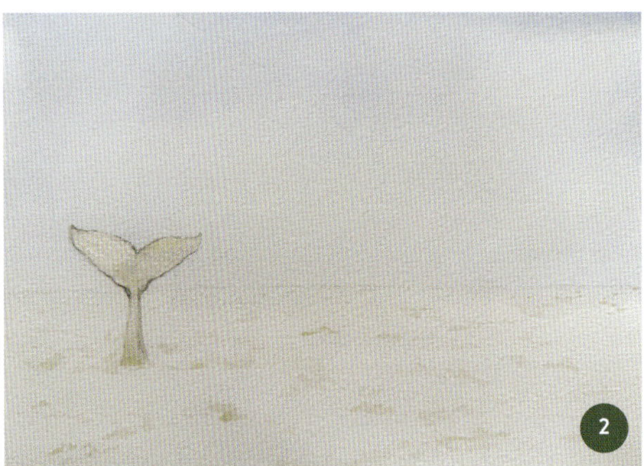

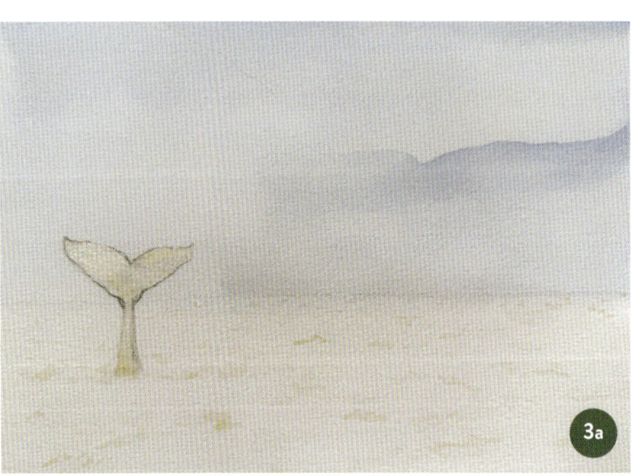

Use a masking fluid brush prepped with soap and masking fluid (page 15) to paint the whale tale, preserving the paper for later. Finally, use the masking fluid to paint choppy sea-foam waves in short, horizontal marks and blocks across the ocean that are larger in the front (toward the bottom of the page) and smaller toward the back (just tiny dots). Let dry for 30 minutes or until tacky.

STEP 2: THE SKY

Layer a wash of clean water across the sky and the mountain layers. Use a size 12 round brush with watery French Ultramarine to paint a warm, pale blue sky. Let dry completely.

STEP 3: THE MOUNTAINS

Mix a bit of Quinacridone Rose into the watery French Ultramarine to get a pale blue-violet, then paint the background mountain, first with paint (along the top ridge), then with water to blend it down, creating a subtle gradient.

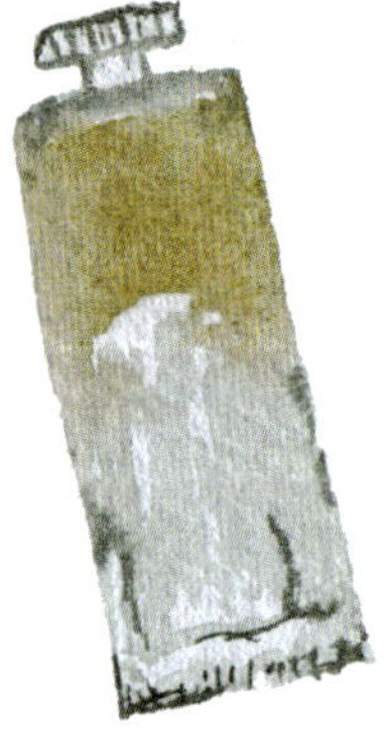

Let dry completely, then use a foliage brush with a slightly darker blue-violet to paint the next mountain layer, which will predominantly be trees. Create a jagged tree-like texture along the ridge by painting short, vertical strokes into the wet wash. Tap a bit of clean water along the bottom of the mountain, pushing away the paint and creating a foggy effect. Mix a dark green (French Ultramarine + a bit of New Gamboge [more blue than yellow]), then use a foliage brush to paint the still-wet tree layer, leaving behind flickers of the blue layer and the white fog along the edge.

Again, while still wet, mix a bit of Payne's Gray with French Ultramarine, and use a foliage brush to tap shadows into the tree layer, this time intentionally using short, vertical strokes with the foliage brush to imply tree shapes shrouded in fog. Let dry completely.

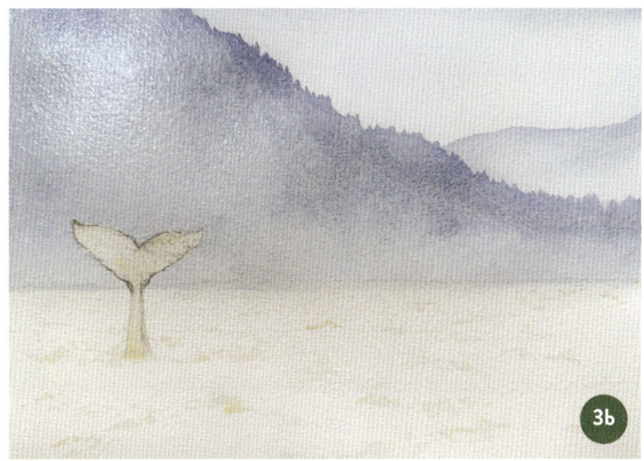

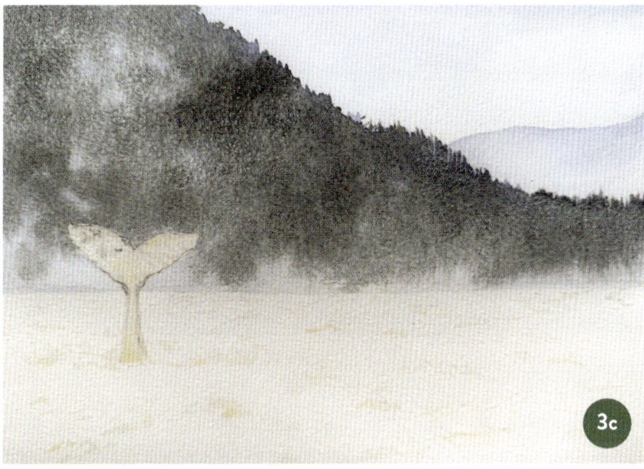

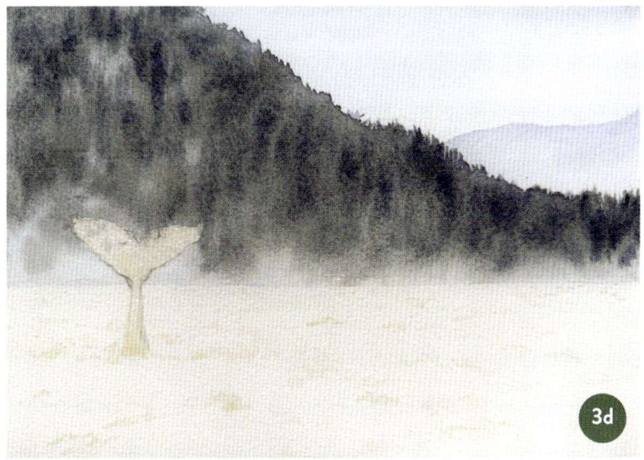

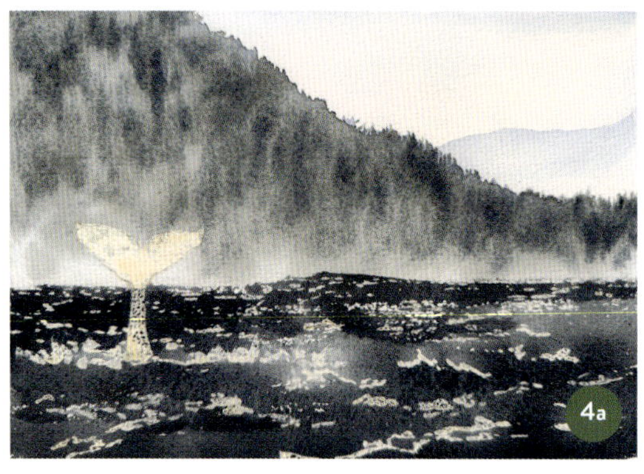

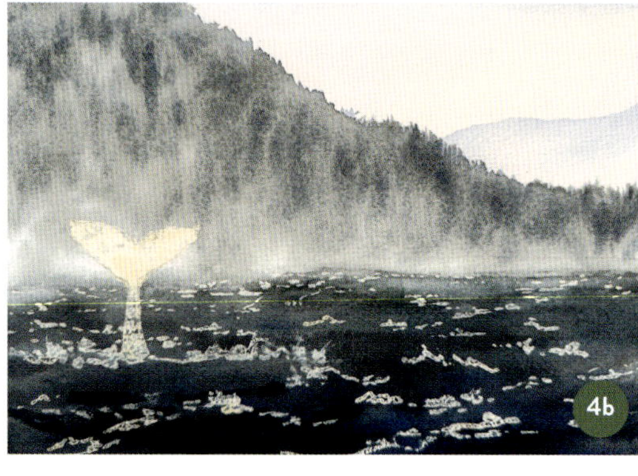

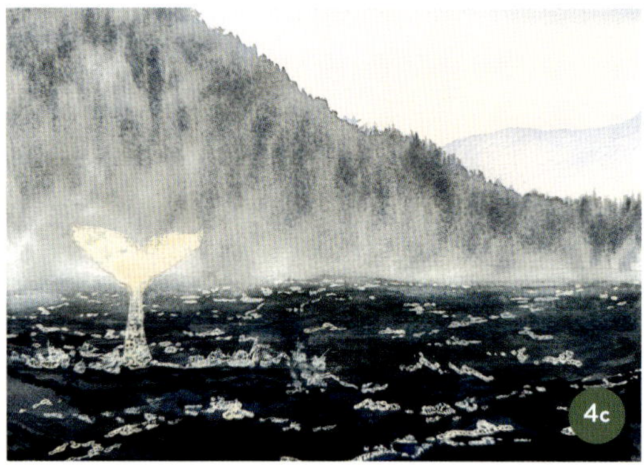

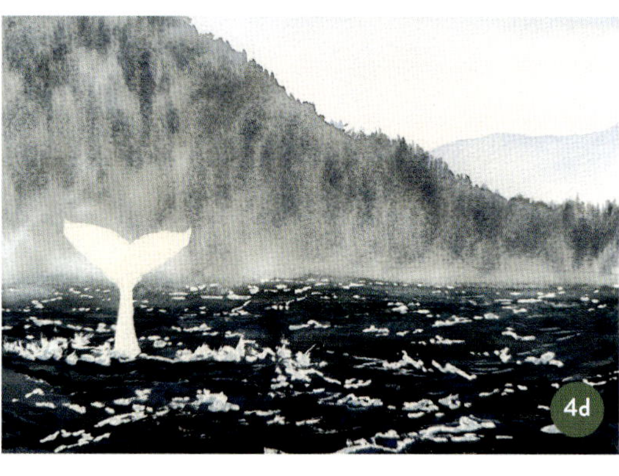

STEP 4: THE WATER

Mix a dark turquoise with Payne's Gray and Phthalo Blue, then paint the ocean layer, making sure not to cover up the fog at the base of the mountain layer. While still wet, use a size 6 round brush to paint Phthalo Blue directly into the wash in loose, horizontal zigzags, adding more color to the water. Let dry completely, then use a size 2 round brush with the dark turquoise mix to add wet-on-dry (page 12) wave marks on the surface of the water, leaving behind strips of dry space for added contrast.

This is choppy water, so we want plenty of texture and movement! Repeat with even darker-value paint (adding more Payne's Gray).

Let dry completely, then remove the masking fluid by gently rubbing it away with your finger or an eraser (page 15). Add a few shadows to some of the sea-foam spots with blobs of quite watery Payne's Gray. Then, add a few thin, horizontal wavy lines of white gouache between some of the waves.

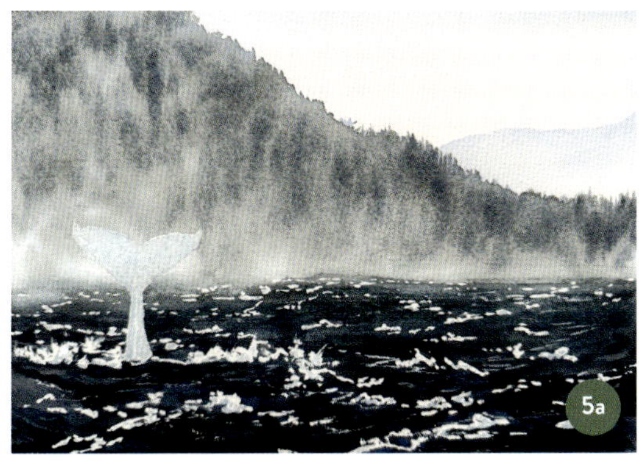
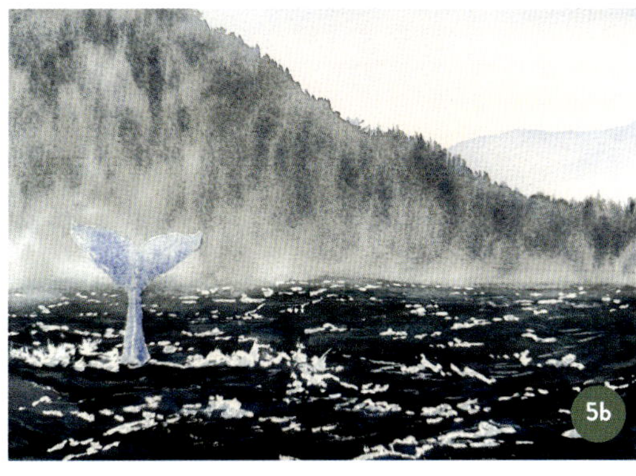
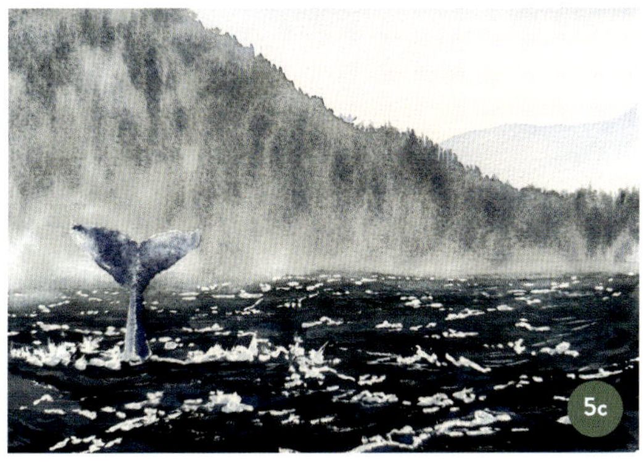
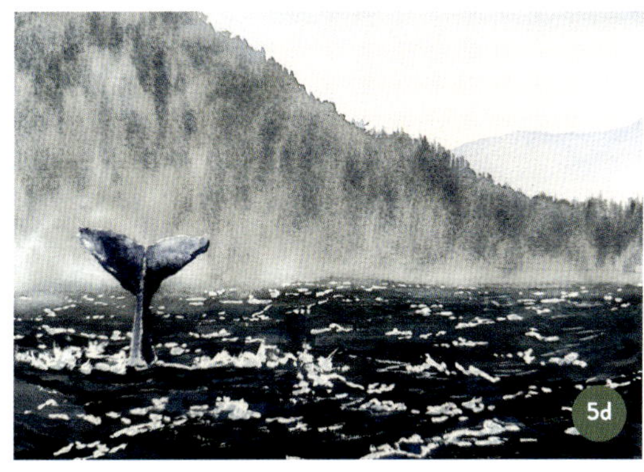

STEP 5: THE WHALE TAIL

Wet the tail with clean water using a size 2 round brush, carefully leaving behind a vertical strip of dry space up the center and along the edges of the tail. Drop a watery French Ultramarine into the wash. While still wet, add a bit more paint to the French Ultramarine mix, and drop it into the wash, especially on the bottom right and top left. The idea here is to create shifting shadows, so as long as some parts are darker than others, that will work. Add Payne's Gray to the mix, and repeat. Let dry, then use a size 2 round brush to paint wet-on-dry (page 12) strokes to darken the shadows even more and sharpen the contrast. Finally, let the paint dry completely, then use

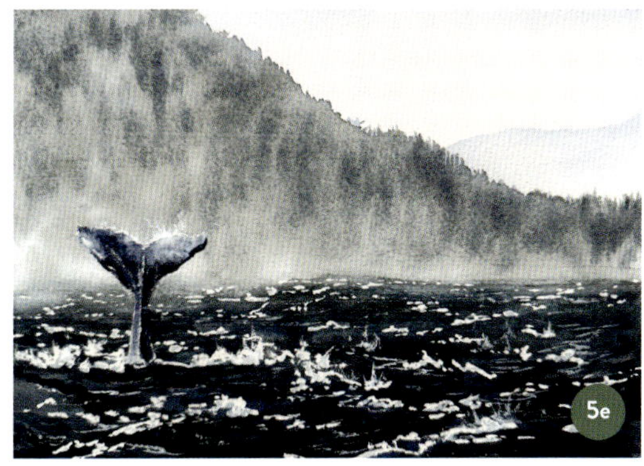

white gouache with a size 2 round brush to add a few highlights and dry brush (page 12) marks, mimicking water running down the tail and splashing upward from the top. Add white gouache anywhere on the ocean as well, mimicking splashes as you see fit.

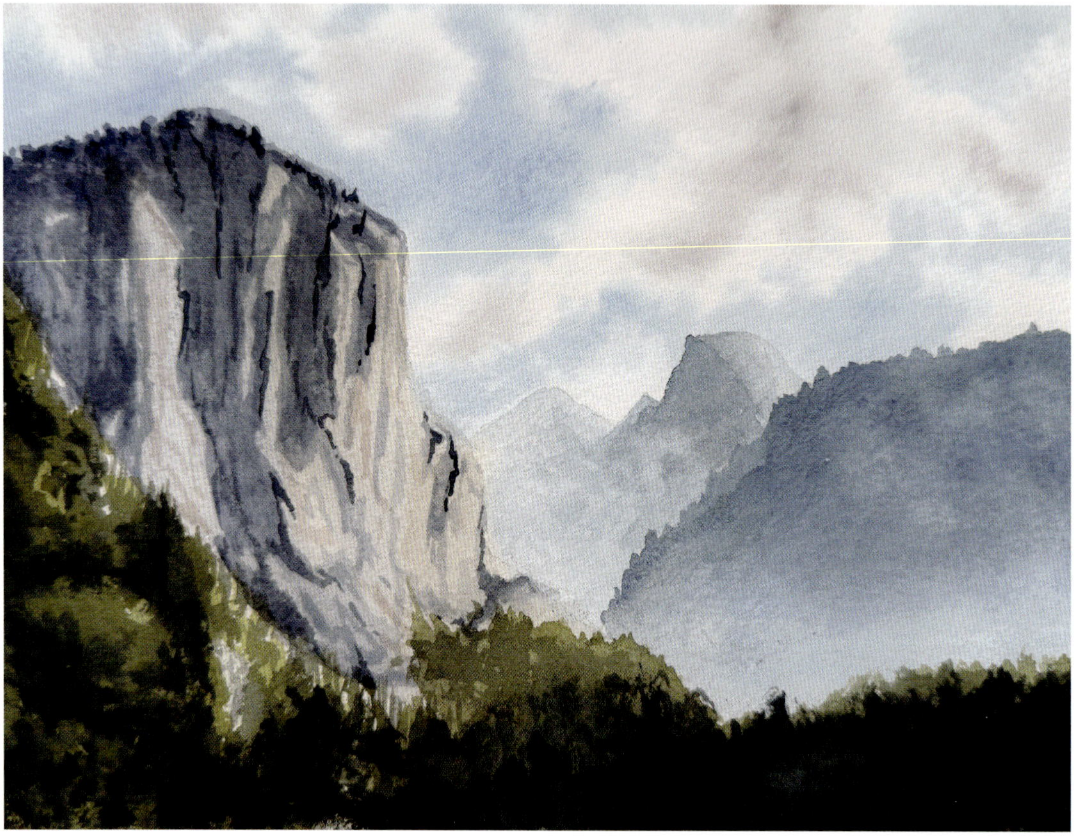

YOSEMITE

BRUSHES
Round sizes 2, 6, and 12; Foliage brush

COLOR PALETTE
Payne's Gray, Pyrrol Scarlet, French Ultramarine, Phthalo Blue (Green Shade), New Gamboge

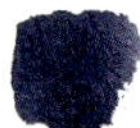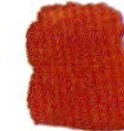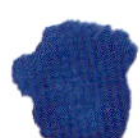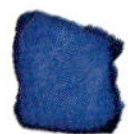

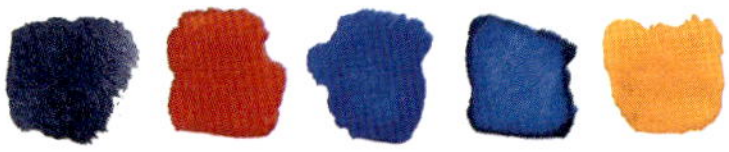

El Capitan in Yosemite National Park is one of those mountains that has inspired humans to search new heights—both within the landscape and within their souls. Let's capture that determination of human spirit with El Capitan standing as a striking sentinel, surrounded by sweeping layers of trees and ethereal mountains spiraling in the distance.

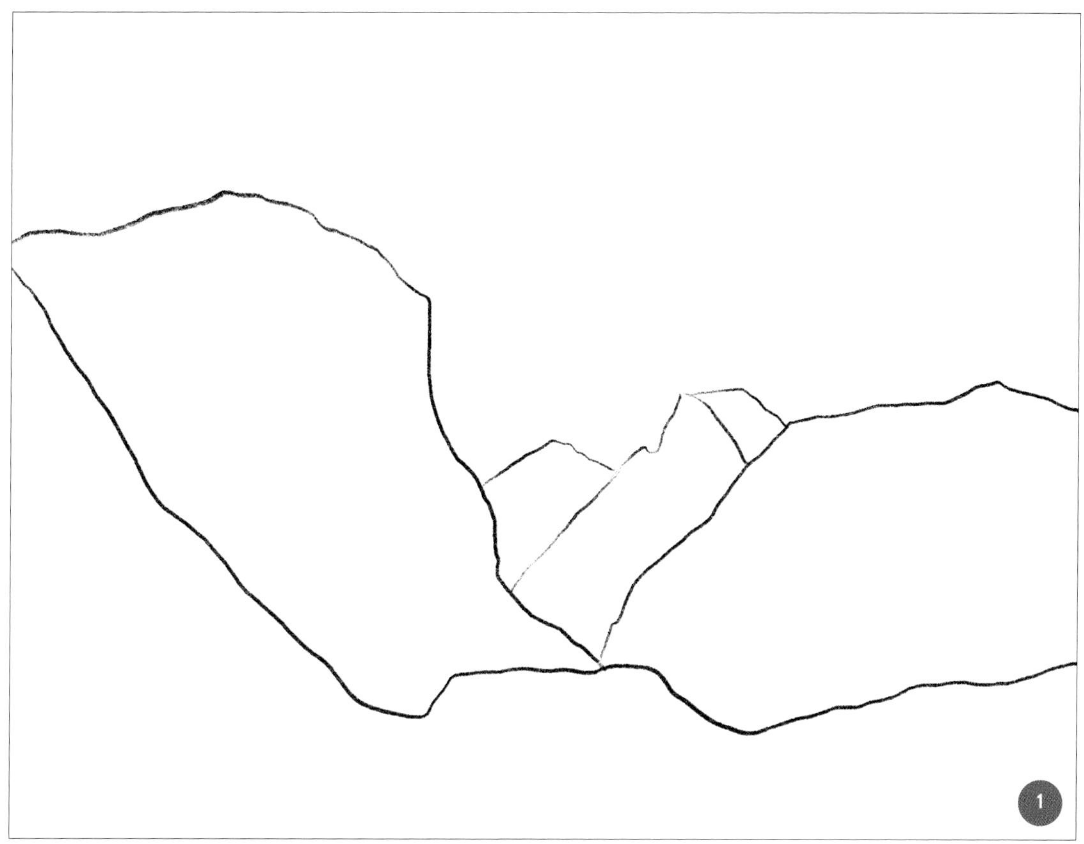

STEP 1: THE SKETCH

Start with a light sketch of El Capitan and the surrounding mountain peaks taking up about two-thirds of the space. Start with El Cap in front on the left side, with a blocky horizontal curve on top, then a sharp turn down for the vertical cliff face. Extend the mountain into the valley below with a few more curves sloping down toward the base of El Cap. Then, sketch the background mountain layers, starting with a large curve on the right side, then smaller curves (especially one making up the iconic Half Dome shape) loosely spiraling smaller toward the center. Add a steep, curved line starting just below El Cap on the left side moving down for a cascading tree layer to frame the scene.

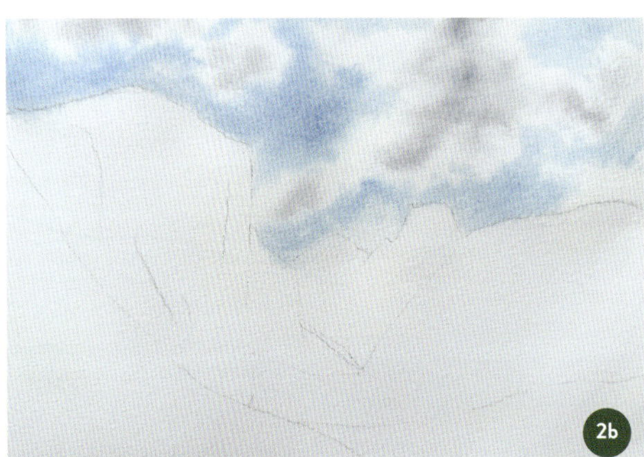

STEP 2: THE SKY

Let's paint a blue sky with fluffy, white clouds to add some background texture. We'll use the negative space technique (page 15) to paint the clouds! Layer a wash of clean water across the sky with a size 12 round brush, feathering (page 12) it into the mountain layers (though we'll try to keep the blue away from the mountains as much as possible. Mix a light-medium value gray (Payne's Gray + a hint of Pyrrol Scarlet—keep it watery), then use a foliage brush to tap the gray mixture into the wet wash in a few spots, making sure the largest gray area is opposite from El Cap. This will be the shadow on the inside of the clouds.

While this layer is still wet, mix a sky blue (French Ultramarine + Phthalo Blue), then use a foliage brush to carefully paint around the gray, leaving behind outlines of white space between the gray and the blue. If the paint is too runny, use a towel to lift the blue away from the white space. Remember, clouds are supposed to be wispy and imperfect! It's okay if you have dried paint lines or muddy mixes. Let dry completely.

Next, layer a light-value underpainting across the rest of the scene. First, create light-value (watery) mixes of muted blue (French Ultramarine + Payne's Gray), light brown (French Ultramarine + Pyrrol Scarlet + New Gamboge), and warm green (French Ultramarine + New Gamboge). Then, wet the areas beneath the sky with a size 12 round brush, and add the light-value mixes to their respective areas: muted blue for the background mountains, light brown for El Cap, and warm green for the forest layer on the right and across the ground.

Let dry completely, then use a foliage brush with slight darker-value muted blue to paint the left shadow of Half Dome (which should be small and toward the center, as it's quite far in the distance from here), using the tapping motion of a foliage brush to kind of blend the wet-on-dry (page 12) shadowy blue into the surrounding mountain area. Let dry, then add a bit more French Ultramarine to the muted blue mix, and paint the next closest mountain layer, using the foliage brush to make the top ridge a bit rough to mimic a line of trees. Rinse your brush and add one or two taps of a clean brush into the wet mix to create a subtle foggy texture within the mountain layer, and use the foliage brush to create a rough blend between the bottom and the green forest layer below. Let dry.

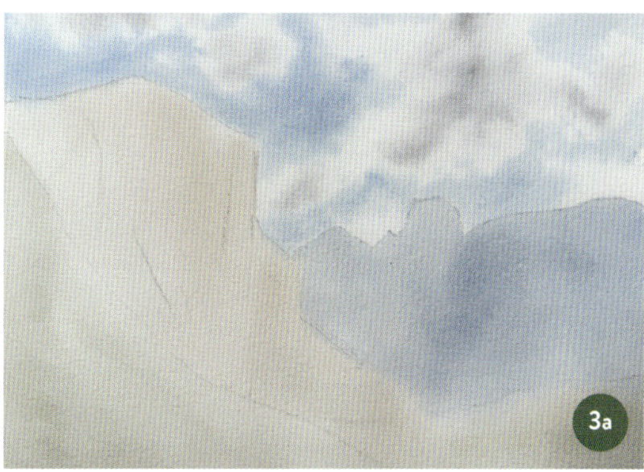

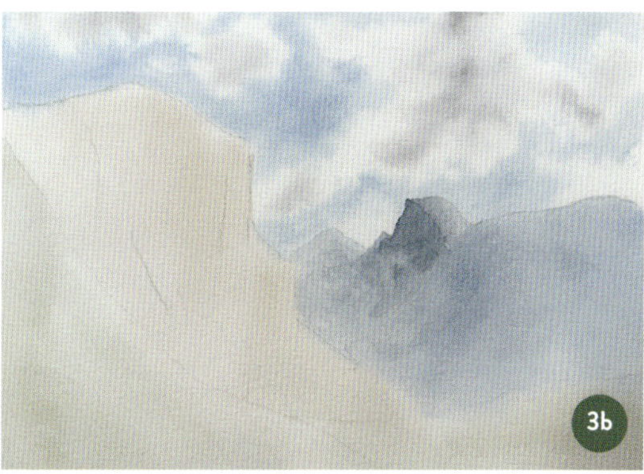

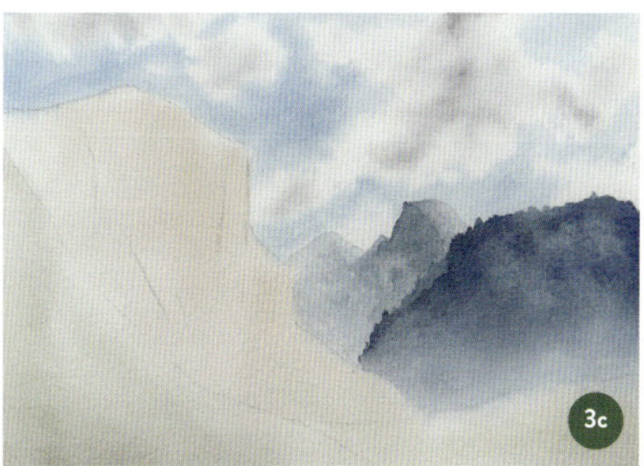

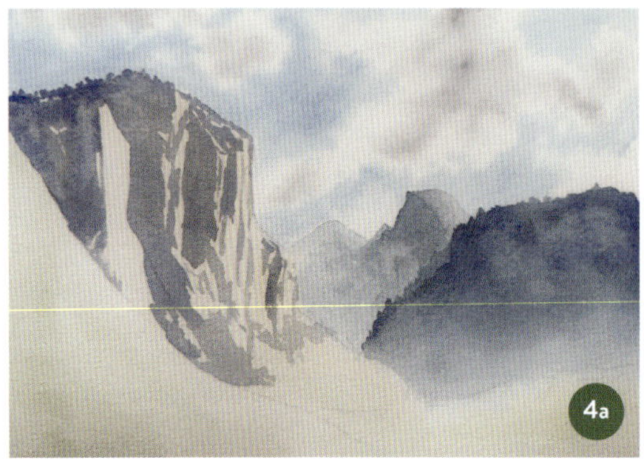

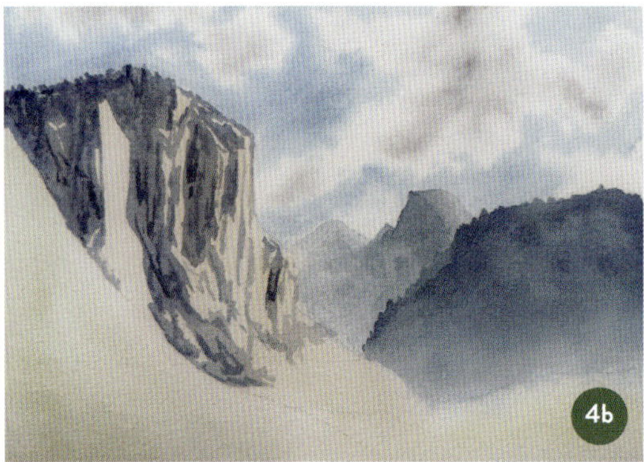

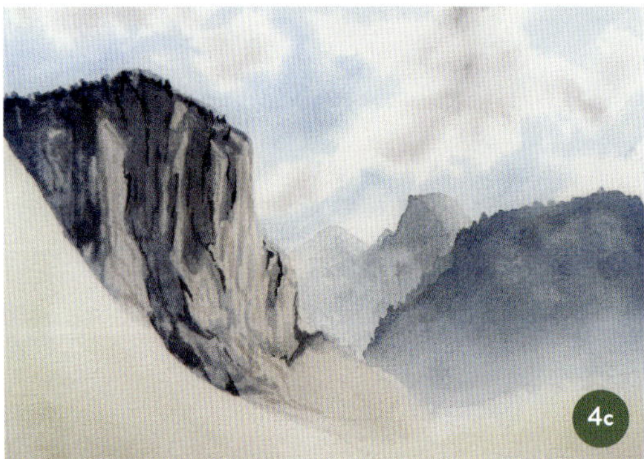

STEP 4: EL CAPITAN

Next, let's paint El Cap with vertical shadows and light cutting into the iconic rocky face. This will be the scary part, and it will feel messy. But don't worry! I almost threw this draft out my first time, but it came together, and so will yours! Create a watery blue-violet mix (French Ultramarine + a hint of Pyrrol Scarlet), then use a foliage brush or a size 6 round brush to paint long, vertical shadows on El Cap—heavier on the left side, then growing lighter on the right. Carve out light, dry spaces, leaving behind thin, jagged, vertical stripes—sometimes small and large in one or two spots. Random is good! Let dry, then use a size 2 round brush with slightly darker-value blue-violet (add a bit of Payne's Gray, but still watery) to add smaller shadows within the shadows, painting in loose, vertical zigzags and adding some rounded texture on top for trees along the mountain ridge. Let dry, then add light brown (watery) vertical zigzags to some of the light areas, using the same mix from the previous step.

At this point, you might look at all of your marks on the mountain and think, *This looks ridiculous.* Keep going! We're going to smooth everything out a bit, then add a few more contrasting marks to sharpen the layers together. First, mix a quite watery Payne's Gray (so pale it's almost clear), and layer it on the entirety of El Cap—even the light areas—tinting everything just a bit. That will loosen the sharp edges but still leave behind the contrasting value spaces.

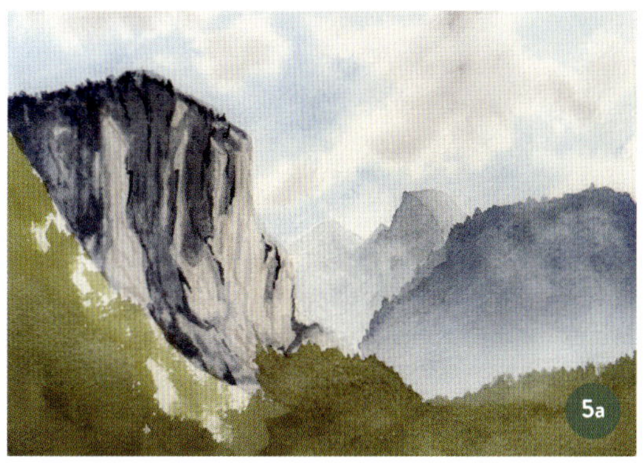

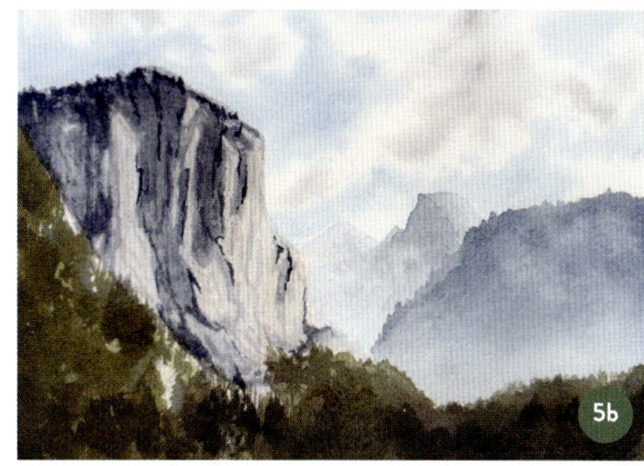

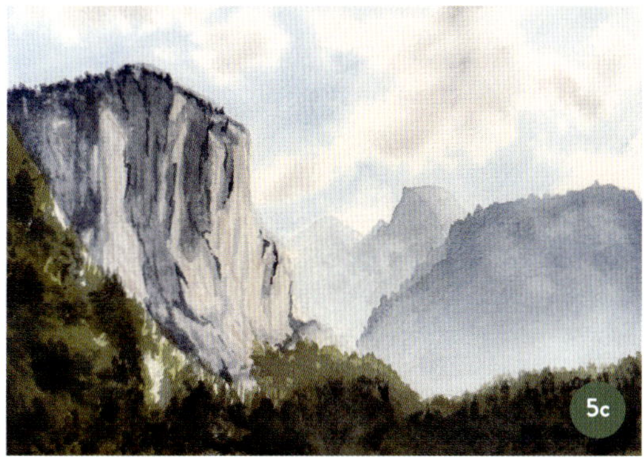

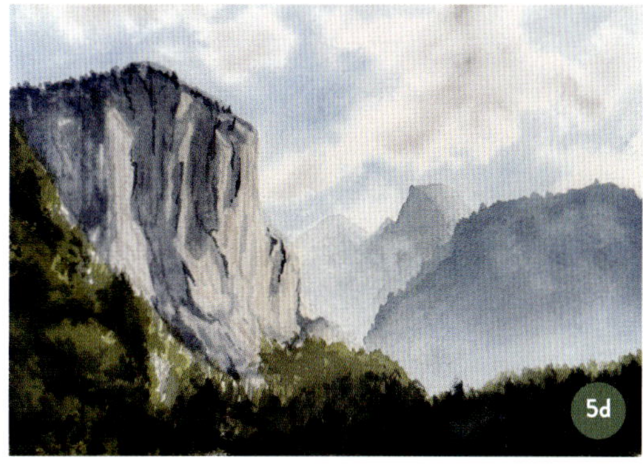

Let dry completely, then use a size 2 round brush with a medium-value Payne's Gray (darker than everything else on the mountain, but not the darkest it can be) to add a few thin, vertical zigzag shadows scattered along the mountain face. Only a few of these dark shadows will go a long way! Let dry completely.

STEP 5: THE TREES

Mix a watery warm green (French Ultramarine + New Gamboge), and use a foliage brush to paint across the mountain layer, leaving behind a few odd spots of dry space for a subtle rocky texture peeking through.

Add a bit of Payne's Gray into the mixture to make it darker, then repeat, leaving behind pockets of the lighter layer and adding more vertical strokes to mimic small treetops throughout the layer. Add a bit more Payne's Gray, then repeat again, deepening the layers of trees. Paint one final round with even more Payne's Gray into the green mix, this time making the right side the darkest and tapering into the left, mimicking the look of a valley cut through with shadows and light. Add a few scattered dark foliage-texture spots on the left side to emphasize the light even more.

acknowledgments

As ever, this book was a labor of love, patience, and no small amount of hope—hope that, somehow, by making watercolor and creativity more accessible, we can make the world just a bit brighter (necessary right now for so many reasons).

I'm so grateful to the wonderful team at Page Street for continuing to believe in my work. This one took me a little longer than the others, and their steadfast patience and support made it possible to bring my vision for this book to life.

As I am a human who has a laundry list of weaknesses, I also have to thank the family and friends who rallied around me this year—a lot of worlds are falling apart, and finding strength in each other is hopefully how we piece them together again.

Finally, and perhaps most important, I have to thank YOU—the reader, the painter, a fellow artist and creative. Without you, books like this would be squarely filed away in the "maybe, someday" part of my imagination. Truly, creative works are a team effort, and I hope you're receiving as much out of it as I am.

about the author

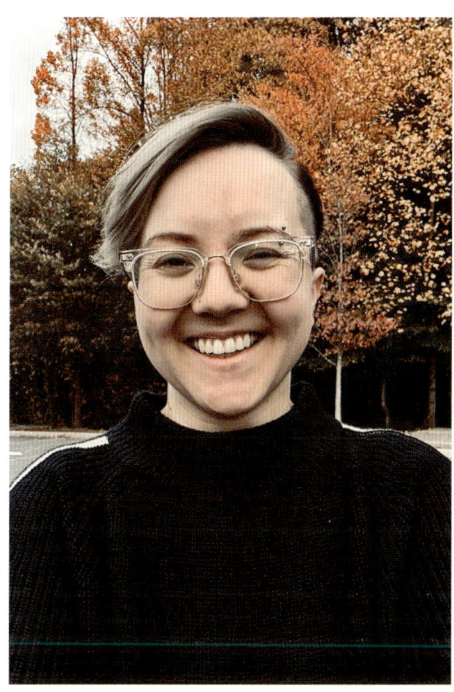

Kolbie Blume is a queer and neurodivergent hobby artist turned creative entrepreneur who really loves to help people discover just how magical watercolor can be. You can find more of Kolbie's classes at thiswritingdesk.com.

When not working or painting, Kolbie loves to walk aimlessly, read obsessively, and make waffles with their son.

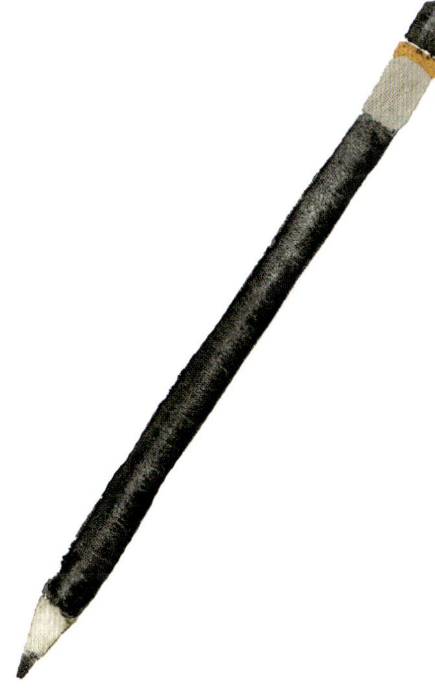

index